Life Journey
A Family Memoir

Serge P. Petroff

iUniverse, Inc.
New York   Bloomington

Life Journey

A Family Memoir

Copyright © 2008 by Serge Petroff

iUniverse books may be ordered through booksellers or by contacting:

iUniverse
1663 Liberty Drive
Bloomington, IN 47403
www.iuniverse.com
1-800-Authors (1-800-288-4677)

ISBN: 978-0-595-51115-0 (pbk)
ISBN: 978-0-595-51165-5 (cloth)
ISBN: 978-0-595-61770-8 (ebk)

Printed in the United States of America
iUniverse Rev. 11/25/2008

Contents

*For Bunny, who encouraged me
to write it, and for Paul, Buzy,
Greg, Andy, and their children*

"Let us not burden our memories
with heaviness."

William Shakespeare

PREFACE

This book grew through time out of a reflection on the need and relevance of a family memoir. My wife, a native-born American whose New England roots go back to the XVII century, had been urging me for years to write an autobiographical sketch of my life because it was so different from that of other Americans. She wanted our four children to have a better understanding of how their paternal grandparents came to California, why they left Russia, and what kind of influence they had on my upbringing. I welcomed the idea, but could not decide on how to structure the memoir. Should it be a short sketch written specifically for my children and grandchildren, or should it be a more ambitious full length book written for a wider English-speaking readership whose interests include recent history and biography? I opted for the second option. I felt my family's story was sufficiently unique and interesting to warrant my writing a full length book.

In the past twenty years a number of excellent memoirs written by descendants of Russian exiles have appeared in the United States and the United Kingdom. Alex Shoumatoff's *Russian Blood: A Family Chronicle*, Nicholas Daniloff's *Two Lives, One Russia*, Serge Schmemann's *Echoes of a Native land*, and, more recently, Michael Ignatieff's *The Russian Album*, winner of the prestigious Royal Society Literature Award, escorted readers through several generations of their Russian ancestors, recreating their lives before, during and after the Russian Revolution. All had one distinctive thing in common. They were accounts of Russia's elite forbears and their descendants who left Russia through her western portals and settled in Europe and the eastern United States. My story is different. Neither of my parents were part of the titled nobility, nor did they leave Russia by way of Europe. They escaped through Siberia and China after nearly four years of civil war in which my father played a significant role. Also, when they finally settled permanently, it was in California and not London, Paris or New York. To my knowledge no one has to this date produced a family chronicle centered on the exodus of Russian immigrants through Siberia, through what my father called his "long and twisting journey from the Bay of Finland to the Golden Gate."

The past is never simply what one thinks it is or what one remembers of it. This is especially true of the early years of life. It is hard to separate one's own recollections from the rousing stories told by doting parents and family friends. It is also difficult to unchain one's psyche from the experiences of early adulthood. More often than not, we remember only what we wish to remember, and have to rely therefore on family photographs, letters, and diaries. Fortuitously, my parents left a plethora of family remembrances. My father, whose lifetime hobby was photography, had a vast collection of photographs that went back all the way to my childhood. He also left eighteen notebooks containing autobiographical materials and two published memoirs. My mother, an inveterate saver of correspondence with her children, left some important letters that were extremely helpful in recalling a number of significant experiences. Without their help, I don't think I could have written my memoir. They helped me focus on many details in full color and intensity. Also, I could not have completed the memoir without the help of my son, Paul Petroff. He painstakingly reformatted the manuscript and prepared it for the publisher.

Complicating the task is also the realization that we all wear a mask which hides what we have secretly buried in the remote regions of our brain and don't want to reveal in fear of being misunderstood or criticized. Identifying and sorting out this repressed hoard of stored memories is a taxing travail, especially when the social and cultural fabric of one's life lacks continuity. Most people, who are raised and come to adulthood as citizens of one country under an established set of nationally accepted values and aspirations, tend to follow a uniform path through early life, even in the worst of circumstances. Those who don't are an exception. I did not have the luxury of growing up in one country. My early life history twisted and swirled through five different life experiences. I was born in China to White Russian émigré parents and received my earliest upbringing in a milieu dominated by vanquished warriors who had not yet lost their hope of returning to their native land. I grew up and matured as a stateless expatriate in the international setting of pre-World War II Japan and the difficult war years that followed it. After years of wandering and searching, I arrived in the United States at the age of twenty-four and spent five full years as an immigrant waiting to become a citizen. Finally, I became a U.S. citizen, not just out of convenience, but because I genuinely longed for permanence and wanted to become an American.

As I look back at my long life and think about the uneven course of its journey, I see myself transiting through five very different worlds each of which left its mark, its stamp of approval or disapproval, its permanent imprint on the course of my life. *Life Journey* is the story of those five stages of my life against the background of twentieth and early twenty-first century history, and our family's sinuous traverse through the labyrinth of every day life.

1
EMIGRE IN CHINA

I argue not against heaven's
hand, nor bate a jot of heart
or hope, but still bear up, and
steer right onward.
Milton

I

I was born in Harbin, China on November 1, 1922, five days after
the Red Army marched into Vladivostok and occupied the last White
anti-Bolshevik stronghold in eastern Siberia. My mother (Mama) had
unwisely failed to leave the besieged city during the massive exodus
hoping that I would be born on Russian soil. Some of our family
friends have said I was fortunate to have been born at all as the political
and military situation in Vladivostok during my mother's last days
of confinement was extremely precarious. In October 1922, the Red
Army had successfully broken through the White defenses, cutting off
the only land escape route out of Vladivostok. Thousands of White
Army families and refugees, including Mama, were now stranded in
Vladivostok. The city was in a state of intense panic, awash in rumors of
impending looting and rumors that the more prominent White Army
personages remaining in the city could expect a bloodbath. As the wife
of a White Army general who was chief-of-staff of the defeated White
Army, Mama was a conspicuous target whose life was most certainly
in peril.

The military situation in Vladivostok was very similar to that of
the Crimea a year earlier when tens of thousands of White troops and
families were anxiously waiting to be picked up by British and French
warships and ferried to Constantinople (Istanbul) or Varna, Bulgaria.
With the land route out of Vladivostok cut off by the advancing Red

Army, Mama had only two avenues of escape. She could either board a Russian naval vessel of the Siberian Flotilla that was still at anchor in the Bay of the Golden Horn, or hope to be rescued by the Japanese navy. Like the British and the French in the Crimea, the Japanese navy was standing by in Vladivostok to help the Whites evacuate the city.

Escape on a Japanese ship looked safer to Mama than what the Siberian Flotilla could offer. The Japanese were ferrying refugees to Korea while the destination of the Siberian Flotilla remained uncertain. Admiral Iu. K. Stark, commander of the flotilla, was still trying to decide what was best for the men under his command. In the end, the Siberian Flotilla left Vladivostok via China to the Philippines where the ships were scuttled in 1923. Mama made the right decision. She wisely accepted the Japanese offer, and twelve hours before the Red Army secured the city, she left Vladivostok aboard a Japanese destroyer. With only an overcoat on her back, her remaining jewels sown into its lining, and her diploma from the Radionov Institute in her pocket she arrived in Genzan (Wonsan), Korea where she boarded a train for Harbin, arriving there on October 29. In Harbin, she pawned some of the jewels, bought a bed, a table, two chairs, an assortment of household utensils and baby paraphernalia, and set up house in a room she had rented near the apartment of Uncle Volodia, her mother's first cousin, and his wife who had fled Russia in 1919 during the early stages of the civil war. Two days later, I was delivered safely by Dr. Kazen Bek, the military surgeon with whom Mama had worked as a nurse in the southern Urals. She often retold the dramatic story of her escape from Vladivostok. Sparing no detail and with a certain amount of disdain for the gravity of her situation, she described how she and the wives of two junior officers who accompanied her at the insistence of the destroyer's commander, boarded the ship at night to the sound of hooting horns and beaming searchlights only a few hours before the Red Army entered the city. Asked by us children how she had endured the journey. She would say in all seriousness that "I felt like a queen with two ladies-in-waiting caring for all my needs and wishes."

Father (Papa) was not present when I was born. He was somewhere between Novo-Kievsk and the Chinese border with the remnants of the White army that was slowly retreating south toward the border. For most Russians who chose to oppose the Bolsheviks the civil war in Siberia had ended two years earlier. They crossed the Chinese border at Station Manchuria in November 1920 after nearly two and one half years of incessant fighting under the most intolerable conditions across the vast expanse of eastern European Russia and Siberia. With no place to go and no other prospects for survival, approximately 20,000 veterans of the long campaigns did not halt in China but traveled to Vladivostok where they continued to serve a variety of changing anti-Bolshevik governments. Papa and Mama did not move to Vladivostok immediately. Trying to establish a bastion of anti-Bolshevik opposition in eastern Siberia did not seem like a viable option to Papa. He did not believe that an anti-Soviet government could survive on Russian soil without American, British and Japanese help, nor did he want to become involved in the pathetic and pointless debates and in-fighting that had become part of the Vladivostok political scene. Instead, they remained in Harbin, China, the headquarters of the Chinese Eastern Railroad built by the Russians to connect the Baikal region of Siberia with Vladivostok. There was also a tragic personal side to his and Mama's decision to stay in Harbin. I was not my parents' first-born child. A daughter -- baby Tata -- was born in January 1921 during their stay in Harbin. She lived less than nine months, dying a terrible and heartbreaking death in the meningitis epidemic that swept through northeastern Asia that year. Papa and Mama were devastated by the loss of their baby daughter. The White defeat in the Civil War, the dreadful hopelessness of their personal situation and Tata's death were especially hard on Mama. It took months before they could contain their grief and again confront the fickle demands of their uncertain lives.

But the passions of the Civil War and the flames of carrying on the fight did not die out. In Papa's case, they really never were completely contained. They continued to flare up from time to time during most of his long and active life. The Kronstadt uprising, the spreading peasant rebellion in central Russia and the success of the White veterans who crossed over to Vladivostok in pushing the Red Army nearly 600 kilometers from Vladivostok to Khabarovsk raised hopes that the fragile Soviet government would collapse under the pressure of popular rebellion, bringing an end to the communist experiment. Inspired by the excessively encouraging news of a possible Soviet collapse, White officers who remained in Harbin during 1921, flocked to Vladivostok to resume the struggle. Papa was no exception. Against better judgment, hoping against improbable odds that it was still possible to oust the Bolsheviks from the Far East, he accepted the post of Chief of Supply of the White Army. He had held that hopeless post during the last stage of the White retreat from central Siberia, and was now again being recruited to feed and clothe not only the army but everyone else who arrived with it in Vladivostok. In the summer of

1922, when General Diterichs took over the reins of the Vladivostok government, championing the convocation of a popular Land Assembly in the hope of establishing a permanent anti-communist enclave in the Russian Far East, Papa agreed to be his chief-of-staff. The army was his life – his extended family – and he could not turn the offer down, especially since it came from General Diterichs under whom he had served before. Mama at first stayed in Harbin, but did not remain there long. In June she also left for Vladivostok to join Papa.

In the meantime, the political and military prospects of holding on to Vladivostok as a bastion of anti-Bolshevik struggle took a turn for the worse. Freed from the burden of waging war with Poland, the Red Army resumed its push to bring all of Siberia under Soviet control. The Japanese attitude toward intervention in eastern Siberia was also changing. Tokyo was beginning to question the benefit of maintaining troops in the Russian Far East, and on June 24, 1922 announced that Japan was pulling out all of its military forces from the Maritime province by the end of October 1922. Assured of Japanese non-interference, the Red Army renewed its offensive toward Vladivostok, and on October 10 broke through the White defenses, forcing what was left of the White Army to retreat toward the Chinese border. Discouraged and totally overpowered, on 15 October 1922, General Diterichs issued the order to commence the evacuation of all White Army troops and families from Vladivostok and other urban centers of the Maritime province. Continuing the struggle on Russian soil in the hope of establishing a Taiwan-like nationalist state in the Russian Far East was no longer an option. The primary objective now was to hold the Red Army at bay for as long as possible to assure an orderly evacuation of the refugees and White Army families remaining in Vladivostok. Writing about that last stand many years later, Papa recalled that "we withdrew in a sea of mud and water under a continuous downpour which lasted for days, without food and cover, especially hard on the families and the children of the border regions who chose to flee Russia with the army. For all of us who survived the ordeal, it was an exhausting and desperate flight without any hope of ever seeing our native land again." At the border, the army laid down its arms and set up temporary refugee camps with the approval of the Chinese government. Father finally reached Harbin in February 1923, this time leaving Russian soil for good. There, he learned that Mama had escaped safely and for the first time saw his baby son Seriozha, christened and named after St. Sergius of Radonezh, Russia's highly esteemed saint who championed Muscovy's insurrection against the

Mongols in the fourteenth century. Papa and Mama believed that the choice of St. Sergius as their son's patron saint was fitting considering the uncertainty of the times in which he was born.

They did not stay in Harbin very long. Papa did not like Harbin when he was there in 1921 and he found it again not to his liking. It was too artificial, too complacent for him after the devastating experience of the civil war. It reminded him of Pushkin's short story *Pir vo vremia* chumy (Feast during a Pestilence). Situated on Chinese soil, Harbin was in all respects a Russian city. Built in the 1890s by the Russian government to serve as the administrative center of the Chinese Eastern Railroad operated by Russia through northern Manchuria under a lease agreement with China, Harbin was a railroad town with all of the trappings that come with running a railroad. It had repair shops, coal yards, technical schools and thousands of railroad workers and families living in a typical setting of a pre-revolutionary Russian city with churches, stores, schools, entertainment centers, and a provincial press that kept Harbin's citizens abreast of what was taking place in Russia. The Revolution of 1917 and the ensuing civil war changed everything. Thousands of refugees from Siberia and eastern European Russia -- academics, professionals, businessmen, politicians, Cossacks, army officers and enlisted men from the defeated White Army -- arrived in Harbin, swelling its Russian population to nearly 250,000. On the positive side, the railroad -- still managed by Russians with strong anti-Bolshevik sentiment -- offered the newcomers employment and ancillary business opportunities, making their life considerably better than that of their less fortunate brothers and sisters who were forced to settle in Berlin, Paris and other large centers of Europe. Almost overnight, dozens of new restaurants, theaters, cabarets and hotels sprang up throughout the city, giving it a heady and intoxicating atmosphere of bogus affluence and debauchery. As far as Papa and Mama were concerned, this was not what they were looking for. To them Harbin was permissive, grotesquely unreal and unscrupulously unconcerned about the fate of thousands of White soldiers -- officers and enlisted men -- who were now refugees, many of them still quartered in the refugee camps of northern Manchuria. I suspect there was also another reason why Papa found Harbin an unwelcome haven. His closest army friends -- the field commanders with whom he had fought against the Bolsheviks -- did not stay in Harbin. Generals Moltchanoff and Puchkov left while it was still possible for the United States, General Voitsekhovskii accepted a senior military position in Czechoslovakia, General Bangerskii returned to his native Latvia where in the early 1930s he became the Minister of Defense, Generals Diterichs and Virzhbitskii stayed in China but chose Shanghai and Tientsin instead of Harbin, Diterichs becoming President of the Far Eastern Division of the All Russian Military Union, the émigré military organization with headquarters in Paris. The White leaders who settled in Harbin and stayed there through World War II were predominantly political and paper generals, politicians of the Kolchak government, Ataman Semenov with his Cossack retainers, and sundry White Russians who later collaborated with the Japanese. Papa never thought much of them, and it is not surprising that he preferred to steer clear of the tangled politics that they brought with them to the Harbin émigré scene.

But remaining inactive was out of character for Papa. Shortly after arriving in Harbin he agreed to act as a liaison officer with the Chinese and Japanese authorities in Manchuria on matters pertaining to the White Russian refugee camps in Kirin (Chilin) and Hunchun. In that capacity he often had to travel to Mukden (Shenyang) and Peking (Beijing). Mukden was closer to the Chinese and Japanese government centers with which he had to deal on matters pertaining to the resettlement program. There, he also found a more permanent position. Boris Ostroumov, the Russian director of the Chinese Eastern Railroad, offered Papa an administrative position at the railroad's Mukden terminus. He had known Papa during the Civil War when Papa was Chief of Supply of the White Army, and was certain Papa could handle the tangled logistics of the Mukden terminus. In our family album there is a photograph of Papa, for the first time in mufti, sitting behind a desk with a large map of Manchuria and the railroad network at his back. In December 1924 the family permanently moved to a large comfortable house in Mukden belonging to the railroad.

For the first time in four years, Papa and Mama began living a life that Papa liked to call "normal." After nearly five years of separations, fleeting reunions, and days of grinding and paralyzing anxiety about each other's fate during the Civil War, they were now together raising a family and trying to make the best out of what was in reality still a very unstable situation. They were married on July 19, 1919, in Cheliabinsk on the eastern slope of the Ural Mountains a few days before the crucial battle of Cheliabinsk that sealed the fate of the White movement in eastern European Russia and Siberia. They had originally met some months earlier in Asha on the western slope of the Ural Mountains after the unsuccessful White spring offensive that same year. Mama was a twenty-seven year old army nurse dispatched to Asha from Orenburg to escort a contingent of wounded soldiers to the Orenburg Military Hospital. Papa, ten years older, was chief-of-staff of the retreating 6th Ural Corps. In early July of 1919 fate had thrown them together again, this time at my maternal grandfather's town house in Cheliabinsk that served as a temporary White Army command post. Mama was on home leave from her work at the Orenburg Military Hospital. Papa had just been promoted to Major General and was waiting for an assignment to a new post. As marriages go, it was a shake of the dice. There were no joyful rides for them on a troika that were so much a part of the Russian courting custom, no romantic walks in the park, no family festivities, no engagement balls. The White spring offensive had ended in failure and the White Army -- still 75,000 to 80,000 strong -- was in retreat hoping to make a stand in the Cheliabinsk highlands. The honeymoon -- if you want to call it that -- lasted but a few days with Papa rushing to the front and a separation that continued until December when they were again reunited during the harrowing "March of Ice" through the Siberian wasteland. Through blizzards, snowdrifts and sub-zero temperatures, sometimes on horseback, at other times by sled, they moved east with the remnants of the White Army through the most inhospitable expanse of central Siberia. Describing the experience, Papa would often remark that Pasternak's depiction of the Siberian winter in *Doctor Zhivago* did not even come close to their ordeal. At Krasnoiarsk, during the battle for the city, Mama managed a front line first aid station and, on the river Kan, marched shoulder to shoulder with the exhausted troops and the sleds carrying the sick and the wounded. Describing the retreat from Krasnoiarsk, Mama colorfully noted in a memoir that "the army was like a tired-out wolf driven by borzois whirling around in the snow and looking for an escape route." A few days before the spent army reached Lake Baikal, together with thousands of other White soldiers and fleeing civilians, she was stricken with typhus. Papa gave up his command responsibilities and for the next three weeks personally nursed his delirious wife to health.

II

Mukden, the largest city in Manchuria where they settled after leaving Harbin, was Marshall Chang Tso-lin's headquarters. The "Old Marshall," as he was often referred to in the foreign press in contrast to his son, the "Young Marshall", was a bandit warlord who had risen since 1911 to the top of the Chinese military leadership under the aegis of the Japanese. He was unfailingly anti-communist and sympathetic to the needs of the recently arrived White Russian refugees, many of whom were artillery officers who easily found employment in his munitions factories and as artillery instructors in his army. In 1924, when Papa and Mama settled in Mukden, the Japanese had a sizable presence in the city, but on the whole still maintained a low profile by staying out of the day-to-day direct control, carrying garrison duty on the Southern Chinese Railroad that they had built in southern Manchuria. The local government remained in the hands of Chang Tso-lin.

Papa's position with the Chinese Eastern Railroad did not last long. In mid-1924, the Chinese annulled the old lease arrangement and agreed to manage the Chinese Eastern Railroad jointly with the Soviet Union. For many of the railroad workers the change of ownership had little visible effect on their lives, even though they now had to take out Soviet passports or accept nominal Chinese citizenship. The vast majority, because of their technical knowledge and lack of other opportunities, stayed on and continued to run the railroad. For Papa staying on was out of the question. Even if he had agreed to accept Chinese citizenship he would not have been acceptable to the Soviet partners because of his marked anti-Bolshevik record during the Civil War. Nor would he have agreed to remain with the railroad because of his obvious hostility toward anything that had even only a perfunctory connection to the Soviet Union. The comforts of the large house and the tenuous security of the job with the railroad were now history. He had to find a new profession, a new undertaking, a new way of making a living. Making life even more uncertain was Mama's new pregnancy. On November 4, 1924, Mama gave birth to another son, Nickita, who eventually became known as Nick to friends and family.

Unlike many others who suddenly found themselves without any employment prospects because of the change in the railroad's ownership, Papa was fortunate. For about a year he worked for a private foreign company that was importing heavy industrial equipment to Manchuria, and then opened a photo studio. He had an interest in photography since its early days when as a young officer stationed in Finland he had been testing new photo processes and experimenting with color photography. At the turn of the XXth century, the Russians had a substantial lead in the field of developing color prints. Photography was Tsar Nicholas II's hobby. The famous Russian writer and playwright Leonid Andreyev was taking stereoscopic photographs in color as early as 1909, using the technique patented by the Lumiere brothers. As an intelligence officer on the eastern front during World War I, Papa pioneered aerial photography, actually flying over enemy lines in an open Farman, built by the French for observation purposes. Over the years he had accumulated a large and important collection of photographs which would have been priceless had it survived the Civil War. Unfortunately, together with all his military decorations and Mama's and his personal documents, the collection was lost during the fateful battle for Krasnoiarsk in central Siberia. The hobby now became the means to his family's livelihood. Selling Mama's remaining jewels and borrowing all he could get from friends and former colleagues, Papa opened a photo studio. I was too young to remember the early years of the new endeavor, but by the age of five or six, I was very much aware of what Papa was doing. Located on Chiyodo Dori in the Japanese section of Mukden, the studio proudly displayed in English the name " P. P. Petroff Photo Studio" on the marquee over the entrance to the building.

The business prospered. Papa was the only European photographer in Mukden and his clientele included not only Russian immigrants in the city, but almost all foreign business representatives -- Americans, Englishmen, Germans, Czechoslovaks and the French -- who sold automobiles, munitions and heavy industrial equipment to Chang Tso-lin. Papa also had the patronage of the Old Marshall and his son who would periodically call on him to take an official state photograph for release to the foreign press. I have a clear recollection of Marshall Chiang Hsueh-liang's arrival at the studio. In dress uniform, with all his medals and ribbons, the Young Marshall pulled up one day in a large chauffeur-driven Packard in front of the building, entered the studio and sat in for a portrait session. It was probably sometime in early 1928. My brother Nick and I hid behind the back door of the studio savoring every minute of what looked to us as a most auspicious occasion.

By Mukden standards life was pleasant, comfortable, and even gracious. By 1927 we had a cook and an amah. Our family quarters were above the studio, warm even in the midst of the bitterly cold Manchurian winter. The summers were hot, often terribly humid, much like the summers in our American Midwest. On weekends we traveled -- sometimes by hired taxi, at others with friends who had access to a private auto -- to what was generally referred as "the river," the Hung Ho, a narrow waterway that cascaded swiftly over the flood plain in the spring, but ran sluggishly in the summer. There I first learned to swim, to appreciate the outdoors with its sudden summer showers and thunderstorms, and to enjoy the sunsets and informal dinners with *uha* (Russia's quintessential fish soup) made with crayfish that we caught in the river, dark bread, cucumber salad, and a surprise desert that our cook Jan would prepare for the occasion. During the year, we celebrated all of the Christian holidays, according to the old Julian calendar -- Christmas, Easter, Assumption, and the various saints' days. I remember the decorated tree on Christmas, but the details of the Christmas festivities escape me now. For some unknown reason I have a much more lucid and unclouded recollection of Easter, that most mysterious and grand holiday which connotes for all Russians not only that "Christ has Risen," but also reminds them, just as it did their pagan ancestors, that winter had passed and spring has finally broken out of its long and wintery mantle. To this day my recollection of holy week in Mukden remains vivid: the candlelight church procession at the evening service before Pussy-willow Sunday,[1] the traditional family fast during the last week of Lent, the panic and trepidation of my first confession and communion, the mournful a cappella music of the Saturday liturgy, and the resplendent crescendo of the midnight Easter service in the magnificent rotunda of the church that had been specially illuminated and decorated for the occasion. I have not kept up the faith of my Russian ancestors, but the centuries-old Orthodox ritual which I first witnessed in Mukden somehow refuses to desert my memory even today. Spring, especially late Spring, was our worst season. Unprotected by mountains or rolling hill tops, the Manchurian plane has a way of spawning powerful wind storms in the spring with massive clouds of fine dust from which there is no easy escape. Dust gets into everything: fingernails, hair, clothing, windows, the internal workings of the house, and even one's nose and mouth. I remember days in Mukden when the dust was so thick that you could not even see the sun.

I have a less vivid recollection of the Mukden émigré community, but from conversations with parents and from reading and archival collections, I believe that Russian Mukden in the early 1920s was a community of about one thousand families, almost exclusively military, whose customs and traditions were followed meticulously by the entire enclave. Religious life, centered at first around the stately white marble church at the Russian military cemetery, followed the age-old rituals of the Russian Orthodox faith. The cemetery had been built in 1905 to bury the Russian dead at the Battle of Mukden during the Russo-Japanese War. As the most senior military officer in the community Papa was an honorary elder of the church and we participated actively in most of its activities. Other churches were built later to accommodate the growing Russian population. Schools were opened as early as 1924, and by 1927 Russian Mukden had a fully operating *real gymnasium* which was coeducational and included military training for the senior boys. Wearing the traditional Russian high neck uniform and leather belt with a polished buckle, I spent my one and only year in a Russian school as a *prigotavishka (preppie)* in 1929-1930, enviously watching the older boys drilling with rifles in the school playing field. Mama, who had been an early devotee of Maria Montessori, opened a Montessori school for the younger children and, with the help of two young officers who were single, organized a summer camp for the eight to twelve-year-olds. An officers' club was soon opened and regimental holidays were meticulously observed. Convinced that their services would someday be again called for in a new Russia cleansed of its Bolshevik interlopers, most young officers attended courses in military science organized by their senior colleagues. Except but for a few members of the émigré community, the Russian enclave had very little contact with other Europeans most of whom lived in segregated compounds in the international section of the city. The annual Invalids Ball that the Russian community staged in Mukden to raise money for their old and disabled was the sole means of contact with other foreigners living in Manchuria. A gala affair -- often costumed, with guitars, balalaikas, fancy Russian cooking and the proverbial vodka -- it was always well attended by the non-Russian foreign community of the city.

Our family was a closely knit circle, organically bound by blood and firmly fused together by the unique circumstances arising out of the White defeat. There were no grandparents, uncles, aunts and cousins to enrich our family life. They were left behind in Russia never to be seen again. Papa had last seen his family in the spring of 1918, Mama in the late summer of 1919 when, together with the 4th Infantry Division that Papa commanded, she left Cheliabinsk for the front. Communication by mail was at best limited, and after 1927, nonexistent. With the scrapping of the NEP, the launching of the massive collectivization program, and the onset of relentless reprisals and arrests in 1928, our relatives in Russia wrote Papa and Mama begging them not to write because each letter from abroad led to a confrontation with the CHEKA, the predecessor of the KGB, and the risk of being branded an "enemy of the people." In April 1927, there was another addition to the family with the birth of my youngest brother Dmitri, Mama's and Papa's youngest son who became known first as Mai, then

11

Mike, and finally Michael D, a name that many years later he formally adopted when he graduated from University of California in Berkeley. According to the family official chronicle, our Chinese cook Jan was responsible for that transformation. As the story goes, it was Jan who used to call out "Mai" (come in Chinese) to the little fellow, rewarding him with a cookie when the boy made several steps forward. When someone asked my baby brother what his name was, he said "Mai," and the name stuck, giving him a new identity.

The Petroffs were an unusually large family as émigré families went. Most couples in Mukden were childless or at most had one or two children because they did not feel secure enough to bring children into the chaotic and unstable life in immigration. Papa and Mama did not feel that way. They maintained a positive attitude despite the uncertainty of their lives and insisted after losing everything they owned and treasured that their children were their real capital, their precious inheritance and gift to future generations. They nurtured this inheritance lovingly but firmly, relying on traditions that they had inherited from their parents. In an environment that at times looked almost artificially created to justify the idea that it was still possible to return to Russia and recapture the lost Zeitgeist that they had left behind, we read epic folk tales about herculean Russian heroes of antiquity, children's stories out of Pushkin and the marvelous fables of Ivan Krylov, Russia's La Fontaine. There was no radio, no television. Reading was the primary source of information, and we learned to read very early in our lives. I remember paging through a large atlas bound in leather that Papa found in a second hand store in Harbin. By the time I was seven I knew the names of almost every country in Europe, Asia and the Americas, an accomplishment that would be much harder to duplicate today. There were no more than sixty nation states in the world to commit to memory in the 1920s, not the one hundred ninety that decolonization and ethnic segregation created after World War II. We were also schooled in the history of Russia's great men and women and in the epic of the Russian Civil War which to Papa and Mama always remained the definitive experience of their precarious lives.

The Civil War was a bitter and unforgiving memory for Papa and Mama. What started with great success on the Volga in 1918 turned into a painful and disastrous rout a year and one half later, rupturing their lives, upsetting their personal goals and ambitions, and separating them from their national roots and family nests. Despite the joyful diversion of raising three boys whom they treasured and loved very dearly, they found it difficult not to look back at what they had gone through during four and one half years of civil strife. The Civil War hung over them like an ominous black cloud that constantly constrained them to internalize their war experiences in an attempt to uncover the real reason for the White defeat. Neither of them blamed the Allies for their indecisiveness and failure to provide the aid they had promised when the outcome of World War I was still a toss-up. They were both honest enough to put the blame where it actually belonged. Mama condemned the command structure, the constant political and tactical bickering of the White leaders, the lack of organizational discipline, and what she liked to call the "whole chaotic mess" that was part of the White central government and headquarters command. Too often, she said "the right hand did not know what the left hand was doing." Papa was more circumspect in his judgment. He ascribed the White failure to the lack of a unified, clearly focused and universally understood White credo in opposition to the distorted slogans of Bolshevik propaganda about a class war that was to put an end to the horrible exploitation of the workers and the peasants. In a war that was not territorial but ideological, he felt that the White leadership failed to articulate a clearly defined belief that they were fighting for. The reconvening of the Constituent Assembly was too abstract a concept for most people. The strongly nationalist rhetoric that the principal objective of the White armies was the restoration of a "united, indivisible and mighty Russia" was also a poor excuse for a unifying principle of the White cause. It was of little interest to many of the fighting men and women in the White Army who came from a diversity of social and ethnic backgrounds. In a more professional vein, Papa also recognized the inadequacy of White manpower, transport, and industrial resources to pursue the war indefinitely. To have won the war, he said, "The White army had to trounce the Reds in the first six months of the encounter. Beyond that, time was on the side of the Bolsheviks, not the Whites." Superior White generalship failed to make up for the lack of manpower reserves and munitions, forcing thousands of White soldiers and officers to leave Russia and seek a political haven abroad.

As children, Nick and I -- Mike was still too young when we lived in China -- heard our parents' discussions, eavesdropped on their debates with visiting colleagues, soaked up the pathos of their experience, fantasized and acted out the events of their long and exhausting march to the Chinese border. They, on their part, did not discourage our interest in their experience. They had not yet lost the hope of returning home to Russia and recapturing their way of life. In the family album there is a wonderful photograph of my brother Nick and me standing at attention in play military uniforms made of paper. I am wearing the shoulder straps of a major general with two stars on a zigzag background and a St. George cross on my chest. Nick, wearing the shoulder straps of a junior officer, holds his right hand in a military salute.

There were teas, dinners, and holiday galas – congenial segments of Papa's and Mama's uncertain lives – that we witnessed with a touch of curiosity and gratification as they entertained their Civil War colleagues and friends. Invariably, the guests would address Papa as "Your Excellency," an honorary title reserved in pre-revolution Russia for high ranking civil servants and generals. When that happened, Papa would usually wave his hands and say in all seriousness: "What kind of excellencies are you talking about ...the honorary title is a thing of the past, cast away a long time ago by the Revolution and what we went through during the past decade." But they could not put a stop to that old-fashioned practice. It was part of their upbringing since the days when they were young cadets in military school. It was second nature to them; in a way it defined not only Papa, but also their own lost status as officers and military professionals. Mama, on her part, enjoyed the solemnity and exaltation and found unrestrained pleasure in the title. To her Papa was a hero, a courageous leader who brought his men out of Bolshevik captivity She often talked to us about it, and reminded us that we were special -- sons of a general and therefore different from other children. Like Papa, we were destined to be leaders who someday would also have to overcome adversity. Our goal in life was to set an example for other children and learn to be leaders like him, quite a trip to lay on youngsters whose main interest in life was unrestricted play.

It is not at all surprising therefore that a strand of this early experience became part of the fabric that defined my life. I accepted the special status very early in childhood and many years later when adversity threatened, I almost always thought of Papa and how he would react to the situation. His reaction to confrontations that could easily get out of hand was distinctly disciplined. He was calm, reserved, and unusually polite even when there was really no ostensible need for politeness. Recalling her finishing school code of ethics, Mama called his reserved behavior "*bonne mine a mauvais jeu* – showing good face to foul play." We were brought up on that exhortation. We were encouraged to remain well mannered and cordial regardless of how unsavory and rude we found our opponent. It was not always an easy rule to follow. Sometimes, I failed miserably, but it was a worthy goal to aspire to, and it served me well throughout my entire life.

My interest in the Russian revolution and civil war also never faded. For a long time it remained in a state of hibernation, but as I neared retirement I began to read widely on the subject, taking every opportunity to acquaint myself with what was being published in the West and the Soviet Union. Upon retirement, I returned to college, earned undergraduate and graduate degrees in history with emphasis on 20th century Russia, and after nearly five years of research wrote a comprehensive history of the Russian Civil War in Eastern European Russia and Siberia.[2]

I dedicated my book to my parents. I don't think I could have written it had I not personally witnessed their soul-searching and grief over the failure of what they considered a just cause. My work grew to fruition under the virtual tutelage of their recollections and reminisces without them ever knowing that their experience became an inspiration for me. Psychologically, those early years in exile were an extremely difficult time for them, but they somehow managed to make our young lives not only an extension of their own unique experience during a terrible civil war, but also were able to provide the underpinnings of a stable and sound life for us. They did this in an orderly and meaningful manner that was full of love and disciplined care. Mama would often read to us before bedtime and Papa amused us with Gogolesque stories out of his peasant past. Crying was not allowed in our family. It was looked upon as a sign of debility that had to be always kept under control. Our upbringing was stoical in the full sense of that dispassionate word. We were expected to observe the traditional and uncompromising aims that most military families followed everywhere: duty, honor and the flag. Because we were émigrés torn away from the land of our ancestors and cut off from our cultural capital, the flag was somewhat more abstract and less ubiquitous, but it did not prevent Papa and Mama from reminding us of its proud legacy. Many years later, I could understand their feelings better when I saw how émigré Cubans in Miami or Vietnamese in California venerated their national flags. The concept of duty was inculcated systematically, both through discussions and by example.

We did not resist the rigorous discipline, nor the emphasis on honor and duty. We accepted them as part of our upbringing largely because there were no other ideals, standards or diversions that competed with our way of life. As a child, I did have a nasty temper that occasionally got in the way. When I exploded, Mama tried to sweet-talk me, while Papa appealed to reason and jokingly called me "Yozhik (little porcupine)." I sulked, but it rarely lasted very long, and in the end I usually blamed myself and apologized. Both Papa and Mama had a deep sense of social responsibility. In Mukden and everywhere else where we lived prior to our coming to America, they never forgot their obligations to the less fortunate Russian immigrants who found themselves disbursed by the Revolution throughout the non-Communist world. In Mukden, our home was a constant haven for displaced Russian refugees who stopped in for a few days and sometimes stayed longer waiting for the right moment to move again. The travelers' room, as we learned to call it, was almost always occupied by someone. Why I did not rebel against the excessive discipline and rigidly structured way of life, I find difficult to explain. It was probably because I adored my parents, empathized with them, knowing what they had to give up and how hard they had to work, and recognized that they always thought first of our needs in an environment that was far from conducive to what most people would call normal family life. They loved us unconditionally and treated me as an adult from the very first days that I can remember.

Papa put in long days in the studio. The dark room was his inner sanctum and we were forbidden to enter it. But as boys everywhere, we sneaked in occasionally to see for ourselves what was taking place in that mysterious room with red lights, black curtains, fancy equipment and the powerful smell of photographic chemicals. The neatly hanging film drying after development, the trays with floating prints, and the large enlargement camera were objects of great curiosity to us. Papa would often demonstrate how photography worked, but seeing for ourselves the various ingredients that went into making a picture was much more exciting, especially when it was done clandestinely and in the absence of parents.

Mama managed the household with an iron hand and directed, what seemed to us children, myriads of charities and social undertakings that were staffed by women volunteers. Telephones were a rarity in Mukden and most of the organizational work had to be done in person. When Mama was away attending meetings or running errands, we were entrusted to the care of the maid, a lilliputian Chinese woman wearing black pants, a white over blouse and tiny pointed cloth slippers covering her diminutive feet that had been tightly wrapped since childhood to prevent their growth. She spoke haltingly in pigeon-Russian, calling me Yozha, and my brothers, Nika and Maika. Mama was universally respected and got along with all kinds of people. She treated everyone with the same amount of concern and deference, the conceited and unassuming, the cultured and backward, and the old and young. The festivities on July 24, her saint's day, were a tangible proof of that respect. A procession of friends, volunteer coworkers and community elders came to pay their respect on that day. Bearing bouquets of gladioli and boxes of chocolate which Nick and I always waited to raid, they came to taste the pirogi and the other Russian delicacies that Jan had created for the large table set for the occasion in the garden behind the studio. The warm July night that seemed to last forever, the sound of cicadas, the laughter, the toasts, and Mama in a silk summer dress with an over-sized corsage of white carnations pinned to its bodice is a tableau I find even now hard to forget.

I believe Mama always had a following. Outgoing, self-assured and at ease in the most diverse of social encounters, with a boundless energy for volunteer work that most people tried to bypass, she was a natural leader. She was born into a family of merchants, industrialists, and bankers whose ancestors had migrated from central Russia to the southern Urals after the Napoleonic wars in the early years of nineteenth Century. Her hometown, Troitsk, was founded in the XVIIIth century on the river Yui in the southern Ural region as a military outpost for a system of fortifications built to protect the streaming wave of settlers from the nomadic Kirghis and Kazakh hordes of Central Asia who, from time to time, pushed northward, trying to stop Russia's expansion into Asia. By the second half of the 19th century Troitsk was a bustling frontier town – a Russian stop on the Silk Route where caravans of as many as 4,000 camels came to trade silk, lustrous taffetas, ornamental rugs, and spices for metal utensils and armaments produced in the Ural foundries. The annual fair with its colorful crowds of Tatars, Bashkirs, Kirghis in native costumes, Cossacks in embroidered shirts and flowing bloomers, soldiers in dress uniform, and settlers in their Sunday best, was the third largest fair in all of the Russian empire. Vestiges of that splendor are still to be found in the old section of Troitsk with its old trading yards, wide tree-lined avenues, imposing mansions of local merchants, and shaded city squares where horses could be tied to hitching posts in front of baroque style hotels and government buildings that looked like they had been lifted from the streets of Paris. The house in which Mama was born still stands on the corner of Monastyrsky and Markov streets, renamed by the Soviets in 1919 to Rosa Luxenberg Street – in honor of the famous German revolutionary -- and Pavel Poprugi Street. Who Poprugi was I never could find out when I visited Troitsk in 2005. The widow's walk is gone, the glass in the large intricately carved windows is badly damaged, the imposing granite entrance looks like someone had used a sledge hammer to make the stone stairway impassable, and the roof has been patched up many times by galvanized iron and copper plate. It's a far cry from its days of 19th century grandeur, although I was told that a local entrepreneur had purchased it recently from the government, and plans to convert in into apartments, an emerging capitalist endeavor that is taking place today all over Russia.

Mama had a privileged and enlightened upbringing. Her father studied in Germany at the University of Heidelberg, traveled widely, and had friends in high places. Upon returning to Russia in the early 1890s, he took control of the family business interests that included a steam-powered flour mill with a capacity of producing 48,000,000 kilograms of flour per year, a lumber mill, and the construction of a railroad that ran through Troitsk from Chelyabinsk to the cities of Central Asia. A loyal supporter of Count Sergei Witte, he pushed for more rapid industrialization and strongly resented the conservative influence of Russia's leisure classes at the courts of Alexander III and Nicholas II. Having personally witnessed what was taking place in Germany during Bismarck's stewardship, he represented a new species of Russian entrepreneur who sought reform, criticized government corruption, and strongly believed in universal education.

At the tender age of eight Mama was packed off to Kazan and the Radionov Institute which, like the Smolin in St. Petersburg, occupied a very special place in the life of Russia's upper class women. There she received a first rate classical education, acquired a strong feeling of *noblesse oblige* and polished up her German and French which she had learned from a tutor in early childhood. She graduated in 1908, second in her class, with a silver medal for excellence, and returned to Troitsk where she immersed herself in volunteer social work at the local hospital. In 1913 the University of Kazan -- Lenin's alma mater -- opened its doors to women and Mama returned to Kazan to study medicine. World War I put an end to her studies at the university. She joined the newly formed Army Nursing Corps, spending most of the war on the Galician front and at the Orenburg Military Hospital in the southern Urals. Small, athletic -- she was an excellent horse woman -- she was independent, reform-minded and not afraid of standing up for her beliefs. Had she been born an American instead of Russian she would have probably been an active supporter of Susan B. Anthony, the tireless American suffragette leader of the early 20th century.

Papa's background was very different. His parents were hard-working semi-literate peasants eking out a living in Pskov province, a region with a long history of wars and resistance against military invasions from the west. He was born only a few kilometers from Lake Ladoga, on whose frozen expanse of ice and snow, immortalized in the world of music by Sergei Prokofiev's polyphonic cantata, Prince Alexander Nevsky made a stand against the Teutonic knights in the thirteenth century. During the Livonian War in the sixteenth century, Pskov and its surroundings were invaded by the Polish troops of Stefan Batory, and not far from Pskov, in the first years of the eighteenth century, Peter the Great stopped Charles the XIIth of Sweden from making any further incursions into northern Russia. The twentieth century did not put an end to invasions by foreign armies. During World War I and World War II, the region was occupied by the Germans. In World War II, the occupation lasted more than three years, and when the defeated Nazis left Russian soil, they poisoned the wells and burned Papa's village down to its stone foundations. When Bunny and I visited the village in 1989, it had been rebuilt, but only the old folks remained in the restored village. When I asked an old man who had survived the war how it was during the German occupation, he scratched his head saying: "During the day we had to cope with the Gestapo and, during the night, with the partisans. It was not a life I would want to lead again."

Pskov and its surroundings escaped serfdom; nor did it witness the Mongol invasion that lasted nearly 300 years in the rest of Russia. It was too far north of the black earth regions of central Russia for massive agricultural exploitation through serfdom, and the Mongols never succeeded in reaching Russia's northern settlements beyond Moscow. Tall, blond, independent, probably with a trace of Swedish, Finnish and Estonian blood, Pskovites raised flax and a poor quality of wheat – the region was too far north for high grade wheat – tended livestock, and went to church. Papa's mother was devoutly religious and often made the nearly sixty kilometer journey on foot to pray and meditate at the Pechory Monastery, one of Russia's most famous ancient cultural centers that still stands today completely refurbished and restored , a shining example of ancient Russia's artistic heritage. His father, a stern disciplinarian who drank only on feast days, raised flax and wheat during the spring and summer. In the winter, he tailored, using a Singer sewing machine that was looked upon as a wonder of wonders by the peasants of the neighboring villages. He had bought it on credit from a traveling Singer Company salesman at the turn of the 19th century.

The village was Papa's early childhood provenance. In the autobiographical sketch he left to me and my brothers, he noted that the "village was badly in need of literacy and enlightenment. Whatever was of value came from the church, passed by word of mouth from generation to generation, through strict adherence to an established order of life and tradition. Unfortunately, the church concerned itself more with ritual and not with the education of its parishioners." It was from such a beginning that Papa crossed over into the ranks of Russia's pre-revolutionary elite, through hard work, superior intelligence, an advanced military education, and a certain amount of good luck. A precocious village lad who learned to read early, by age ten, he became the assistant to the school's only teacher, helping him with the younger children of the village. At the age of fifteen, Papa made his debut in the administrative apparatus of rural Russia by being appointed clerk to the head of the regional Zemstvo, the local administrative and judicial organ of rural Russia. Thus began a transformation which five years later led him to the equivalency exam and the prestigious *Vladimirovskoye Voyennoye Pehotnoye Uchilishche* (Vladimir Infantry Military Academy) in St. Petersburg from which he graduated in 1906 ninth in his class as cadet master sergeant. He could have probably done better, he often explained, if he had early training in French and German, but lacking that experience, languages were always a problem for him. Commissioned second lieutenant at Tsarskoye Selo at a commencement exercise attended by Tsar Nicholas II, he was now an officer and gentleman. In the autobiographical sketch he left to us children, he recalls with a certain amount of levity how on returning to his village after graduation to see his parents, he was startled to hear the coachman whom he had known since early childhood address him as "your honor," a formal greeting with which he was not yet entirely comfortable. The salutation was, of course, not egalitarian, but that was the way the class structure worked at the beginning of the Twentieth century, not only in Russia but in most of Europe. Too late to serve in the war with Japan, Papa was posted to Finland where, at the turn of the century, Swedish culture was still de rigueur.

In 1910 he returned to St. Petersburg invigorated by the experience but unconvinced that what he saw in Finland would work in Russia whose population was still predominantly peasant and only recently emancipated from serfdom. Citing episodes from his early childhood, he would argue convincingly through most of his life that before Russia could seriously consider western-style democracy Russian peasants had to discover a new identity as responsible yeomen farmers capable of managing their own economic and political lives. The Stolypin reforms of 1906-1910, he would often say "were a step in the right direction, despite the criticism leveled at them by the revolutionary parties of the left. They created hundreds of thousands of new independent peasant farmers, not enough unfortunately to achieve democracy in the Russian countryside." The post-Soviet Russia of today is still struggling with the same problem, complicated by seventy-five years of collectivization and absence of land ownership.

In Finland, he developed a taste for art, music and theater, and a compelling ambition to succeed. He did not want to spend the rest of his life as a forgotten subaltern at some remote outpost of the Russian Empire in the Caucasus or distant Siberia. Two years at the Imperial War College[3] guaranteed his aspirations. He graduated from the Imperial War College in 1913 and was appointed to the Russian Imperial General Staff in St. Petersburg. To make us children understand what that appointment meant to him, he would show us the Faberge-designed silver emblem with the double-headed eagle that the Tsar personally handed out to each graduate at a gala reception upon graduation. "Right or wrong," he would then comment, "this insignia was my *carte blanche,* my entry ticket to the inner chambers of Russia's upper social strata." The defeat in World War I and the October Revolution brought Colonel Petroff to First Army Headquarters in Samara, where in the wake of the spreading Civil War he joined the People's Army of the local anti-Bolshevik Socialist Revolutionary (SR) government, and, when it collapsed six months later, the White Army of Admiral Kolchak. He could not accept the October Revolution. Like many other thinking Russians he recognized the ineptitude and backwardness of the Imperial government, but he could not justify what was happening in Russia in the name of liberty and freedom for all. To him the Bolshevik coup d'etat was morally reprehensible and in opposition to the Provisional Government's promise of a Constituent Assembly to determine what kind of rule Russia should have. He often said that he could serve any form of democratic government -- including socialist -- but Leninism and its latter day derivative of Stalinism were anathema to him. Deliberate, analytical, with a high tolerance for physical and psychological discomfort, Papa liked to arrive at his conclusions carefully and did not enjoy small talk. "The less said the better," he would often comment, "most people are not interested in long and tedious explanations." Mama, on the other hand, made her decisions quickly and almost instinctively, accompanying them by lengthy and intense arguments to make her point.

Despite the contradictions of their dissimilar upbringing and differences in personality, Papa and Mama made an excellent team. Mama's spontaneity and electrifying fervor complemented Papa's more deliberate and balanced approach to life. Politically, they were moderates who eschewed extremism. Unrelenting monarchists committed to the restoration of the Romanov dynasty[4] and fascists of the far right, or radical Social Revolutionaries and Mensheviks on the left were not people they admired or trusted. They fought the Civil War under the mantle of the Constituent Assembly that Lenin had dissolved in 1918, and they were still committed to the same idea. "Russia's future," they said, "must be decided by a democratically elected Constituent Assembly, not by a contentious party or political faction that was interested only in power and unwilling to function democratically in a climate of political pluralism." They had adapted themselves to life in exile better than most émigrés, but this did not mean that they were completely reconciled to that life. They tried to live in the present for the children, but this was not always possible. There were days when, for one reason or another, they could not avoid turning back to their roots in the native land that they left behind. They longed to see again the Russian countryside depicted so well in the oils of Isaac Levitan, the groves of fluttering birches, and the bright blue church domes with their golden crosses glittering in the sun. Papa, especially, missed the quiet charm of the Russian countryside; it's not surprising that a reproduction of A. I. Kuinzhe's famous oil painting "The Birch Grove" hung in our dining room. Both also longed for the good-natured revelry of family holidays and the rich city life that they had left behind. Mama missed the untroubled elegance of the family mansion in which she grew up, the graceful vista of the undulating spaciousness of the southern Urals, and the exhilarating morning rides on horseback through the boundless steppe bordering Asia. Papa found it difficult to adjust to civilian life and its lack of hierarchic structure. Like most married couples they often had differences of opinion, but they would almost always find common ground. "*Devant les enfants* (In front of the children)" Mama would say in French to Papa, implying that their conversation was not for our ears. They would then either stop their discussion or switch into Mama's rapid-fire French and Papa's halting rejoinder to conclude what they had started to say in Russian. There was one discord, one bone of contention however, that they found increasingly difficult to negotiate. Exploiting every spare hour away from the photo studio on the affairs of the community and the émigré military alliance, Papa continued to play an active role in a number of world-wide émigré organizations that were involved in the struggle against the Soviet Union. His contacts in these organizations brought him in touch with White Russian leaders in Europe, the United States and Australia, and reinforced his hope of some day returning to Russia. Mama, on the other hand, was slowly losing that hope. More practical and pragmatic than Papa about the nature of their exile, she was beginning to feel that the portals to Russia were permanently closed and that even if they did open, they would find a very different and alien Russia from the one they had left behind. She wanted a more permanent domicile. She did not want her three boys to end up like so many other émigrés, driving taxis or waiting table; she wanted them to be properly educated and permanently settled to experience a more satisfying life. Papa resisted, arguing that it was too early to make any long-term commitments, that the political situation in Russia was still fluid and, under favorable conditions, a return was still possible. "Not to recognize that is to throw in the towel prematurely," he maintained, "admit defeat and move away to a distant land from which there would be no chance of return." The dissension on this crucial issue did not diminish. Papa stubbornly stuck to his position, Mama steadily moved away from it. An inescapable estrangement was gathering steam.

In the meantime, the political situation in Mukden was becoming less stable. Under the influence of growing Chinese nationalism, Marshall Chang Tso-lin gradually moved farther and farther away from his Japanese handlers toward a rapprochement with Chiang Kai-shek. By 1928 Chiang Kai-shek had unified most of China proper and was now looking to Manchuria as the next step to achieve China's full unification through the containment of the warlords who had been ruling the peripheral regions of China since 1916. For obvious reasons, the Japanese Kwantung Army[5] did not look kindly at the rapprochement. It remained in southern Manchuria after the War with Russia, allegedly to protect Japan's investment in the Southern Manchurian Railroad, but in actuality it was doing everything possible -- politically and economically -- to make Manchuria an integral part of Japan's expanding empire. Its leadership -- especially a small group of the army's firebrands --envisioned Manchuria as an autonomous buffer state under Japanese protection shielding Japan and China from neighboring Russia and the threat of communism. Their plan recognized that Manchuria could be an important supply base of raw materials, a human outlet for Japan's burgeoning population and a major market for her finished goods.

On June 28, 1928, Chang's train was dynamited near Mukden, fatally injuring the Old Marshall. The Western press generally placed the blame on Japan and its operatives in Manchuria, but the opening of KGB archives in Moscow since the break-up of the Soviet Union suggests a different story. It appears that the dynamiting of Marshall Chang Tso-Lin's train was the work of Soviet agents who were ordered to kill the Old Marshall because of his intense anti-communist posture in Chinese internal politics. The elimination of Chang Tso-Lin was obviously in Japan's interest. It created a political vacuum in the region that made it possible for the Japanese to move into Manchuria. The full take-over did not come about until March 1932 when Japan finally proclaimed Manchuria an independent nation and placed P'u-yi, the last Ch'ing emperor of China on the throne. However, the assassination of the Old Marshall started a chain of events that eventually led to 1932. It set aside all local political constraints almost immediately and allowed the Japanese military to act as they pleased. As more Japanese businessmen, colonists, and government officials arrived in Manchuria, the Kwantung Army dropped all previously disguised pretenses of carrying out only garrison duty and openly began working for the annexation of Manchuria. Mukden was suddenly swarming with Japanese soldiers and the Hinomaru -- Japan's national flag -- now brazenly flew throughout many districts of Mukden. Standing in front of our studio on Chiyodo Dori, I often saw Japanese soldiers marching through the city's streets. One scene has left a particularly indelible imprint. I remember how a Japanese regiment in parade uniform with its regimental colors in front passed by our studio. What amazed me was the condition of the regimental standard. All that was left of it was the outer border with its gold cording frayed by time and dulled by the sun. To a little boy of six or seven its damaged condition did not make sense. I remember turning to Papa for an explanation. "The Japanese whipped us in the Straits of Tsushima," he replied casually "but on land, our lads made their victory in Manchuria a costly venture. That standard was probably ripped by Russian bullets at the Battle of Mukden."

As far as our family was concerned, there did not seem to be any immediate repercussions arising out of the assassination of Chang Tso-lin. Orders for photographic work continued to pour in as in previous years. In the summer of 1929, we even managed to spend a full month vacationing in Rakkotan, a small village outside of Dairen (Dalien) on the shores of the Ta Lien Bay. Playing in the sand, walking at low tide through the shallow waters, hiding behind huge boulders that peppered the shoreline, and eating dinner outdoors on the veranda of the Chinese farm house that we rented for the summer was a pleasant diversion from the hot and sultry summers of the Manchurian plain. But in the fall of 1929, the political situation in Mukden worsened, and our family's good fortunes again came under assault. Ignoring the demands of the League of Nations to cease aggression, Japan refused to jettison its plans for the subjugation of Manchuria. Anyone who followed the deteriorating political situation now knew for certain that it was just a matter of two or three years before the Kwantung Army would overrun all of Manchuria. American and European firms in Mukden closed down their offices, Papa's photo business began to falter and, by the summer of 1930, we were for all practical purposes again out on the street. Other than working directly for the Japanese, there were no other opportunities remaining in Mukden.

III

General Diterichs, the White Army's last field commander during the Civil War in Siberia, had been urging Papa to relocate to Shanghai since the beginning of 1930. As head of the Far Eastern Division of the All-Russian Military Union, the émigré military organization with headquarters in Paris, Diterichs needed an assistant, a deputy who could help him with the organization's affairs in Shanghai. Established in Paris in the early 1920s, the All-Russian Military Union was a White Russian émigré veterans organization to which most World War I and Civil War veterans belonged. Its main purpose was to preserve Russia's military traditions, provide a central source of communication, and continue the struggle against the Bolsheviks. During the early years of its existence it remained relatively inactive in the fight against the communists, but in 1930, after nearly ten years of political hibernation, White Army generals again began to agitate for a more vigorous and direct campaign against the Moscow government. On January 26, 1930, General A. P. Kutepov, the highly respected head of the All Russian Military Union, was kidnapped in Paris and, although the case was never fully solved, it was generally conceded by the French that it was the work of the Soviet secret police. The assassination of Kutepov gave rise to wide-spread indignation among the White veterans of the Russian Civil War, triggering an upsurge of new enthusiasm for reopening the struggle against the communist dictatorship in Moscow. News from the Soviet Union also spurred new anti-communist activity, especially the news about the growing conflict between Stalin and the more democratic elements of the Communist Party. The massive collectivization program was uprooting millions of peasants and producing immeasurable suffering and loss of life. Dissenting party officials, the literary community, and even some Red Army generals were openly defying Stalin and urging a retreat from collectivization and a reinstatement of Party democracy. Many senior White officers were convinced that the unfolding struggle might lead to an internal destabilization and the possibility of an anti-communist insurrection in the Soviet Union. Agents of *Soiuz Spaseniia Rodiny*, a White Russian anti-communist liberation front, returning from the Soviet Union called for more active participation in the anti-communist underground, and there was even talk of establishing contact with the Red Army Marshals, many of whom served in the Czarist army and were graduates of Czarist military schools. The new developments called for more active participation, increased anti-Soviet propaganda, and a campaign to establish anti-communist resistance within the Soviet Union itself.

Papa had been wrestling with the idea of moving to Shanghai since the beginning of 1930. Shanghai, according to him was for Russian émigrés "another Harbin on a smaller scale" with all of the same internal bickering and name calling that he found in Harbin during his stay there in 1923 and 1924. But the changing political situation in Manchuria and the challenge of reactivating the anti-Bolshevik struggle helped him make up his mind. In August he wired General Diterichs that he would accept his offer. Mama's reservations were more personal and family related. She feared that, in accepting the Shanghai assignment, Papa would again become so involved in the affairs of the All Russian Military Union that everything else would take second place. She felt certain, however, that Shanghai offered better schooling opportunities for the children, the prospect of a nursing job for her, and a more favorable "jumping off point" for a permanent home in Europe, Australia or the United States. Everything considered, she was in favor of the move. In the fall of 1930, Papa and Mama liquidated the photo studio, sold most of their possessions and took a Japanese steamer to Shanghai.

The largest city in China and one of the world's greatest seaports, Greater Shanghai had its origins in the Treaty of Nanking which opened China to foreign trade in 1852. The British and the French, joined by the United States a few years later, established the International Settlement in 1854. Claiming that it was being dominated by the British and the Americans, France withdrew from the joint arrangement in 1862, creating a separate French Concession south of the International Settlement and southeast of the Chinese city. Japan also entered the field some years later, and by World War I, Greater Shanghai consisted of four separate municipalities: the International Settlement governed by the British and Americans, the French Concession administered by a specially established commission of the French colonial government, Chapei governed by the Japanese, and the vast independent Chinese City that surrounded the foreign concessions to the south and southeast. The foreign settlements were originally intended only for foreign merchants, but with time -- especially after the Taiping Rebellion which created a great deal of insecurity in the lower Yangtse region -- Chinese refugees and other nationals were allowed to reside within their boundaries. The Russian Revolution and the ensuing civil war brought a stream of anti-Bolshevik White Russians most of whom settled in the French Concession. Greater Shanghai became an international city and, for the arriving Russians, a city within a city, with Russian schools, churches, theaters, restaurants, night clubs, newspapers, and shopkeepers -- a teeming Russian diaspora where Russian was the primary language and Russian culture the dominant influence of every day life.

The physical center of Shanghai was the British Race Course on Bubbling Well Road, a spacious green oasis located in the International Settlement with massive grandstands and club facilities where English businessmen watched the running of their prize horses, played cricket and traded gossip over gin and tonic. It was a symbolic monument to Western power and wealth. Ordinary Chinese and émigré Russians were not officially banned from entering its premises, but on the whole stayed away in awe of its grandeur and specter of wealth. The Chinese Communists were not unaware of its symbolic importance. When I visited Shanghai in 1988, I discovered that they had converted it into a city park with their own dominating fetish, a large "People's Square" in the middle, for festivals and special occasions. Spreading from the race course in all directions were streets, avenues, parks and the business and living compounds of Shanghai's foreign dwellers. After Mukden with its wide streets, sparsely settled neighborhoods, modest architecture and absence of water, Shanghai was a *"monstrum horrendum"* of incredible size. The Bund along the Huangpu River with its agglomeration of majestic buildings -- banks, steamship companies, trading firms -- built mostly by the British, the river with thousands of flat-bottomed sampans and freighters flying flags of many nations, the crowded department stores and shops on narrow and busy Nanking Road, the tree-lined Avenue Joffre, the French Concession's main thoroughfare, were imposing spectacles that I had never seen before. Teaming with people of different ethnic and national origins -- British and French colonial servants in white fedoras and sun helmets, U.S. Marines, Sikh and Senegalese traffic policemen in colorful uniforms, Vietnamese soldiers in native campaign helmets, Russians, Cossacks, some still in uniform, and of course thousands and thousands of Chinese -- Shanghai was a Babel of confusing sounds and voices, a multicolored and multilingual city of millions of people, a grimy international metropolis in a sea of Chinese. It is not surprising that some Russians called it "Babylon on the Huangpu." To a little boy of eight it was something out of a fairytale, bizarre, chimerical and immensely intimidating.

Our first home in Shanghai was a comfortable colonial bungalow with five bedrooms, central heating, modern plumbing and a servants' quarter that Papa and Mama quickly converted into the habitually used "travelers' room" saved for the itinerant and homeless who needed a temporary roof. Located on Route Joseph Frelupt – I never found out who Frelupt was -- on the French Concession across the street from the French Colonial barracks and rifle range, it was exceptionally well situated as far as Shanghai's Russian community was concerned. Many years later, traveling through China as a tourist, I located the bungalow on the renamed Jianguo Road to find to my surprise six or seven families living on the premises, chickens running around in the garden, and the whole structure in utter disarray. The colonial barracks also had a new occupant. Flying the Red Flag of the Chinese Revolution, the barracks were the headquarters of the regional branch of the Communist Party. My brothers and I loved living on Route Frelupt. We were awakened by the sound of the bugle blowing the reveille in the morning and went to bed in the evening to the sound of the French version of taps. We also liked to watch the changing of the guard in front of the barracks, especially on holidays, when the Vietnamese and Senegalese guard details in full parade uniform accompanied by drum and bugle corpsmen went through the intricate military ritual of posting the new guards.

We arrived in Shanghai too late to seek admission to one of the French or English schools. The fall semester had already started and there were no openings available until the following academic year. There were a number of Russian schools in the French Concession, but Mama categorically refused to consider them. "There is too much smoking and drinking in the Russian schools," she claimed, "and the level of instruction is also inferior," she argued to convince Papa that a Russian school would be a grave mistake. For someone who smoked like a veteran trooper, her protestation against excessive smoking seemed to me a little out of place, but Papa agreed -- somewhat reluctantly -- and we were therefore home-schooled during our first year in Shanghai. When I say home schooled I am not suggesting that Papa and Mama took over the entire responsibility for our education. In fact, our schooling arrangement was much more complex. Some subjects Mama taught herself, others were taught by Mrs. Diterichs, a diminutive and imperious Russian lady of French ancestry who was more interested that Nick and I receive a proper Christian education -- Mike was still too young to be included -- than master what we were supposed to learn. Math was the province of one of the older girls in the Diterichs household who was a member of a small informal orphanage that the Diterichs organized for the children of White officers and soldiers killed during the Civil War.

The Diterichs occupied an old Victorian town house surrounded by a large and overgrown garden on Route Pere Robert, not more than four or five blocks from where we lived. Belonging to the French municipal government, the property had been leased to General Diterichs to serve as an informal headquarters for the White Russian military émigrés in Shanghai. Despite the presence of many other White Russian leaders and community organizations, the French looked to Diterichs for help in dealing with thousands of former officers and soldiers who had settled in the French concession since 1923. During World War I he commanded a Russian division in the Balkans, was a Cavalier of the coveted French *Legion d'Honeur,* and in the Russian Provisional Government after the February Revolution was Quartermaster General of the Russian Army. They trusted him and did everything possible to make his life more comfortable in Shanghai. The town house contained the living quarters of General Diterichs and his family, the orphanage, the General's study, Papa's office, and a private chapel. General Diterichs was an intensely religious individual who never lost faith in his Christian upbringing and believed in seeking solace in prayer and meditation. He had a private chapel in his command rail car when he was Commanding General of the White Army during the Civil War, and he had one built in his Shanghai residence. Tastefully decorated in the style of the Russian far north, the chapel could hold fifty to sixty worshipers, mostly close friends, former military colleagues and their immediate families. Services were held regularly on Saturdays and

Sundays and the Diterichs meticulously observed all Orthodox feast days and saints days. There were only a few boys of my age in the General's entourage, and it did not take long before I was recruited to be an alter boy. As I look back at the experience, I am inclined to think that I performed my duties somewhat mechanically without any sincere regard for religious enthusiasm. Mama insisted that I had the makings of an agnostic very early in childhood. I did not have any interest in Christian dogma, she claimed, only in what was morally right or wrong. If that were indeed the case, it is not at all surprising that as I grew to adulthood I gradually drifted toward a more secular view of human behavior away from what the Russians called *Zakon Bozhii*, the Orthodox equivalent of the Roman Catholic catechism. The alter boy service was not an altogether wasted experience, however. In the two years that I served as an alter boy I learned enough Church Slavonic -- the root basis of all modern Slavic languages -- to be able to decode years later nearly sixty percent of all written passages in Ukrainian, Polish, Bulgarian, Serbo-Croatian, Slovak and even Czech.

My life during the first year of our domicile in Shanghai was centered almost exclusively around our bungalow on Route Frelupt and the Diterichs' town house further uptown. At home we did our home work, played with the few toys that we owned, and had our morning and evening meals. The rest of the day we spent on Route Pere Robert, studying and playing in the large overgrown backyard of the Diterichs' town house. Wandering alone beyond the bungalow and the town house was strictly *verboten,* and the Chinese City whose western gate was only about half a mile from our home was off limits to us. The one time that I wandered beyond the gate exposed an expanse of dark and filthy alleys teeming with humanity and indigenous social and commercial life. I saw emaciated beggars with all sorts of frightening skin deceases and invalids with grotesquely swollen limbs disfigured by acute elephantiasis, dried-out old men and women who looked like they were on their last breath, odd-looking men poking metal darts into the bare backs of squatting patients, sweating coolies carrying immense loads of pressed soy bean, and street merchants hawking strange foods and sundry wares. It was summer, and the alleys were strewn with water melon rind, rotting vegetables, newspaper and human excrement, and swarms of buzzing flies and grimy maggots. The stench was overpowering. It did not take long before I raced back to the less contaminated sanctuary of the foreign concession, never to return again to the Chinese section of Shanghai. To give credit where it belongs, we should recognize that the Chinese communists not only erected statues of Mao but also cleaned up this appalling blight and brought even the remote areas of China into the 20th century.

There were also other prohibitions. We had to give our word of honor that we would never buy or accept anything that was sold by Chinese street merchants. Sanitation on the streets of foreign Shanghai was infinitely better than in the Chinese town but it, too, was outrageously poor and in some areas even non-existent. Vegetables and fruit had to be washed with a solution of potassium permanganate, hands had to be washed many times a day and strange foods, according to Mama, had to be avoided lest we picked up some dreadful parasite or, even worse, contracted trachoma -- a contagious eye disease that caused an extreme form of conjunctivitis. Having survived the typhus epidemic during the Civil War, Mama displayed an almost uncontrollable anxiety about cleanliness. We were checked daily for ticks and flees, regularly purged and medicated against parasites, and marched off at least once a year to the oculist for an eye examination.

As far as our moral and intellectual upbringing was concerned it was not very different from what we experienced in Mukden. The emphasis continued to be placed on duty, honor and patriotism, only in larger doses because in Shanghai we were subjected not only to the counsel of our own parents but also to that of the Diterichs and their immediate entourage. White Russian Shanghai in 1931 was a study in contradiction. It was at the same time a bastion of dedicated White Russian elite -- officers and political leaders --who continued to keep up appearances, passionately championing the anti-Bolshevik cause, and a hideous cesspool of poverty, despair, and degradation that underscored much of the community's every day life.

Memorial church services for the war dead were regularly celebrated and the pre-Revolutionary national anthem continued to be sung at all community gatherings just as it was sung by the White Army during the Civil War. Officers attended lectures on military tactics and strategy and the Shanghai Volunteer Corps made up exclusively of young Russian men -- many of whom were veterans of the Nechaev Brigade and the Shantung Russian Military Academy -- drilled regularly in anticipation of a possible insurrection or disturbance caused by the Chinese population of Shanghai. Local newspapers carried proclamations of solidarity against communism, and the Brotherhood of Russian Trust, like Radio Marti in Miami, beamed anti-Soviet propaganda at the cities of eastern Siberia. I found out about the radio station by accident. I had mistakenly showed up for a dental appointment with Dr. Panchenko at the wrong time and found him to my great surprise with a microphone in his hand broadcasting to Russia. I never noticed the broadcasting equipment previously; it was expertly stored away out of sight during regular office hours.

But beneath the formal and patriotic trappings was the tragic bustle of everyday life. Widows and young women prowled bars and dance halls in the hope of meeting someone who could offer them some semblance of security. Prostitution, drunkenness and corruption were rampant, children were left unattended to play on the streets because their mothers had to work. Living conditions for most people were intolerable; several generations of one family often had to live in excruciatingly limited space. As more and more White Russian émigrés arrived from Manchuria, Tientsin, Hankow and other cities of the Chinese interior, White Russian Shanghai took on the face of a dysfunctional society experiencing a great deal of strain from within and without.

As a family we were spared most of the pain and discomfort -- especially during our first two years in Shanghai. We were not entirely unaware, however, of what was taking place in the Russian community as Papa and Mama were deeply involved in helping the less fortunate immigrants arriving in Shanghai. Nineteen thirty-one was a good year for the Petroff family. Escaping the heat of Shanghai's summer, we sailed -- together with the Diterichs -- to Dairen (Dalien) and spent most of July and August at a large working farm owned by a former Russian diplomat and early settler in Manchuria. Located half way between Dairen and Port Arthur at Ying Chen Tza, a whistle stop on the Dairen-Port Arthur railroad spur, the farm produced and marketed milk, eggs, pork and all sorts of fruit and vegetables to wholesalers in the greater Dairen area. For a little boy of almost nine who had never seen fruit trees and animal life before, the Ying Chen Tza experience was something out of the ordinary. Although we were not permitted to handle the animals we had a free run of the entire farm and were allowed to pick fruit, cucumbers, tomatoes; only grapes were not to be touched. As the summer progressed, we sampled every fruit the farm produced, including the prohibited grapes. I liked to munch on pears and apricots; Nick favored apples and peaches and Mike, who was only four in 1931, was especially fond of honey.

Life at the farm followed a definite pattern. After morning chores and prayers, breakfast, consisting usually of fruit, porridge, fresh bread and milk for us children, was served in the dining room by eight. Lunch was optional and was available in the kitchen. Dinner was the big meal and was generally served on the patio of the big house. The owner of the farm, a confirmed vegetarian with a lively interest in health and nutrition, had collected hundreds of recipes that featured a variety of vegetables from his own farm. We feasted on *pirogs* (pies) stuffed with egg plant, pumpkin, carrots, leak and potatoes, ate cottage cheese, drank fruit juices, savored fruit compotes, all in the name of better nutrition and a healthier life. The owner sincerely believed in the therapeutic qualities of a balanced non-animal diet, and, prodded by an adult, would occasionally expound with examples from biochemistry on how primitive societies thrived on plant protein and lived to old age despite the absence of medical care. His lectures did not make me into a true vegetarian, but I like to think that the Ying Chen Tza experience may have had something to do with my preference as an adult for fish, fowl, fruit and vegetables instead of animal fat and red meat.

Ying Chen Tza also offered opportunities for long walks, occasions to learn something about nature and to contemplate on the mystery of life itself. Papa, unfortunately, could not stay with us during the entire summer --three weeks was all that he could spare -- but while he was there, I made sure that we spent as much time as possible together. We took long walks through the neighboring hills and valleys, sometimes returning only at dusk. We talked about people, about faith and worship, about the obligations of everyday life. He was a deeply spiritual person who continued to hold on to the Russian Orthodox canons of his childhood, but he was also a free thinker above religious partisanship who could easily worship in any church, any temple, or for that matter, on a Manchurian hilltop far away from his ancestral home. He loved the outdoors and had a keen interest in nature -- undoubtedly, the result of his early life experience in the Russian countryside. He knew his trees and flowers and could identify many of them with a great deal of accuracy. During that summer I learned the names of wild flowers, birds and insects, learned how to whistle and how to use a knife. That summer we also visited Port Arthur, the ill-fated Russian fortress that was seized by the Japanese during the Russo-Japanese War. I have an exceptionally clear recollection of the visit to Port Arthur that Papa must have arranged in advance. We were met at the entrance by a Japanese officer who came to attention, saluted Papa and, in passable Russian, said "You are welcome to Port Arthur, Your Excellency, I will be your guide. You will have to take your hats off, however, in honor of the Russian and Japanese soldiers who fell on this hallowed ground." We spent close to two hours climbing the ramparts, exploring tunnels, and examining the fortifications that had been breached by the Japanese in 1905. The Port Arthur visit was a lesson in history and civility that I don't think I will ever forget. It was too poignant, too heart-rending, too epiphenal to slip out of the memory of a nine year-old boy. On a broader scale of growing to adulthood, the entire Ying Chen Tza experience was an important building block of my early development.

We returned to Shanghai relaxed and psychologically refurbished. Even Mama, who had been troubled by the enormity of the privation experienced by many Russian immigrants was now more hopeful that something could be done to alleviate their difficult lives She was also elated to find out that Nick and I were admitted to College St. Jean D'Arc, a primary school for boys located in the French concession not too far from where we lived. The school was bilingual with instruction in French and English, although the Catholic nuns who ran the school were French and spoke English with a pronounced accent. St. Jean D'Arc was housed in a complex of clean modern buildings, but the instruction, as I look back at it now, left much to be desired in terms of our modern approach to the education of children. We were drilled on our multiplication tables, learned French and English poems by rote, memorized whole paragraphs of children's literature, and in parrot-fashion recited what we were taught. The only thing that I can say about my two years at St. Jean D'Arc is that I can still recite the Lord's Prayer in French. The student body was international. There were boys whose parents were English, American, French and Portuguese from Macao. There were also a few Chinese boys who came from well-to-do Chinese families, a number of Eurasians and a few Russians, sons of Russian businessmen and restaurateurs. For the first time in our lives, Nick and I found ourselves in a new environment trying to communicate in a new tongue. Nick -- our family's natural linguist -- seemed to do a better job of adapting to the new environment. We found ourselves in many ways in two separate worlds. What was especially confusing in that first year at St. Jean d'Arc was the discovery that there were two Christmases and two Easters - a Russian Christmas and Easter and a Catholic and Protestant one. Mama tried to explain that Russian Orthodox believers used the Julian calendar which placed Christmas not on December 25th, but thirteen days later, while Catholics and Protestants had accepted many years ago the modern Gregorian calendar used throughout the world. I don't think we understood fully what she was trying to tell us. The distinction seemed too abstract in its construction, but it did reveal to us that there were other religious and cultural worlds beyond the boundaries of our strictly Russian way of life.

Fall flew by with astonishing swiftness bringing scores of new friends, new insights and new school experiences. On the whole, I think we adapted rather well to the new course of our education and upbringing. Every day, except Sunday, from 9:00 AM to 3:00 PM we studied and played in the international setting of College St. Jean d'Arc, spoke haltingly in French and English, sang French songs and soaked up the multinational ingredients of Shanghai's distinctly international culture. After 3:00 PM we returned home to speak and think in Russian and to continue the way of life that had been devised for our parents by history and many years of social acculturation. There were no serious divergences between the two daily experiences but that did not mean that they were totally free of contradiction. I can remember a number of occasions when I questioned the appropriateness of a teacher's response that seemed to be opposed to what I had assimilated from early childhood. Conversely, there were also occasions when I challenged Papa's and Mama's reactions to what I had recently learned from teachers at school. There were also some unforeseen benefits to our bifurcated system of education. For example, that year we celebrated two Christmases -- one at school during the week leading to December 25th and the other at home on January 7th, the nuns graciously allowing us to stay a few extra days from school to observe the Russian version to its full extent .

IV

The new year began with darkening clouds on the political horizon. On a more general political level, we saw the final stage of the Japanese thrust into Manchuria and its effect on the Russian émigré population in China. We also observed the first military confrontation between the Japanese and the Chinese in China proper, and witnessed a change in the attitude of Shanghai's French authorities toward the anti-Soviet activities of the All Russian Military Union. These political developments had an influence on our lives and state of mind. There were also more personal family developments that suddenly surfaced to complicate our lives.

The Japanese intrusion into Manchuria and the disbandment of the Nechaev Brigade[6] sent thousands of Russian émigrés to Shanghai. The most tempting haven sought by Russian émigrés in China, Shanghai -- especially its French concession where most Russians settled -- was bursting at the seams with destitute immigrant families from all corners of the Far East. According to unofficial estimates, from 1930 to 1933, the Russian émigré population of Shanghai had doubled from twenty thousand to almost forty thousand.[7] The new arrivals had to be housed and gainfully employed, their children educated and the families assimilated into the communal life of the Russian enclave. The Russian Chamber of Commerce, the Cossack Union, Russian professional societies, all tried to help the new arrivals, but the greatest burden fell on the shoulders of the All-Russian Military Union because the majority of the arriving immigrants were White Army veterans of the Civil War. Papa literally slaved on two fronts that year, helping the new arrivals settle on the French concession and laying the ground work for a more active clandestine anti-Soviet activity in eastern Siberia. The anti-Soviet activity was clothed in secrecy, but there were rumors that General Diterichs was trying to establish contact with Marshall V. K. Bliukher, Commander of the Far Eastern Red Army.[8] Unlike Tukhachevskii and six other Soviet marshals who were summarily executed in 1937, Bliukher died in prison a year later after undergoing torture for several months. It is conceivable that his execution may have been held up by the NKVD in an attempt to find out if in fact he did establish contact with the All-Russian Military Union in Shanghai. Stalin was obsessed with the idea that a plot against him was being organized by senior Red Army commanders and White Army generals. In a cloak-and-dagger game between spies and counter-spies Hitler nurtured Stalin's paranoia by circulating false revelations about alleged pro-German leanings of the Soviet marshals. In 1937, 1056 senior Army and Navy officers were executed, leaving the Red Army virtually naked without any experienced commanders to conduct the war against Nazi Germany.[9] Russian archival collections do not hold any hard data about a military coup d'etat against Stalin. General Diterichs died in 1937, leaving his personal archive to the Russian National Archive in Prague where, after World War II, it fell into the hands of the NKVD who parceled it out to four different archival collections in Moscow. As of this writing, the Diterichs archive has not been located despite several search attempts by me and the Curator of the White Army Civil War Collection at the State Archive of the Russian Federation. Papa's personal archive which has been turned over to the Hoover Institution in Palo Alto, California also does not contain any information about the alleged conspiracy. The possibility that Marshall Bliukher actually participated in an anti-Soviet plot thus remains a mystery until post-Soviet Russia declassifies all of its KGB files.

On a closer and more personally-touching political level we witnessed the first Sino-Japanese armed confrontation that took place in the outskirts of Shanghai. On January 28, we woke up to the distant sound of artillery fire coming from the direction of Chapei, Shanghai's northern suburb under Japanese control. For a number of days rumors had been circulating in Shanghai that the Chinese were massing troops outside of the city in a patriotic protest against the Japanese occupation of Manchuria. The bombardment confirmed the rumor, leading to the closing of Shanghai's international borders from the rest of the city. Fearing that the hostilities would spread to the International Settlement, Shanghai's municipal authorities prepared for the worst. Fortifications were constructed along the border between the International Settlement and the Chinese sections of the city and machine gun emplacements built out of sand bags were erected at the principal intersections of the International Settlement. U.S. Marines and members of the Shanghai Russian Volunteer Regiment were put on full alert. I remember walking with an older boy from St. Jean d'Arc to see for myself what a gun emplacement looked like, only to be sternly warned by a U.S. Marine guarding a fortified intersection on Avenue Eduard VII that I had no business being there and should go home. There was also a mad rush to buy supplies and provisions as food prices climbed out of control. The "Undeclared War," as it became known in the international press, lasted five and a half weeks to March 3rd. After seventy thousand Japanese troops had battled a surprisingly vigorous Chinese resistance, both sides accepted an armistice in fear that the Chapei encounter would expand into a real war. The "Undeclared War" was not without tangential consequences. While it lasted, the blockade of the Huangpu River and the port facilities made it impossible for Shanghai's foreign residents to obtain fresh food supplies. Those who stocked up early when the clash first started weathered the crisis without any serious discomfort; those who did not, had a very difficult time. We were fortunate, as Papa and Mama anticipated the curtailment of food supplies and stocked up canned food in advance. For nearly four weeks we lived on canned goods, condensed milk, a full head of Dutch cheese that they bought on the black market, home baked bread, and tea. The "Undeclared War" -- Japan's first armed conflict in China proper in the twentieth century -- was a wake-up call for Shanghai's foreign community. It confirmed what most people always feared that Shanghai, despite British, French and American protection, could easily find itself in the boiling caldron of a more protracted and extensive war.

The "Undeclared War" did not create any long-term complications for White Russians in Shanghai, but the Japanese occupation of Manchuria split the White Russian community in China into two camps: a Manchurian clique that turned pro-Japanese and a China proper group, steered by the leadership of the All Russian Military Union, that refused to collaborate with Japan. Those who turned pro-Japanese believed naively that Japan would help them in overthrowing the Soviet regime. Those who refused to collaborate were convinced that Japan had ulterior motives and was trying to win the support of the White Russian community in China to pursue its own ends in Manchuria and the Russian Far East. In Shanghai, unlike Harbin and other urban centers in Manchuria, there were very few pro-Japanese supporters. Most Russian émigrés in Shanghai were confident that they had the protection of France, Great Britain and America that would allow them to maintain their neutrality in the event of a local political emergency or even war.

While the "Undeclared War" was still raging, Shanghai's French authorities modified their policy with respect to the White Russian émigré community in favor of a more uncompromising and fixed course of action that affected especially the political activities of the All Russian Military Union. Why this occurred is not at all clear. It's possible the replacement of the intensely anti-Soviet Laval government in France in February 1932 by a more conciliatory Herriot-Blum social democratic coalition that did not want to antagonize the Soviet Union may have had something to do with it. It may have been also the result of pressure from the Chinese nationalist government and the ruling Kuomintang party who made no distinction between pro-Japanese Russian émigrés and those who refused to collaborate with the Japanese. As far as the Kuomintang was concerned all White Russian émigré associations in China were suspect of pro-Japanese feelings and therefore had to be regulated and restrained. The local French authorities may have also decided with the backing of the British and the Americans on the International Settlement to tighten the control over the White Russian population on the grounds that some of its organizations had become politically too independent and were using the sanctuary offered by Shanghai authorities as a means of carrying on clandestine activities and propaganda against the Soviet Union.

Whatever may have been the real reasons, the French authorities established new controls to curtail the activities of the All-Russian Military Union in Shanghai. The clandestine anti-Soviet radio station was shut down, White Russian organizations were directed to secure permission for all public meetings and, what was especially annoying to our family, we were ordered to vacate the house on Route Frelupt that the French authorities had provided when we first arrived in Shanghai. No concrete reasons were given for our eviction, but community hearsay claimed that the French municipal government did not like the constant coming and going of itinerant immigrants whom it suspected of being anti-Soviet agents of the All Russian Military Union. I was too young to grasp the full significance of the changes in local French policy, but old enough to recognize that something new was happening and we were moving into a new phase of our life in Shanghai. Papa became more close-mouthed about what he was doing, more security conscious and more concerned about the safety of those with whom he had to work. Looking back at what transpired in the spring of 1932, I believe the new policy came about as a result of pressures from many different sources, including Moscow. The new policy was not heavy-handed, nor did it affect everyone the same way. In fact, it appeared to be a trivial "bone of appeasement" thrown by the local French authorities to the Chinese rather than a locally forged policy to curtail the activities of the All Russian Military Union in Shanghai. General Diterichs, for example, did not lose his municipally-owned residence and most activities of the All-Russian Military Union continued as before.

For all practical purposes, our family became the only real victim of the new policy. We were forced to move to less favorable quarters -- a small apartment in the heart of Russian town in the French concession on Avenue Joffre. The move weighed heavily on Mama's morale. For some time, she had been telling Papa that it was time to stop playing soldiers and instead begin thinking about the family and its long term needs. Immigration to the United States was out of the question. Friends and former colleagues in San Francisco wrote about the Great Depression and how difficult it was for newly arrived immigrants to live in the United States. They had a hard time keeping their own body and soul together, let alone take financial responsibility for an additional family of five. The negative news from San Francisco did not satisfy Mama; she continued to press for emigration to Australia, Chile, Argentina, anywhere out of the "hell-hole" that she considered Shanghai. Caught in the mesh of the All Russian Military Union's clandestine activities, Papa refused to listen or to examine the alternatives raised by Mama. Complicating their disagreement was also Mama's strong dislike of Mrs. Diterichs whom she considered a pathetic neurotic who meddled into her husband's and Papa's work.

Mama resented Mrs. Diterichs's outbursts of uninvited righteousness, her super nationalism and her outpouring of intense religiosity. I suspect that the feelings of resentment were probably mutual, making Papa's relationship with General Diterichs more difficult than it could have been without the clashing personalities of their wives. In May, Mama joined the nursing staff of St. Luke's hospital, partly because we could use extra money to pay for our schooling at St. Jean d'Arc and partly because Mama needed a diversion from the drab monotony of daily life. She was thirty-nine, still strikingly beautiful, full of excess energy and zest for life. Papa, on the other hand, ten years older, had somehow retreated into the arcane and secretive world of the All Russian Military Union and its unrelenting pursuit of trying to liberate Russia instead of being a responsible and loving husband to a younger wife. It was a disaster in the making; there did not seem to be any alternative in sight.

In 1932, we did not go to Yen Chen Tza for the summer as we did the previous year. Instead, we stayed in Shanghai enduring incredibly muggy and sweltering one hundred degree temperatures that never seemed to subside. The nights were especially brutal -- hot, stuffy, mosquito-infested, sleepless, and terribly confining in the cramped quarters of an apartment that had only one open outlet to the outside street. Nick and I tried to get daytime relief at the public municipal swimming pool in the International Settlement, but Mama was vehemently opposed to our using it. She was certain that it was swarming with all kinds of germs that could give us anything from hepatitis to cholera that were so prevalent in China during the summer months. We had to promise to stay away from the municipal pool, but whenever there was an opportune occasion we snuck out to swim and frolic, knowing that we would get a lecture when we returned home. Papa and Mama did not believe in corporal punishment and we were not afraid to face up to a scolding. In the arithmetic of our personal gratification, a swim in the soothing cold water of the pool when the outside temperature was 105 degrees Fahrenheit was not something to pass up in the interest of avoiding a sharp reprimand.

Mama tried very hard to get night duty at the hospital in order to spend the daytime with us, but this was not always possible. In the summer when we were out of school we had a lot of spare time during which we could get into mischief on Avenue Joffre, French Shanghai's principal street of commerce, entertainment, and outdoor play. Mama tried out several Chinese amahs, but this was also not a solution. It worked reasonably well for Mike who was only five at the time, but not for Nick and me who were nearly eight and ten. We were too old to be supervised by an illiterate nanny, too rambunctious, too "street-savvy," too independent to be deterred by an amah from doing what we wanted to do. Finally, in desperation, Mama found a young man to watch over us when she was at work. About thirty, blond, in excellent physical condition and rakishly good-looking, he was the son of an elderly general whom Papa had known during the Civil War. Too young to have taken part in the Russian Civil War, he had attended the Shantung Military Academy and, in the 1920s, served in the Nechaev Brigade during the War of the Warlords in northern China. In Shanghai, he was a member of the Russian Volunteer Regiment, a corporal who sometimes arrived at the apartment in his uniform which gave him an added aura of authority in his relationship with us. We liked him at first. He was full of riveting stories about the exploits of the Nechaev Brigade; he was also young enough to play soccer with us in the small park that was not far from where we lived. His name was Petr Ivanovich Tsumanenko, but we called him simply Uncle Petya.

For Mama, finding Uncle Petya seemed like an ideal solution. She could now go to work knowing that the children were properly cared for. She could also participate in volunteer work that she had always enjoyed. Papa also approved the arrangement -- it made life easier for him, knowing that Mama now had more free time and did not have to worry about us children when she was working at the hospital. We too enjoyed the new association, but found with time that Uncle Petya was somewhat of a bully who could become very physical when he was frustrated and not averse to using force in trying to discipline us. Freed from constant exhaustion and the responsibility of caring for three children under conditions that were far from ideal since our move from Route Frelupt, Mama came alive again. She made new friends, had time for reading, and occasionally was even able to go out for an evening of fun. When that happened, Uncle Petya usually acted as escort, and we did not think that there was anything wrong with that. It was a chance for Papa to take his turn with the children, helping Nick and me with spelling and math or reading a story to Mike. But what started with an occasional escape from household boredom for Mama somehow blossomed into a dangerous liaison. It was obvious that the conflict that Papa and Mama experienced regarding their children's future and his over-involvement in the activities of the All Russian Military Union had deeper roots than what appeared at first glance. Men and women strive not merely for survival, but for a meaningful existence out of an innate need to be materially and emotionally whole. Papa and Mama had overlooked this dictum and, in the course of their difficult and taxing struggle for existence, had somehow drifted apart. "Every unhappy family is unhappy in its own way." Tolstoy wrote in *Anna Karenina* and, as in the novel, both Papa and Mama were obviously unhappy, each in their own peculiar way. He buried his unhappiness in work that he must have known was intrinsically hopeless; she sought relief in the arms of a younger man. It was a replay of unrequited passions and suppressed instincts straight out of Tolstoy's complex masterpiece, except that the mental pain and the insults were milder, the times were different, and Papa was not an Alexander Karenin. He was not the coldly righteous husband that Tolstoy made out of Karenin in his novel, nor was he particularly concerned about the social consequences of Mama's affair. Looking at it now as an adult, I think deep down in his heart Papa blamed himself as much as Mama, and therefore chose to disregard her indiscretion in the hope that time would resolve the temporary crisis. Nick and Mike were too young to understand the unfortunate entanglement and its consequences on our family life. I, on the other hand, felt betrayed, angry, and terribly hurt. I cried my heart out, accusing Mama, but above all, I blamed Uncle Petya. I wanted to strangle him for what he had done to our family life. Mama's affair with Uncle Petya was not something that a ten-year old who loved and idolized his parents could easily ignore. Mama's relationship seemed to me catastrophic, disheartening and beyond any imaginable hope of coming to an end.

The rest of the year flew by swiftly with the speed of a rushing hurricane. Again, we celebrated two Christmases, but we had become accustomed to that from the previous year. At St. Jean d'Arc, Nick moved into second grade and I into fourth. Our French had improved immensely, but we were still struggling with English, especially the syntax which we found to be a bore. Mama's affair with Uncle Petya remained in an ambiguous state of what "will be, will be." We, children, could not do much to force a resolution, and Papa wisely continued to close his eyes to it. Everyday life in the cramped quarters of our small apartment on Avenue Joffre did not show any improvement, but we had somehow acclimated ourselves to its inadequacies. The winter of 1932-1933 stretched lethargically without any hope for better times.

The All Russian Military Union in Shanghai was also experiencing difficulties. Global depression and the influx of thousands of Russian émigrés to Shanghai from Harbin and other areas affected by the Japanese intrusion into Manchuria severely affected the ability of the Shanghai Division of the Military Union to provide welfare funds for new arrivals. The decision to participate more actively in propaganda and underground operations within the Soviet Union brought about by the growing conflict between Stalin and the more democratic elements of the Communist Party also placed increased pressure for additional funds. Membership dues were not enough -- there was an urgent need for a new source of money. One such source were the 22 boxes of gold bullion and coin deposited by Papa for safe-keeping with the Japanese Military Mission on the Sino-Russian border in November 1920.

The twenty-two boxes of gold had an entangled history.[10] Nearly two-thirds of the Imperial Russian gold reserve -- the largest in Europe prior to World War I --had been moved to the city of Kazan in May 1918 by the Bolshevik government as a precaution against the possibility of a German take-over after the signing of the Brest-Litovsk Treaty with Germany. Consisting of gold coin, gold bullion, silver, platinum and silver and gold objets d'art, it had a value of 651 million gold rubles, a sum that in today's market would be valued in billions of dollars. On August 7, 1918, the combined forces of the KOMUCH[11] anti-Bolshevik government and the Czechoslovak Legion seized Kazan and with it also the gold reserve. The gold was immediately moved to Samara, the KOMUCH capital, but as the Russian Civil War in the central Volga region expanded and the Red Army moved east toward the Ural Mountains, it was shipped first to Cheliabinsk and then Omsk, Admiral Kolchak's White Capital in Siberia. There it lay idle until May 1919 when the Kolchak government began shipping it in separate consignments to Vladivostok for the purchase of war materials from British, French and Japanese suppliers. One such shipment of October 18, 1919 consisting of 722 boxes of gold valued at 42,251,000 gold rubles never reached Vladivostok. It was seized by Ataman Semenov, the renegade leader of the Trans-Baikal Cossacks, who had established his own stronghold in Chita under the aegis of the Japanese. In Chita, it was sequestered in his treasury, most probably with the blessing of the Japanese military authorities who were convinced that the Kolchak regime was collapsing and there was no longer any need to buy war supplies through Vladivostok. While the Japanese remained in the Trans-Baikal region Semenov used the gold for his government's civilian and military needs. In November 1920, when the Red Army resumed its campaign against the retreating White Army, Semenov transferred 7,700.000 gold rubles to Papa, who at that time was Chief of Supply of the White Army. 5,380,000 gold rubles were used for army salaries, supplies and forage, and 1,050,000 gold rubles were turned over to four unit commanders, Generals Bangerskii, Maievskii, Molchanov and Smolin to cover the cost of billeting troops under their command after they crossed the border to China. The balance, consisting of 20 boxes of gold coin and 2 boxes of gold bullion valued at 1,270,000 gold rubles were deposited by Papa for safekeeping with the Japanese Military Mission at Station Manchuria on the Sino-Russian border. The White Command considered it safer to place the remaining gold in the temporary custody of the Japanese Military Mission rather than shipping it to Vladivostok in unarmed rail cars through the bandit-infested area of northern Manchuria. A formal receipt signed by Colonel R. Isome, Head of the Japanese Military Mission on the Manchurian border, confirmed that the 22 boxes were handed over for safekeeping and were to be returned to Major General P. P Petroff upon request. Copy of that receipt is in the Petroff Collection of the Hoover Institution Archive on Russia at Stanford University, Palo Alto, California.

The Japanese never returned the gold that was left with them for safekeeping. An attempt to recover it by the White government in Vladivostok in 1922 failed, so did two other tries in 1923. The launching of a new attempt in the early 1930s seemed more promising, especially since a timely window had suddenly opened to make the return of the gold more feasible. In 1933, conservative anti-war political groups in Tokyo were organizing to reduce the dominance of the Japanese military and were interested in assisting the White Generals, seeing in this move the opportunity to embarrass the Kwantung army officers, who had used the gold to finance the Japanese incursion into Manchuria. The 1931 Mukden incident that was staged by junior officers of the Kwantung army and led to the Japanese takeover of Manchuria was severely criticized by the more conservative generals and ministers of the Japanese cabinet. Prime Minister Inukai, who was later assassinated by navy firebrands, was enraged by the army's usurpation of the decision-making functions of the cabinet. What kind of assistance the All Russian Military Union could count on was not clear, but it was hoped that it would include both financial and political support once the request had been formally filed with the Japanese government.

In March of 1933 Papa left for Japan to coordinate the recovery effort. It was a tearful parting for us children, but his departure was probably in everyone's interest. Both Mama and Papa could now examine the origins and consequences of their marital dilemma in private and think through what could be done to save their marriage, especially since Mama's liaison with Uncle Petya was beginning to unravel. The children always came first for Mama. Their lives had been obviously affected adversely and she was now desperately trying to disengage, but was not quite sure how to attain a satisfactory denouement. Uncle Petya, on the other hand, was becoming more demanding and I think Mama was afraid that he could become violent if she were to seek a clean break. There was a dark side to Uncle Petya's character which often surfaced when he was frustrated or things were not going his way. Papa's departure gave Mama the excuse of spending more time with us children. As a result of that we were seeing less of Uncle Petya – he was still welcome, but he was no longer entrusted with our care. A Chinese amah was hired to baby-sit Mike during school hours and I took over when Nick and I returned from school. The same arrangement lasted through summer, except that it was more flexible because of Mama's varying work schedule.

I hated everything connected with that spring and summer, the ambiguity of Mama's relationship with Uncle Petya, the beastly July and August heat, the solitude of being left behind when most of my friends were away on vacation, Papa's absence, and the crushing constraint of having to take care of my younger brothers who did not enjoy being bossed by an older sibling. Papa maintained that I was born an adult, that I liked to use long and difficult words and often spent hours listening to adults as they talked about art, literature and politics, but the experience of that spring and summer was very different. I had to behave not only as an adult, but also run herd over two active younger brothers, argue with them over insignificant bauble and order them around when everything else failed. I am convinced that their tendency as adults to oppose what they called my "big brother dogmatic opinions" sprang from our anomalous relationship during the summer of 1933. They never understood that, had I the option, I would have preferred to remain a child instead of having to act as a surrogate parent in a relationship that was full of hidden behavioral traps. Psychologically speaking, it was one of the worst experiences of my early upbringing, full of tension, angst, and feeling of betrayal.

But entanglements and crises have a way of dissolving, often on their own without an explicit attempt by anyone trying to influence their seemingly uncontrollable path. And so it was with our family crisis -- it ended abruptly on a positive note. Originally, Papa had left for Japan on a temporary assignment hoping to file an official demand for the return of the gold with the help of Japanese connections in Tokyo, return to Shanghai and manage the return process by proxy. In Japan he found that this was not a viable option and that he would have to stay there much longer to win the political support he needed to negotiate the return of the gold. The delay was a godsend -- it offered a perfect solution for both Mama and Papa to end the painful imbroglio that threatened to tear the family apart. In a long letter to Mama, Papa told her he wanted her and children to relocate as soon as possible to Japan. He described the availability of more favorable living conditions, the educational opportunities at St. Joseph's College, one of the most respected educational institutions in the Far East, and the security that the children would have in Honmoku, Yokohama, where he was planning to lease a house. Papa's letter was exactly what Mama needed. It gave her the endorsement to end her relationship with Uncle Petya and a new basis for getting the whole family together again. During the last days of August we packed our modest belongings and in the first week of September sailed for Japan.

I have a most vivid remembrance of our departure, probably because I wanted to put Shanghai and everything else related to it behind me. Our ship, a Japanese liner whose name I can not remember, weighed anchor in the early afternoon and slowly moved through the congested and muddy Huangpu River to the estuary of the great Yangtse and from there to open sea. It was not until we were a whole hour out of Shanghai that the water finally lost its dirty brown color and abruptly turned a clean dark blue. Standing on the outside deck at the ship's rail I watched the transformation with great fascination. There was something almost symbolic about that sudden change in the color of the sea, as if we were leaving behind all that was sad and distressing to open a new chapter in our lives in Japan.

The two day passage was not entirely flawless. It was taifun[12] season and the East China Sea was exceptionally rough, with huge swells that pitched the small ship in all directions, making it very difficult for anyone to move. Poor Mama was seasick almost throughout the entire journey and six-year-old Mike had to be tethered in fear that he would get washed away if he stepped out on deck. The ship's cuisine was Japanese -- our first exposure to *o miso*, a hot bean soup for breakfast and smelly *daikon*, the yellow pickled radish, served at lunch and dinner with lots of rice. We somehow survived the voyage, sleeping on *tatami*, the hard and compact straw mats that were standard floor covering in every Japanese home. The ship's officers were cordial, respectful and unusually concerned about our safety on board, while the steward continually served hot green tea to Mama which she received politely but never touched in fear that it would make her even more sick. In the early morning of the third day out, the sea calmed down and we saw land again -- the southern tip of Honshu, Japan's largest island.

2
EXPATRIATE IN JAPAN

All things that are, are with more
Spirit chased than enjoyed.
William Shakespeare

I

Our ship docked in Shimonoseki under cloudy skies in gentle and intermittently falling rain that enveloped what looked like an agglomeration of ugly western contemporary buildings and small thatch-roofed Japanese houses that did not seem to belong together. There was almost something surrealistic about the scale and incongruity of the architecture. After Shanghai with its massive and extravagantly appointed buildings, broad avenues, and tall foreigners dressed in western attire, everything and everybody in Shimonoseki – buildings, streets, shop fronts, and people – looked small and strange, straight out of a Japanese wood block print from the early Meiji era that one could find in a trendy antique shop at the Imperial Hotel in Tokyo. I was too young to grasp the full significance of that first impression, but as I grew older I discovered that the outwardly visible incompatibility of native and western architecture that I first saw in Shimonoseki applied to almost everything in Japan, to ideas, mode of thinking, expression of emotion, and even to the ethical precepts of everyday life. Japan had emerged from its feudal past in less than two generations, borrowed and copied Western technology, arts and political institutions, but psychologically, socially and intellectually had continued to follow beneath the surface of modernization its old established traditions molded by centuries of isolation from the West. Some of the native ingredients are now disappearing, but the underlying framework is still a dominating reality today, just as it was when our family first stepped on Japanese soil in 1933.

At the dock we were met by a uniformed officer of the *Kempeitai* – the Japanese Military Police – who spoke Russian, and obviously knew who we were and why we came to Japan. He welcomed us, inquired about the journey, asked Mama if we needed a *jinrikisha* to take us to the railroad station and, when she declined, escorted us on foot to the rail depot which was not too far from the wharf. Our baggage arrived an hour later in a two-wheeled cart pushed by a man in a short dark blue jacked, close fitting "tights," and rubber-soled cloth shoes that had the big toe separated from the rest of his toes, footwear used by the working-class in old Japan. For some reason, the construction of the footwear stuck in my mind, perhaps because it was so different from anything I had seen before. After boarding the train we sat down in our compartment together with the military police officer who asked our names, dates and places of birth, and other pertinent details, all of which he carefully entered into a small black book that he casually produced for the occasion. I suspect that he already had all of the necessary information, but was following a protocol that was standard procedure, repeated many times during our stay in Japan, sometimes cordially as in Shimonoseki, at others, rudely with a fair amount of annoyance. He stayed with us until the next stop, where he excused himself politely, thanked Mama profusely for allowing the interview, and disembarked, undoubtedly, to inform headquarters that Mama was not a communist agent traveling with children to provide cover, but was indeed the wife of Major General Paul Petroff who was already living in Japan.

Relieved that the arrival formalities were over, Mama sat riveted to the window of our compartment watching the pine-studded mountains, the well-groomed paddy fields, the grey tiled roofs of the village temples and dwellings, and sundry advertisements for tonics, sake, cosmetics and other mysterious commodities, streaming in front of her through the Japanese countryside. We also looked out of the window, but our primary interest centered on tunnels, railway stops, and what looked like thousands of people jamming the railway platforms of the stations through which we passed. As the train raced through the tunnels we tried to count them, but there were so many that we lost count. We also tried to learn the names of the cities that we passed through, but they were too foreign, too difficult to pronounce, despite the bellowing public address system that announced each city as the train came to a stop. Among the multitude of people at the larger railway stations, we were especially interested in the *bento* (box lunch) hawkers who plowed the station platforms peddling their wares. Shouting at the top of their voices *"o bento, o bento,"* they walked by the windows of the railway carriages displaying elegant-looking boxes made out of very thin pieces of natural wood that contained an assortment of boiled rice, pickles, fish roll and sweet beans. Passengers opened their windows to purchase the box lunches, usually together with a pot of tea, We, too, wanted to try out a *"bento;"* it looked so enticing that Mama finally gave in to our entreaties and we lowered our window to purchase a box for each one of us. I remember Mama saying on opening her box how colorful and beautiful the contents looked. "It was almost a shame to ruin the colorful arrangement by eating it," she told us, but we dug into the *"bentos"* and devoured everything except the exotic looking pickles that we found too tart.

In Kobe we moved to a sleeping compartment, arriving at the Yokohama Main Station early the next morning. There, we were met by Papa and Suzuki-San who promptly took charge of everything, baggage, transfers to Sakuragi-cho station on the electric line closer to the center of town, and transportation to our final destination in Honmoku on the outskirts of Yokohama. Our meeting with Papa was noisy, joyous and full of questions, although both Papa and Mama remained surprisingly reserved. After months of emotional alienation and nearly six months of physical separation, it took several years for them to regain their self-confidence in front of each other and become spontaneous again.

Papa's choice of Honmoku for our first home in Japan was either a very astute decision or an amazing stroke of good luck. Honmoku offered not only an unsurpassed location to raise the family, but also gave all of us – parents and children – a unique opportunity to come into direct contact with Japanese culture, its people and their way of life. Had we settled in the international section of Yokohama where most *gaijin* (foreigners) lived, we would have had less occasion to interact with an authentic Japanese community, to learn Japanese, and get a feeling for the Japanese way of life. Honmoku was our prep school, our introduction to Japan.

Situated on the Bay of Tokyo about twenty minutes on the Number Four city tram line from Yokohama's business and international districts, Honmoku was at one time a sleepy fishing village famous for its fresh fish market and dry seaweed production. Foreign trade and rapid industrialization after the opening of Japan to foreigners in 1858 transformed Yokohama into a huge port city that gradually swallowed most of the small communities on its periphery. One such small community was Honmoku. By the time we arrived in Japan, it was a prosperous Yokohama neighborhood with its own modern business center, stores, including a French bakery, professional offices, post office, police station, and the famous Sankei-en Garden known for its three-storied pagoda, lotus ponds and chrysanthemums, considered one of Yokohama's main tourist attractions even today. Side by side with this newly built western-looking section of Honmoku was the old fishing village with its assortment of thatch and tiled-roofed houses with barred wooden frontages, intermingled with vacation cottages and larger villas situated closer to the hills. Untouched by modernization, it remained an authentic fragment of the old Japan that Lafcadio Hearn wrote about when he first arrived at the end of the nineteenth century.[13] Here, on the corner of the broad thoroughfare running along the Bay of Tokyo and the main commercial street of the old village, we settled into a cottage that was at one time a vacation home owned by a businessman living in Tokyo.

With its narrow cobbled streets, shoji-screened houses, little shops with dark blue draperies accented by beautifully scripted white or crimson lettering, paper lamps in different styles and sizes, noodle shops, picturesque tea houses with their gilded and lacquered sign-boards advertizing the establishment, and small Shinto shrines with offerings, old Honmoku had an almost mythical aura to it. Many of its inhabitants – fishermen, craftsmen, local workers, merchants, diminutive men and women – still wore the traditional Japanese attire The fishermen wore raincoats and sandals made of straw. The workers were in short blue coats with large ideograph lettering imprinted on the backs of their costumes, proudly telling everyone their craft, trade, or place of work. The women were dressed in flowering kimonos, with their babies strapped to their backs with scarves in a variety of pastel shades. The village sounds were also distinctly Japanese. During the day, one heard the noisy clatter of the *geta* (wooden clogs) worn by Japanese men and women since time immemorial, the chanting of the fishermen pulling their sharp-prowed boats ashore, the beating of drums and the trance-like droning of the sutra that reverberated softly through the paper-thin shojis of Buddhist temples and private homes. At night, we listened to the sound of waves smashing gently against the breakwater and the clanging of iron rings set in motion by the night watchman as he made his rounds pounding his metal rod against the hard pavement of the empty streets. In the air was a faint scent of sake, soy sauce, dried fish and *daikon* (pickled radish), accented by the smell of salt and seaweed gently drifting from the bay. We loved everything about Honmoku, the ambiance, the strangeness, and the proximity to the bay.

The house that Papa rented was a two-storied residence that was neither entirely Japanese nor European. Fronted on both floors by glass-covered balconies featuring polished overhead beams of cypress and hardwood floors finished in cherry, the house – like many other built by westernized Japanese in the 1920s and 1930s – was an airy and practical combination of both. Looking eastward toward the vast expanse of Tokyo Bay, the house captured the early light of sunrise and the turbulent force of prevailing winds. On a clear day we could see from the upstairs balcony fishing boats returning with their daily catch of fish and huge ocean liners moving slowly in and out of the Yokohama harbor. With strong binoculars one could even identify their flags. The balconies extended through the entire front of the house and were large enough to serve as regular rooms. Mama converted the downstairs balcony into a parlor, decorating it with rattan furniture, potted plants, hanging greenery, and a large Japanese paper lamp that hung over a square table covered with a green table cloth. She loved the parlor and its open view into the landscaped Japanese garden that separated the house from a handsome wooden fence weathered by wind and rain that gave us a feeling of privacy from the hustle and bustle of the adjoining main thoroughfare. She said it reminded her of a favorite veranda that was part of her family home in Russia. The upstairs balcony, a more open replica of the one on the first floor, became our playroom where to Mama's consternation we took turns sliding on the polished hardwood floor. The rest of the house, except for the downstairs study that was furnished in western style with built-in bookshelves and a large window looking out at the garden, was typically Japanese with *tatami* (straw mats), large built-in closets and handsome grass paper covered sliding doors separating the rooms. The largest room on the first floor had a *tokonoma* (place of honor), the traditional alcove for a flower arrangement, a *kakemono* (wall hanging), or a collection of prized family artifacts and memorabilia. Mama promptly purchased a beautiful *kakemono* from an antique merchant on Benten-dori, Yokohama's fashionable street where tourists shopped, and hung it to the satisfaction of everyone in the *tokonoma*. The prized possession – a nineteenth century ethereal rendition of a fisherman casting his net in a cascading stream – still hangs in our California home. The entrance to the house via the downstairs balcony had a recessed vestibule where, like all Japanese families, we took our shoes off and put on slippers for inside use.

The house utilities were very marginal. We did not have hot running water or modern plumbing. Our only source of hot water was the *o-furo*, the Japanese hot tub made out of pine and strips of copper, fired up each day in the late afternoon. Like all traditional Japanese houses, ours was also without a central heating system, although we did install a wood-burning stove downstairs after spending our first winter literally half frozen. There were no sewers, no leaching fields, and the night soil had to be physically removed weekly by the *gomiya-san* (night soil carrier), *a Burakumin*,[14] who cleaned out toilets and carted the night soil away to be sold for fertilizer. Despite its functional inadequacies to which we became accustomed with time, the house was a find, architecturally a gem. Many years later, when my wife and I built our home in the hills overlooking the Bay of San Francisco, we used the Honmoku house as a model to satisfy our desire for space and a view of the bay.

We were not the only *gaijin* in Honmoku. There were at least forty foreign families living in the village, many of them with children who became our playmates as time went on. The foreign enclave was truly international – Americans, Brits, French, Germans, Portuguese, and even a Spanish family of mixed Spanish-Japanese blood. Signor Planas, the Spanish Consul General in Yokohama, came to Japan in the first years of the twentieth century as a representative of a European automobile company, fell in love with Japan, married a Japanese woman, and raised a family of five children – three strikingly beautiful daughters and two sons, one of whom was one of my classmates. Except for two American Standard Oil Company families whose breadwinners were in Japan on temporary assignments , the rest of Honmoku's foreign families – many of mixed European and Japanese blood – had been living in Japan for twenty or thirty years, some even longer. Like Signor Planas, the men came to the Orient when Japan was still in need of foreign experts to install modern machinery, produce Western merchandise, and run the shipping and import and export companies. Some brought wives with them, others married Japanese women. Some continued to work in their original capacities, others opened their own businesses, mostly connected with consumer goods and foreign trade. The Laffins came to Japan from the United States at the turn of the century and built a soft drink empire. Monsieur Eymard arrived in Yokohama before World War I as an importer of French wines, married a Japanese woman and became a prominent wine merchant and official purveyor to the Japanese Imperial court. Herr Wolshke came to teach the Japanese how to make sausage, also married a Japanese woman, and stayed on in Japan running a delicatessen shop. The Helm brothers originally came from Germany, married women from a variety of countries, and over the years built a real estate empire that included hotels, warehouses, and commercial buildings in the Yokohama-Tokyo area. The foreign residents of Yokohama were very different from those living in Tokyo – missionaries, college professors, members of the diplomatic corps and foreign press, who returned to their home countries when their time of service was over. They were expatriates, in the full sense of that word, who held foreign passports, but had no intention of ever returning to their homelands because Japan was their permanent residence and, for their children, the only home they knew.

There were no White Russian families in Honmoku; in fact there were very few in central Yokohama, perhaps because so many perished in the 1923 earthquake that new arrivals were afraid to settle there. Most Russian émigrés lived either in Tokyo or the larger provincial cities in Honshu or Hokkaido. Although the total Russian émigré colony in Japan was sizable – perhaps as many as a thousand families – the majority of Russian families had a very different background from ours. They were headed by former non-commissioned officers of the White Army, by wealthier peasants from Russia's eastern provinces and by railroad workers of the Chinese Eastern Railroad. Arriving In Japan in the early 1920s, they became itinerant salesmen of imported woolen cloth and men's furnishings, traveling the small provincial towns of Japan. They were entrepreneurial, hard-working, and frugal. In the ten years since their arrival after the revolution, they adapted themselves exceptionally well to local conditions, showing very little interest in Russian politics or prospects of ever returning to their homeland. Some became quite prosperous, opening stores in provincial cities; some even owned a chain of retail stores. There were very few Russian immigrants who were military professionals and members of the intelligentsia; one could literally count them all on the ten fingers of one's hands. There were two or three field grade officers, one working for the Shell Oil Company, two professors, two musicians who came to Japan to beef up the national symphony orchestra, two or three engineers, one of them a representative of Otis Elevator Company, a fishery expert, and Dmitri Ivanovich Abrikossow, charge of the old Russian Embassy in Tokyo. He had stayed at the embassy until February 1925 when Japan finally recognized the Soviet Union. His greatest contribution to the Russian refugee cause was that he succeeded in securing a guarantee from the Japanese Foreign Office for all Russian émigrés in Japan that they could remain as stateless citizens under Japanese protection if they refused to accept Soviet passports.[15]

A confirmed bachelor and scion of a wealthy Russian family with funds and connections abroad, Dmitri Ivanovich could have easily left for New York, London or Paris, but he decided to remain in Japan, acting as an informal intermediary between the Japanese Foreign Office and the White Russian community in Japan. To many who knew him, his stay in Japan remained a mystery. Some said he had a secret Japanese mistress, others claimed he was a rejected suitor of Countess Natalia Brasova, later wife of Grand Duke Michael, brother of the Tsar. I found many years later that there was indeed some validity to the story about Countess Brasova. Paging through a copy of *Michael and Natasha*,[16] I came across a photograph of Dmitri Ivanovich and Grand Duke Michael lounging in the garden at Gatchina, on the outskirts of St. Petersburg. Abrikossow and Papa became good friends and soul brothers, often playing chess and having tea. With no children of his own, Dmitri Ivanovich was very generous with us children at Christmas, spoiling us with expensive presents our parents could not afford.

The first weeks of our stay in Honmoku were somewhat disorganized and hectic. Mama had to find furniture, linens, china and cooking utensils, no easy job in the Japan of the early 1930s. She had to learn how to use the local market for fish and produce – beef and chicken were a rarity – and how to shop at Gibbs & Company on Moto-machi in the international section of Yokohama for tea, coffee, dried fruit, cereals and canned goods that were unavailable in native Japanese stores. She also had to get accustomed to a new standard of measurements. In old Japan, one did not buy grain, flour or sugar by the kilogram or pound, but by the size of a square wooden box filled to the top.

All of that was new and very perplexing, although Suzuki-san, a junior member of the law firm that was helping Papa recover the gold from the Japanese government, did everything possible to make the adjustment easier for her. He did not speak Russian and his English was limited. Mama, on the other hand, did not speak Japanese and her English at that time also left much to be desired. They often communicated in sign language or on paper, each drawing what they wanted to say. It was really quite comical to see them working out their individual predicaments. I don't know what Mama would have done without him during those early weeks in Honmoku. He was indispensable in all respects.

Papa and Mama also had to make arrangements for our education. In mid-September, Nick and I were marched off to St. Joseph's College for an interview with Brother Joseph Gaschy, the school's principal, an Alsatian who had spent almost his entire adult life in Japan. When he found out that Mama spoke fluent French, there was no end to his pleasure, and we were enrolled that same day in the fall semester that had already started a few weeks earlier. Brother Gaschy gave us a short oral examination, told us that we spoke better French than English, and suggested to Mama that I should be placed in Fourth Grade and Nick in Second. Mike had to wait another year to attend St. Joseph's College as the school did not take anyone who was less than seven. I was almost eleven and Nick was nine, and we probably should have been placed a year ahead, but Brother Gaschy was very diplomatic, saying that the extra year would not hurt us and that it would actually allow us to concentrate on English without worrying about math, geography and history, subjects in which he was sure we were already proficient. Mama agreed with Brother Gaschy and the next day we started school. Papa accompanied us on that first day to St. Joseph's and took a photograph to commemorate the event. In our family album there is a photograph of the two of us dressed in blazers, formal shirts and ties, standing in front of the students' gate to St. Joseph's on our first day.

St. Joseph's College occupied a very special place in the affairs of the foreign community in Yokohama and to a lesser degree in all of Japan. A boy's prep school founded at the turn of the nineteenth century by Marinist brothers, a Catholic teaching order originally established in Alsace, France, St. Joseph's was run by Alsatian and American brothers, some of whom first came to Japan in the late nineteenth century to teach in Japanese universities and private schools. By the time I became a student at St. Joseph's, a practical division of labor had been established between the Alsatians and the Americans. The Alsatians taught the first four grades, foreign languages, and Japanese history which became a requirement for graduation in the 1930s, and the Americans taught grades five to eleven. The Americans also managed the school's sports program. English was the lingua franca in the Orient, and it was the language of instruction at St. Joseph's College. There was no kindergarten at St. Joseph's. To be admitted children had to be seven and be able to read. Classes were held six days a week, with sport activity taking place on Wednesdays and Saturdays in the afternoon – gym throughout the year, soccer in the fall, basketball in the winter, and baseball and track and field in the spring. In high school, the curriculum was a blend of academic subjects combined with practical business courses that would prepare graduates for the world of business. St. Joseph's boys, unlike graduates of other foreign schools in the Orient, learned Shakespeare, Western history, math and the sciences, side by side with business courses, including accounting, typing and shorthand, so that they could, on graduation, step directly into a job at one of the foreign shipping, engineering and import and export firms in Yokohama or other port cities of the Far East. Because most of the teachers were Americans the boys acquired a fair amount of American popular culture, enough to follow the American baseball series, sing popular American songs, debate on the subject of American elections, and know something about American college life. The student body was genuinely international. I recall one year when the school administration claimed there were twenty-four different nationalities represented on our campus, including a fair number of Japanese. My fourth grade class when I entered St. Joseph's had nine different nationalities, including two sons of French citizens who lived in Honmoku, a son of a Latin American ambassador, three Russians from Yokohama, and the nephew of Admiral Takiijiro Onishi, Japan's most renowned navy pilot and originator of the Kamikaze Corps during World War II.

For Yokohama's foreign community St. Joseph's College served as an intricate recasting system that helped students take on new shape and coloring as they moved from grade to grade. Entering it as Russians, French, Swiss, or Portuguese, they came out of it upon graduation as pseudo-Americans, speaking English with an American accent and thinking as young Americans did. Some graduates went off to American universities, but the majority stayed in Japan as expatriates, working for foreign firms, running their own successful businesses, and entertaining themselves at the Yokohama Country and Athletic Club, a huge sports complex established by local foreign residents where they and their children swam, played soccer and tennis, and celebrated Empire Day (May 24), Independence Day (July 4) and Bastille Day (July 14). Until the looming clouds of World War II cast a foreboding shadow on Yokohama's foreign community, it was not a bad life for those who chose to live permanently in Japan.

I I

Life in Honmoku showed an enormous improvement over what we had encountered in Shanghai. For Mama, the sun literally shone brighter and the birds sang more melodiously than they had during the last years in China. She loved everything about Honmoku, the house, the peaceful walks along the seashore, the quiet life in a small

Japanese village, and the certainty that her children were finally going to receive a decent education. She was interested in everything that was new to her in Honmoku: Japanese art, especially the wood block prints of Hokkusai and Hiroshige, Japanese lacquerware, Japanese customs, and Japanese etiquette and entertainment. Trying to keep up with what we were learning at St. Joseph's she immersed herself with a ferocious passion into the study of English, convinced that Nick and I could help her master what she insisted was a barbaric language with too many exceptions and very few rules. Shortly after our arrival, Papa and Mama hired Kazuko, a friendly country girl from Shizuoka prefecture who took over the back-breaking task of keeping a spotless house. Freed from the tiresome routine of running a household for the first time since she left Manchuria, Mama could now do whatever she wanted without constantly worrying about time schedules and unforeseen intrusions from the outside.

Papa's mental outlook on relations with the family also improved significantly. In the six or seven months that he had lived alone in Tokyo, he had time to think through the problems that had overwhelmed the family, his relationship with Mama, and his parental responsibilities to us. Insulated by distance from émigré politics and the crusading militancy of its leadership in Shanghai and Paris, he had apparently come to the conclusion that there was really very little that the Russian émigré community could do to destabilize the Soviet regime. By 1933 Stalin had a firm grip on all aspects of rule in Russia and it now seemed unrealistic to think that it could be dislodged with anti-Soviet propaganda and internal clandestine activity in Russia itself. This did not mean that he was willing to give up the quest for the gold that brought him to Japan. On the contrary, he was even more committed to recover it because, on the economic front, depression had created large hubs of Russian refugee poverty all over the world, poverty that could be greatly alleviated with the gold the Japanese military had seized at the end of the Russian Civil War. He also decided that it was time for him to play a more active role as a parent, spending longer hours with the three of us. Unlike Mama whose life was always inseparable from ours, even in the most trying of circumstances, Papa had always been somewhat distant and aloof from us children largely because of his less outgoing personality than Mama's and perhaps also due to lack of experience on how to amuse young children or play with them. Growing up in a small Russian village, he had no time for idle play or amusement in childhood and adolescence. He had to become an adult very early in his life, chopping wood, herding ducks, harvesting flax and wheat, working as a young teaching assistant and, at the age of fifteen, acting as clerk in the administrative apparatus of rural Russia. We were delighted with the transformation. With his help, we learned to play chess, recite Pushkin and Lermontov, swim and take long walks in the hills beyond Honmoku where we picnicked and talked about our goals in life. It was wonderful. We enjoyed the comradery and the newly acquired closeness as never before.

I also began to feel better about everything, especially about what we could look to as a family living in Japan, but I never succeeded in reclaiming completely the childhood that I lost in Shanghai. I was too old to become again a carefree child like my brothers. Papa and Mama often said that I was born an adult. There was probably some truth to that. Looking back at my early social and psychological development, psychiatrists would have undoubtedly come to the same conclusion if they had known me as a child. There was just too much adult and parent in my personality makeup. New friends and new experiences in an invigorating climate of play and study helped me in getting rid of that excess baggage, but I never succeeded in jettisoning it completely, no matter how hard I tried.

Papa and Mama recognized that the Shanghai experience was far from ideal and did everything in their power to root out its detrimental influences by making us feel more secure in our new surroundings. During those early days in Japan we did a lot of things together as a family. In the fall we made our first family visit to Sankei-en Garden to view the annual display of blooming chrysanthemums and the magnificent red and orange coloring of maple trees – a family outing that became an annual ritual in ensuing years. We also spent a full day at an amusement park north of Yokohama. I recall the latter experience with a certain amount of rumination and self-reproach. We had a wonderful time riding ferris wheels, carousels and diminutive automobiles specially built for children, but somehow I became separated from the family in the afternoon. It was already dark when the park police, who had been searching for me for several hours, finally found me at the adjoining railway station, tired, lonely, and chilled to the bone. It was no surprise that on our return trip to Honmoku, I received a long and tedious lecture on the inappropriateness of over-zealous self-reliance and the risks of catching a cold. Christmas that year was an exciting undertaking. Papa found a Christmas tree that was tall enough to touch the ceiling, and Mama decorated it with glittering tinsel, colored chain links made of paper, and walnuts that she painted silver and gold. On Christmas eve, we were allowed, for the first time in our lives, to sample a few drops of hot glint wine prepared by Papa specially for the occasion out of red burgundy, lemon juice, brandy, sugar, cinnamon and cloves – a libation he had learned to concoct in Finland. The heart-warming recipe is now our family's traditional drink on Christmas Eve. For the first time also, Mama threw a party on the third day of Christmas for our neighbors and new friends from school. It was a gala affair with party favors, Christmas poppers, colorful paper bags that looked like mushrooms full of mandarin oranges, nuts, and caramel candy. Papa took photographs; Mama staged party games and supervised the children as they milled around the Christmas tree. Mama put on a party that Honmoku's foreign community talked about for months.

That year we also experienced out first *Oshogatsu* (New Year's Day), Japan's biggest and most convivial national holiday. Preparation for *Oshogatsu* started early. A clean-up that the Japanese call *oshoji* (literally translated, a big cleaning up) had been going on for several weeks. Inside, the tatami were aired and mended, and the paper-covered shoji screens carefully dusted and repaired. Outside, the wooden exteriors were washed and patched up to look almost virgin, the gardens were swept, raked, and trimmed of all excess growth. The entrances to the houses were hung with the traditional twisted rope and corrugated white paper, a decoration that some families made themselves while others bought ready-made at outside stalls. Some housewives put out outside displays of pine branches with swigs of bamboo, artistically arranged in stone or ceramic vases and accented by white ribbon elegantly tied around them. On New Year's Eve, at midnight, we heard the temple gongs ringing to drive away, we discovered later, people's evil desires and usher in a virtuous New Year. In the morning, the usually quiet streets of Honmoku were suddenly full of colorfully dressed people – adults and children – exchanging greetings with the traditional *"Akemashite omedeto gozaimasu,"* loosely translated, "the New Year has arrived, Congratulations." Papa and Mama were forewarned that they might have to entertain visitors with sake and rice cakes, but decided – after consultation with neighbors – that they were not yet sufficiently familiar with Japanese customs and etiquette to risk embarrassment by doing something wrong. Instead, they served sherry – vodka was ruled out for being too pedestrian – and small sandwiches with red caviar that everyone oohed and aahed over with immense delight. My brothers and I watched the ceremony with colossal interest as guests – mostly friendly politicians backing Papa's gold recovery effort and new acquaintances – dressed in striped pants, tails and top hats, arrived on

59

jinrikishas to wish Papa and Mama a Happy New Year and present to the family a beautifully wrapped box of candied chestnuts or *kasutera*, a sweet ceremonial sponge cake baked for special occasions.

The first six months of 1934 rolled by swiftly without any noticeable changes in our everyday lives. On May 5, we watched our Japanese neighbors and village fishermen blessed with male children erect long poles outside their houses to hoist one or more huge likenesses of carp made of brightly colored paper to celebrate *Tangu no Sekku* (the Boys' Festival). Floating in the wind against an invisible current, the paper carps were a symbol of male strength, will-power, and long and fulfilled life. In June I finished 4th grade, but my English was still far from perfect and I spent many evenings that summer trying to improve what I had learned during the school year. The summer of 1934 turned out to be a great outdoor adventure. We bought a small row boat that we scrubbed down to its original planking, painted it, and made sufficiently sea-worthy to pass Papa's inspection and ease Mama's anxiety about going out at high tide. The days were not long enough to satisfy even our most modest fancies. We swam, searched the beaches for sea shells and other marine animals, went spear fishing during low tide, and proudly rowed our boat to the neighboring village when the bay was calm. That summer we witnessed our first *O-Bon* Festival, a Buddhist version of All Souls Day during which the Japanese offer prayers for the spirits of the dead who, according to 14th century sacred chronicles, briefly revisit the earth from July 13th to July 15th. The *O-Bon* Festival may have had a past religious connotation, but in Honmoku, it looked more like an ornate carnival that lasted three full days from sunrise on July 13th to midnight July 15th. A huge tower was erected on one of the remaining empty spaces in the village for drummers who pounded out a staccato rhythm from early morning to sundown. In the evenings, men and women danced in concentric circles around the tower lost in a trance of the drumbeats and the wailing sound of distant flutes. During the day, young men in short coats and *fundoshi* (loin cloth) swayed huge palanquins topped by gilded temples, panting, shoving and shouting *"washio washio,"* in a state of utter exhaustion and dubious stupor, as they carried them through the village to send the dead spirits away. With ritual dances, boat races, night processions with dancing girls and lanterns, street peddlers selling everything from candied cotton balls to *yakitori* (barbequed chicken on bamboo skewers), and an upsurge of convivial drinking, Honmoku was aglow in good cheer and *sake*. It was all so new to us, so festive that we stayed up one day to midnight, watching a continuous stream of processions lit by hundreds of lanterns as they moved through the crowded streets of Honmoku.

That summer we also became acquainted with the children of the fishermen. Having found out that we were Russian, they taunted us with what we thought at first was a patriotic Japanese limerick whose origins went back to the Russo-Japanese War. We found out later that it was something they had invented themselves. *Nippon katta, Nippon katta, Roshia magetta* (Japan won, Japan won, Russia lost the war)" they would shout, pointing at us and suddenly disappearing into the dark bowels of their houses. But their intransigence did not last long. Soon we were playing together, shooting marbles, exchanging samurai cards, watching together the weekly *kamishibai* performance, a slide picture show conducted by an itinerant story teller using colored pictures instead of puppets. There were occasional disputes, but they did not last long. They were settled with *Jan-Ken-Po*, the universally accepted Oriental game of "stone-paper-scissors." We also learned from them another fascinating and exciting game that obviously had its origin in Japan's maritime tradition. The Japanese boys called it "battleship, destroyer, submarine." Like "cops and robbers" boys were divided into two opposing groups, each player taking the identity of a battleship, destroyer or submarine. A battleship could sink a destroyer, submarines could torpedo battleships, and the destroyer could sink a submarine. The side that succeeded in sinking all of the opponent's players was the winner, regardless of how many of its own players it had lost in the course of the game during which each side tried to minimize losses by hiding from the opponent.

The friendly play did not last forever. By the time we and our Japanese cohorts reached fourteen or fifteen, we retreated into our own social milieu, playing almost exclusively with Honomoku's foreign children. An interesting comment on our relationship with the fishermen's children and on the Japanese social structure as a whole was that the children of Japanese professionals – lawyers, engineers, doctors – living in Honmoku never played with the children of the fishermen. As we found out later from one of our Japanese upper middle class neighbors, it was beneath their station in the complex hierarchy of Japanese social rules of conduct to commingle and play with them.

Mama radiated satisfaction that summer. She loved swimming and sometimes even joined us on our fishing expeditions. But her primary charge, which she enjoyed immensely, was to entertain the visitors who came to see Papa – lawyers, financial backers, journalists and friends who lent their support to Papa's claim. I cannot recall everyone who visited us that summer, but I remember Papa's lawyers well because they came often and stayed longer than other visitors. I also have a very clear recollection of two other distinguished visitors. Mr. Konishi, president of the Japan Tolstoyan Society, was a wisp of man in his late seventies who spoke excellent Russian and always brought us a mouth-watering confection that looked like our American peanut brittle. What made him so interesting was that he actually lived as a young man at Yasnaya Polyana and personally knew Count Leo Tolstoy. In 1934, I was still too young to have read *War and Peace* or *Anna Karenina*, but I knew who Tolstoy was and had read his *Sevastopol Sketches* that were de rigueur reading for Russian boys because they dealt with the subject of valor in times of war. Talking to Konishi-san about life at Yasnaya Polyana was a unique and unforgettable experience. It was like talking to the great master himself. The other, was William Henry Chamberlin, Tokyo correspondent for the *Christian Science Monitor*, American scholar of Russian history, and author of *The Russian Revolution,* a two-volume history of the collapse of Tsarist Russia that is still considered by experts an important reference work. He often came to play chess with Papa and, I suspect, to solicit his opinion on Soviet-Japanese relations and the most recent news stories emanating from Moscow.

The negotiation for the return of the gold – the *raison d'être* for our Japanese sojourn – were not going well for Papa. His contacts in the Diet and the military were not getting anywhere in convincing the War Ministry that it should recognize the claim and return the gold voluntarily on the basis of preponderant evidence confirming that the gold was indeed deposited with the Japanese Military Mission in Manchuria on a temporary basis and was to be returned on demand. Papa had avoided litigation so far, hoping to settle the claim amicably without taking on the expenses of a long and difficult law suit, but his thinking was changing and, on the advice of his financial backers, he finally decided to sue. I was too young to understand fully all of the implications, but I knew enough to realize that friendly negotiations had failed and we were entering a new phase of direct confrontation with the Japanese government. On June 25th, 1934, with all informal means of recovery exhausted, Papa signed a power-of-attorney appointing Hirohito Hada and Toshizo Yamana, two prominent Tokyo attorneys, as his legal representatives to commence litigation. A few weeks later a law suit, Case No. 2013, was filed by them in Tokyo Regional Civil Court. A copy of the power-of-attorney and other pertinent court documents, including the receipt signed by the head of the Japanese Military Mission in Manchuria, are now part of the Petroff collection at the Hoover Institution, Stanford University in Palo Alto, California.

In September, I started 5th grade with Brother Dames as our home class teacher. Born and raised somewhere near Chicago – I believe it was Gary, Indiana – Brother Dames was a perfect role model for a twelve year-old boy who wanted to find out as much as possible about America, its history and government, and about its every day life. Athletic, pleasantly outgoing – he was also the school's sports director – with a great sense of humor and a streak of independent thinking, Brother Dames literally erased my insecurity in speaking English and substituted in its place a high degree of proficiency that has stood me well for the rest of my life. By the end of 5th grade I knew the capitals of all forty-eight states (Hawaii and Alaska became states later), had a fair idea of how the United States was founded and felt comfortable speaking colloquial American English with people whom I never met before. Brother Dames accomplished all of that, using a methodology that was quite unique. Having discovered that I loved reading, he introduced me to Mark Twain, James Fenimore Cooper, Robert Louis Stevenson, and Zane Grey, whose novels I devoured because they were about the American Wild West We discussed the books as I read them; he explained whatever needed clarification and, if I remember correctly, I wrote four or five one-page reviews about the authors of the books I read. I recall one discussion that turned out to be somewhat awkward. I had finished Zane Grey's *Riders of the Purple Sage*, a story set in the desert of southern Utah in the 1870s, and wanted more information about Mormons and why they were polygamous. Brother Dames, a good Catholic who was celibate, found it a little difficult to explain Mormonism to an inquisitive twelve-year old who wanted to know everything, especially the Mormon predilection for more than one wife. I venerated Brother Dames; as far as I was concerned he was the perfect teacher who could do no wrong. I believe he recognized that I was older than most of my classmates, and therefore should be not only catching up on my English, but also doing work beyond the requirements of the 5th grade curriculum. I learned more from the assigned reading in American literature and my discussions with Brother Dames than from the prescribed subjects in the formal class program.

In the spring of 1935 I joined the First Yokohama Sea Scout Troop. Registered in Great Britain and organized along British scouting standards, the troop was made up almost exclusively of English, American and European boys whose parents lived and worked in

Japan. Until my brother Nick joined the troop a year later, I was the only member of the troop whose family did not have Anglo-Saxon or western European roots. It was a new experience that propelled me further into the domain of the international community and the expatriate culture that prevailed among foreigners living in Japan. The scout precepts of duty, honor and the flag were no different from what I was brought up on as a youngster, except the flag now was the Union Jack. I was not quite sure how to reconcile the new allegiance into the precepts of loyalty that had been inculcated previously in Mukden and Shanghai. I remember discussing the dilemma with Papa and Mama. I don't recall their exact comment, but I think they told me not too worry about it, because some day I would have to pledge allegiance anyway to a country that was not Russian. By 1935, they had obviously given up hope of ever returning to their native Russia and had acquiesced in the reality that their three boys would have to choose a new country affiliation of their own. On January 24, 1936, with the rest of our troop in full scout uniform, I ushered members of the Yokohama foreign community and Japanese prefectural dignitaries at Christ Church in Yokohama during the memorial service for King George V, Queen Elizabeth's grandfather, who died earlier in the week.

I loved scouting and everything that came with it, the cheerful comradery, the discipline, and the feeling of accomplishment. The troop owned an old sailing boat, an eighteen footer, that we sailed on Tokyo Bay. In the summer, we had our annual camp-outs on Lake Nojiri in Nagano prefecture where we also sailed and canoed. There, across the lake, several miles away from our camp, I spent my first night alone in terrifying solitude having canoed across the lake to qualify for the First Class badge. In Nojiri, I also got my first exposure to the mountains which later came to play such an important role in my life. One year, we climbed Mt. Miyoko, an extinct volcano, the tallest mountain in the vicinity of Lake Nojiri. Mr. Dundas, our scoutmaster, became a fellow hiker and mountain climber with whom I climbed in the Japan Alps.

Everything considered, my brothers and I were gradually becoming part of the expatriate community in Yokohama. By the end of 1935 we were not quite there yet, but we were getting close enough to have one foot firmly established in Yokohama's expatriate culture. St. Joseph's College, scouting, visiting and playing with friends who were part of that community changed our tastes, desires, and ambitions. Amongst ourselves we were speaking English instead of Russian, reading American authors and comic books, and becoming quite ecumenical, attending Catholic, Anglican and Methodist services as there was no Russian Orthodox Church in Yokohama until 1937. At home, Papa and Mama conducted Russian classes, generally on Sundays, but there was no regularity to them. Afraid that we might completely lose our competence in reading and writing Russian, Papa and Mama dreamt up a truly remarkable scheme. They sold us on the idea of publishing our own bimonthly journal in Russian under their supervision. It sounded like fun and we accepted the challenge. The first copy of the *Honmoku Dosug* (Honmoku Leisure Times) came out before Christmas of 1934. As far I remember, it was a four page news letter typed on an old Cyrillic-script Underwood typewriter containing articles written by all three of us about our life and adventures in Honmoku. It had art work, a crossword puzzle, and an editorial piece by me on the blessings of living in Honmoku, our wonderful village by the bay. We continued to put out the *Honmoku Dosug* through 1936. Papa and Mama were extremely proud of our accomplishments, often showing copies of our journal to friends who came to visit them. In retrospect, I think the two-year experience of publishing our own journal served a very meaningful end. It allowed me to be literate not only in English but also in Russian, to experience Pushkin, Tolstoy, Dostoevsky, and Chekhov not in translation but in the original Russian. I am deeply indebted to my parents for that.

Nineteen Thirty Five sailed through without any serious political reverberations for the foreign community, despite the gathering clouds of political instability in Japan and abroad. Responding to the January Saar plebiscite, Hitler marched into the Saar basin, while Mussolini launched his ill-conceived Ethiopian campaign. In both cases there were only cursory public outcries against the danger of growing fascism and militarism. The League of Nations censured Germany and Italy, but nothing tangible came out of that. In the Far East, Japan's incursion into Manchuria was acquiesced to without a broad-based protest on the part of Great Britain or the United States. They were too preoccupied with domestic problems, trying to deal with an economy that had plunged into the depths of a crippling depression. On the surface, Japanese society and its economic and political structures seemed imperturbable and not very different from previous years, but beneath the facade of traditional Japanese serenity, there were foreboding signs of economic dysfunction and growing political strife. Japan was also beginning to feel the effects of the world depression. Her exports dropped in 1935 to levels not seen since the 1920s, and poverty, especially in the provinces, was reaching alarming proportions. A cycle of vehement political attacks against the corruption of public officials and financial barons hogged newspaper headlines through most of 1935. Even the conservative *Japan Times and Advertizer*, Yokohama's English language newspaper, took part in the diatribe. In August, the grisly assassination of General Tetsuzan Nagata, Chief of Japan's Military Affairs Bureau, by Lieutenant Colonel Saburo Aizawa resulted in a sensational trial of Aizawa that became the rallying point for reformers seeking to overhaul Japanese society. Behind the scenes, the more socially radical and homeland-directed Kodo (Imperial Way) clique and the zealously expansionist anti-communist Tosei (Control) group in the Japanese military were locked in an unnerving struggle for the heart and soul of the military establishment. Both factions feared the spread of communism in Asia and favored a pre-emptive strike against the Soviet Union. Both also sought economic and social reform at home. But there was a difference in the way they sought to achieve their goals. Imperial Way looked to a curtailment of Japanese expansion in Asia and instead wanted to concentrate on radical social and economic reform at home, even if that meant embracing centralized planning, national socialism and the rest of the socialist agenda that was taboo to the more conservative elements of the Japanese elite. The Control faction was more interested in achieving an industrial build-up for military purposes with little concern for the needs of the people. There was also a generational clash between the two factions. Consisting mostly of senior staff and field grade officers supported by party politicians and business trusts, the Control group was more traditional and status quo oriented in the pursuit of its objectives. The Imperial Way clique with its young and hot-headed junior officers demanded a swift and radical settlement that looked to a clean sweep of the corrupt and rigidly structured dual government steered by the elderly military and civilian leaders.

Yokohama's foreign community watched this struggle with great interest, but did not see the warning signals. Life was good and business was prospering. The community was growing as more Russian émigrés from Manchuria and German Jews escaping Nazi persecution arrived and settled in the Tokyo-Yokohama area. Papa's conservative attorneys and financial backers also did not seem to be overly disturbed. They were certain that the factional contest would pass with time and Japan would return to her "virtuous" ways, just as it did in the 1860s when the "Meiji restoration" ousted the corrupt military government of the Tokugawa Shogunate. There was even a contemporary expression that leaders of the Imperial Way faction used to describe their reform program. They called it the "Showa restoration" in deference to Emperor Hirohito whose reign was known as Showa (Enlightened Peace).

The optimistic assessment turned out to be wrong. In the early morning of February 26, 1936, young pro-reform Imperial Way officers and enlisted men of Japan's First Division stationed in Tokyo attacked central government offices and private residences of cabinet members, killing a number of prominent politicians and senior army and navy officers whom they had fingered as proponents of the status quo. Prime Minister Keisuke Okada, a retired admiral, had miraculously escaped the carnage only because someone else was mistakenly killed instead of him. The rebellion was an attempt to stage a coup d'état that would topple the existing government and bring major changes to the Japanese political and economic system.

February 26th was a cold wintery day with heavy snow falling in the Tokyo-Yokohama area for the second day. Brother August J. Walter, who set foot on Japanese soil in 1896 to teach English in Japanese institutions of higher learning and, in the early 1930s, transferred to St. Joseph's College, said that he had never seen such heavy snowfall in Japan. We had enough snow on our playing field at St. Joseph's to build a six foot high fortress out of snow. I remember the February 26th Incident – the "Ni-Ni-roku" as the Japanese have named it – in minute detail. Instead of bicycling to school that day, my brothers and I took a city tram from Honmoku that got bogged down in the snow en route. We had to fight our way for almost a full hour through heavy and deep snow before we reached what foreigners in Yokohama called the "Bluff (Yamate in Japanese), the abruptly rising acclivity where most foreigners lived and where our campus was situated. At noon, St. Joseph's, like all schools in the Tokyo-Yokohama area, was closed down and we were sent home without any clear explanation of the rebellion in Tokyo. On our way home we had to tramp through a foot of fresh snow for nearly a mile and a half, as all public transportation had come to a halt. I was thirteen, Nick, eleven, and Mike not quite nine. It was an unforgettable adventure getting home on foot. Papa and Mama had no more information about what was taking place in Tokyo than our teachers at St. Joseph's. From a number of different sources, including our maid Kazuko who had been listening to the radio, we surmised that there was a military revolt in Tokyo and that the government was under siege. I remember Papa saying "I hope we will not have to be witnesses to another revolution as we did in 1917."

We found out later that the rebels had occupied the Diet, the War Ministry, the General Staff Headquarters and a number of other government buildings in the center of Tokyo, and were passing out copies of a manifesto demanding reform that called for a socialist reorientation of the Japanese political system. At first some senior army officers considered placating the rebels but, to the surprise of almost everyone, the emperor stood firm on the question of bringing discipline back into the army's divided loyalties. On February 29, troops were summoned from army commands outside of Tokyo and the insurgency was put down by the end of the day. The leaders of the rebellion were quickly tried and executed. The services were reorganized to insure unanimity, and dissenters were transferred to overseas commands in Taiwan and Manchuria or retired from active service. The Control clique emerged out of the "Ni-ni-roku" incident as the undisputed winner of the new military regime. The noted American specialist on Japan, former Ambassador to Japan Edwin O. Reischauer pointed out many years later: "(The) re-establishment of discipline within the army did not mean that the army as an elite had become depoliticized. If anything its voice in Japan became greater."[17]

In the short run, the "Ni-ni-roku" incident did not create any immediate difficulties for our family, even though it was a somber harbinger of things to come. We spent a marvelous summer that year, our best since our arrival in Japan. We joined the Hachioji Swimming Club, a summer family retreat in Honmoku founded by foreigners, and Nick and I passed most of our free time at the club, swimming, playing mahjong, and ogling girls. We were still too shy and inexperienced to flirt with them. We roamed the hills collecting butterflies, insects and beetles. Over the next three years I assembled an impressive collection that I donated upon graduation to the science department of St. Joseph's College. That summer, I also discovered *Haseiden* (The Temple of the Eight Wise Men), an elegantly designed hermitage built in the hills beyond the village by a wealthy Japanese businessman in the 1920s in the traditional style of a Buddhist temple. Devoted to quiet meditation and self appraisal, *Haseiden* stood in a majestic grove of pine trees, tall grass and wild azalea bushes, deliberately hidden from the hustle and bustle of everyday life. Inside, on a slightly elevated platform at the head of an incredibly beautiful but simple hall accented by walls in natural wood stood eight life-size figures of Christ, Socrates, Buddha, Confucius and four leaders of Japanese Buddhism, including Nichiren and Eisai. Who the other two Japanese thinkers were I had known at one time, but have unfortunately forgotten. Nichiren was the visionary

Japanese monk of the 13th century who tried to cleanse Buddhism of the metaphysical interpretations and ritual embellishments, and return it to what he considered to be Buddha's original teaching. An analogy could be made by saying that his following represented the Protestant wing of Buddhism that placed more emphasis on personal faith and achievement of good works. Eisai brought Zen Buddhism to Japan from China. In Japan, it matured into a major philosophic teaching that denied the usefulness of sacred books and writings and maintained instead that enlightenment can be achieved not by the exercise of intellect, but directly from the experience of life through a meaningful dialectic between master and pupil. Separating the foreign sages from the Japanese thinkers, stood a large shining circular mirror, with an inscription in Japanese that could have been straight out of Cervantes' famous saying "Make it thy business to know thyself." Roughly translated the inscription said "Look in the mirror, wayfarer, you are standing in front of the eight sages of the world. Think about your shortcomings and strengths." One did not have to read the inscription to understand the significance of the inspiring display– its message was self-evident. Stimulated by that first visit I often came to *Haseiden*. There was something about it that made me feel better about myself after spending a few minutes in front of the mirror and the eight wise men. Years later, as an adult I recognized that what I really admired about *Haseiden* was its subtle but lucid message encouraging toleration of all creeds and peoples. As I think about my moral and spiritual development, I believe it was in *Haseiden* that I first discovered a predilection that transcended the Orthodox beliefs of my childhood and gradually led me to a more pantheistic view of the universe.

III

It did not take long for the military to increase their voice in the affairs of state after the Ni-ni-roku rebellion. On an early June morning, without any advance notice, Papa was taken into custody by the *Kempeitai* (Military Police), allegedly for questioning in connection with an investigation that pertained to White Russian residents living in Japan. We were petrified. Mama dropped everything she was doing and took the train to Tokyo to consult with Papa's lawyers and friends in the Diet to see what they could do to free Papa from the clutches of the Military Police. He was released the next day, shaken by the experience and convinced that the Japanese military were trying to pressure him to drop his law suit. By September it was clear to Papa's Japanese financial backers that the Ministry of War would never allow the government to lose the gold recovery case. Two months later, the Tokyo Regional Court ruled for the Japanese government, following the instructions of the Ministry of War. The court never questioned the validity of the gold's transfer to Colonel Isome in 1920 – the receipt was powerful evidence that could not be dismissed. It had not only the colonel's signature, but also the official stamp of the Japanese Military Mission at Station Manchuria at the Sino-Russian border. Instead, the court took the arbitrary position that Colonel Isome acted beyond the scope of his delegated authority and that his government could not be held responsible for his action, implying that if the plaintiff wanted, he could bring suit against Colonel Isome. As a final insult to Papa, the court stated in passing that General Petroff represented an entity that had no legal status in international law. Especially damaging to the success of the suit was the testimony of former Minister of War General Sadao Araki who, despite compelling evidence to the contrary, testified that the central government in Tokyo had no knowledge of the gold and its expenditure in Manchuria. The attorneys considered filing a suit against Colonel Isome. They even retained a private detective to check on the colonel's estate in Mito prefecture, but Papa refused to follow that line of attack. He insisted, as the official receipt indicated, that he deposited the gold with the Japanese Military Mission, not Colonel Isome, and it was therefore Japan's responsibility to return the gold. In the spring of 1937, the attorneys filed an appeal in the hope that another judge might take a more favorable view of Papa's claim, an action founded more on hope than the realities of the political situation in Japan. The ruling was a devastating blow for Papa. He had put so much time and effort into the recovery of the gold that he now found it extremely difficult to deal rationally with the problem of whether or not the litigation should be continued.

The verdict was also a great disappointment to the family. Financial help from the All-Russian Military Union was drying up. Convinced that the appeal would never get anywhere in a political climate dominated by the military, Papa's Japanese backers also stopped offering financial aid. For all I know, they may have been enjoined by the military to cease and desist. Our own resources were getting down to where we could consider ourselves lucky if there was enough cash on hand to survive financially for more than two or three months. True to form, Mama came through with a solution, even though it did not last very long. Since the beginning of the year, Rev. Roger

P. Pott, Vicar Of Christ Church in Yokohama and principal of the Yokohama International School, had been trying to recruit Mama for the position of the school's resident nurse. Rev. Pott was a dynamic Anglican churchman in his early thirties, a dashing bachelor who claimed he was first cousin of Queen Elizabeth, consort of King George VI of England. On arriving in Yokohama in the early 1930s, he took Yokohama's foreign community and its upper social strata by storm, promising to open an exclusive school patterned on the British public school model with all sorts of additional fringe activities such as fencing, music, horse-back riding, tennis, and an opportunity to use the school's summer camp facility that he was building in Karuizawa, Japan's prime vacation resort in the mountains. In a typical colonial affirmation of Kipling's dictum that "east is east and west is west," Yokohama International School did not admit Asian students, nor did it have many students of mixed marriages. The majority of the student body came from the upper rungs of the foreign community's British families, although there was a sprinkling of American, Swiss, French, Belgian and Dutch children among the "Brits." The school's objective, according to Rev. Pott, was to raise cultivated ladies and gentlemen without having to send them to a public school in England. The concept appealed to the socially more elitist matrons of the foreign community, and the school prospered, gaining a number of students who had previously attended St. Joseph's College.

Mama resented Rev. Pott's overblown elitism and she was also afraid that differences of opinion on questions of health care might erupt if she went to work for him. Rev. Pott had a laissez faire reputation on the subject of medical care. "Don't worry about it, unless it creates an emergency" was his customary reaction to cases of illness or accidental disability according to those who knew him well. Mama, on the other hand, believed in prevention and an early response to illness, no matter how minor or trivial it appeared at first glance. Earlier in the year she had rejected his offer largely because as a condition of employment Rev. Pott insisted that all three of us transfer from St. Joseph's to YIS (Yokohama International School). It was obvious that he did not feel comfortable from a public relations standpoint to have a staff member's children attending a different school. With the family's financial position threatened, Mama agreed to take the job on the condition that Nick and Mike would transfer, but I would stay at St. Joseph's because there were only a few children of my age in YIS. Rev. Pott accepted the compromise and, in the spring of 1937, Mama went to work for the Yokohama International School, first in Yokohama and then at the summer school in Karuizawa.

Located about a mile away from the center of Karuizawa in the middle of a thick grove of pine trees with an open view of Mt. Asama, one of Japan's most active volcanoes, the YIS campus was a perfect setting for summer school. The physical plant consisted of a main building with Rev. Pott's quarters, administrative offices, dining room, a small lecture hall, and a huge covered veranda where children and adults could play and read. Around it, in a crescent, were rustic cabins, housing students and staff. Mama shared a small cabin with the school's teachers, and the three of us were lodged in larger cabins according to age. Although I was not part of the school's student body, Reverend Pott invited me to help with the chores, hoping I would fall in love with the school's activities and would stay at YIS for the fall term. During the day, life at summer school consisted primarily of individual sport activities – fencing, tennis, swimming, fishing, horse back riding – there was a stable a quarter of a mile away – and piano lessons for those who were interested in music. For those who needed catching up, especially in mathematics, there were scheduled lessons in the afternoon. In the evening, we usually lit a campfire, told stories, sang and performed slapstick skits, all of this often to the rumbling sound and orange glow of Mt. Asama that had a way of erupting almost every day. For us children it was a perfect setting for a long summer holiday. For Mama, it was often hard work as there were accidents, daily staff meetings, and exhausting disagreements with Rev. Pott. Mama was against the English practice of caning based on a weekly totaling of demerits, and she was not afraid to challenge Rev. Pott about what she considered an outrage. There were also differences of opinion on sanitation, but what finally brought her professional relationship with Rev. Pott to a climax was an outbreak of colitis among the students. Rev. Pott, a passionate believer in natural foods, had contracted with a local dairy to deliver unpasteurized milk. Mama told him that she could not take responsibility for the health of the children if they were allowed to drink unpasteurized milk. Pott refused to admit that the outbreak resulted from the unpasteurized milk, and their dispute exploded into a full blown confrontation with Mama insisting on a full investigation of the dairy and the testing of the cows and their milk. The stubborn and overbearing cleric refused to order the investigation. In mid August, Mama resigned her position, demonstratively walked out with us in tow, and left Karuizawa to return home.

The short stay at the Yokohama International School was not a complete waste. It turned out to have a positive side. In Karuizawa, I began tutoring younger boys in arithmetic and simple algebra. I enjoyed tutoring and, on return to Yokohama, began doing it on a systematic basis, sometimes coaching as many as three boys and earning extra money without which it would have been impossible for Nick and me to pursue our interest in sports and the outdoors. Mama also profited from the experience. Having observed the ins-and-outs of running a children's dormitory in Karuizawa, she decided to open one in Yokohama for the children attending St. Joseph's College. Brother Gaschy gave his blessing to the enterprise and assured Mama that he would refer out-of-town parents to her as SJC was in the process of phasing out its boarding school division. During the fall of 1937 we gave up our seaside cottage in Honmoku and moved to a much larger house in Sagiyama within walking distance of St. Joseph's. The new house was totally western in its construction – architecturally very uninteresting – but it was large enough to accommodate the family and as many as ten to twelve additional boarders. The house was redecorated, refurbished with new furniture and, in January 1938, officially opened for business with four boarders, a French boy, son of the assistant naval attaché of the French Embassy in Tokyo, and three Russian boys.

IV

In the meantime, the political situation in Japan was worsening. While we were still in Karuizawa, fighting broke out between Japanese and Chinese troops near the Marco Polo Bridge in Peiking (Beijing). It was not clear who started the fight, but the consequences were calamitous. The military hard liners in Japan demanded an apology, the Chinese demurred, and in no time at all fighting spread to Shanghai, igniting a military confrontation that, by November 1937, turned into a full scale war between China and Japan. Attempts to put a stop to it by the Nine Powers Conference in Brussels got nowhere. Nanking fell to the Japanese onslaught on December 13 triggering a terrible and indiscriminate slaughter of Chinese civilians and soldiers. The Rape of Nanking as it became known after the war was a grotesque act of Japanese militarism at its worst. There was no mention of it in the Japanese press, and we learned about it only after the war.

The fall of Nanking precipitated a temporary breach in Japanese-American relations aggravated by the accidental Japanese shelling of the U.S.S. *Panay* sent up the Yangtze river from Shanghai to evacuate American refugees from the war zone. The Japanese government apologized and offered amends, but the sinking of the *Panay* seriously damaged the already strained Japanese-American relations. Some old-timers in Yokohama recalled the sinking of the *Lusitania* in 1915 and expressed fears that American public opinion would demand a break in diplomatic relations, but the incident was satisfactorily closed when Japan promised that it would do everything possible to prevent any future attacks on American interests in China.

The Chinese surrender of Nanking did not satisfy the Japanese. The military wanted a deeper penetration of China to provide a permanent shield for Manchuria. They also insisted on ending the existing "open door" policy and the establishment of full Japanese control over the economic development of China. This did not sit well with the United States and Great Britain because both nations had substantial trading interests in China. It was clear that Japan and the United States were moving ahead on a collision course. In his diary for December 26, 1937, after the closing of the *Panay* incident, United States Ambassador Joseph C. Grew prophetically noted that "our satisfaction at the settlement of the *Panay* incident may be but temporary and that the rock upon which for five years I have been trying to build a substantial edifice of Japanese-American relations has broken down into treacherous sand.[18]

Ambassador Grew correctly assessed the political situation that prevailed in Tokyo at the end of 1937. In December, under considerable pressure from the military, the Japanese Diet passed the National General Mobilization Law which gave the government powers to control vast areas of life and business, including conscription, labor, capital formation, allocation of resources, and even freedom of speech. The practical consequences of the National Mobilization Law, which resembled Nazi Germany's Enabling Act, was that Japan entered 1938 with definite plans for a more protracted war. It was not surprising therefore that we suddenly saw a new spurt of pro-war rhetoric and propaganda in the first months of 1938. Uplifting themes in justification of the war in China appeared in Japanese cinema, music, magazines, cartoon art, film, and newspaper reportage. Even the conservative *Japan Times and Advertizer*, Japan's principal English-language newspaper, joined the ranks of the war mongers in condoning aggression in China and arguing with a fair amount of sophistry that Japan's move into China proper was necessary to counteract the political chaos brought about by the Chinese civil war.

Almost overnight, cinema, radio, and popular literature became more martial, championing the exploits of Japanese soldiers and extolling the spirit of sacrifice at home. *Chocolate and Soldiers,* a film about a poor Japanese soldier on the China front and his young son waiting for him to come home was the most popular Japanese film in 1938. Hino Ashibei's *Tsuchi to Heitai (Earth and Soldiers)* was a first person account of a Japanese assault on the Chinese mainland – a belabored attempt by army headquarters in Tokyo to drum up civilian support for the war. Civilian government officials also took strong pro-war positions. In his November 1938 speech Prime Minister Konoe openly justified Japanese aggression in China as an essential undertaking against the menace of growing "white imperialism and red Bolshevism in Asia." In the streets and neighborhoods of Yokohama and Tokyo ceremonial send-offs for young men entering military service became a common occurrence. With waving flags, patriotic songs and banners extolling duty and courage, Japan dispatched its youth to military training camps and from there to the Chinese front. Caught up in the tide of fanatic patriotism, the Japanese military was elbowing the nation into a more massive and ruthless war. There were attempts to moderate the war passion. From June 1937 to January 1940, four different cabinets took office and fell prematurely largely on the issue of the war with China. But the war hysteria was beyond moderation. By 1938, the military leadership was committed to an all-out offensive in China in order to install a new central Chinese government that would accept Japanese control.

There were two Japans, however. Side by side with the jingoistic and power hungry Japan dominated by the military was a more serene and conventional Japan that resented the military's interference in government and the prostitution of the parliamentary system that the nation enjoyed prior to 1936. It was a Japan that did not want war with China and was shocked by the barbarism of the Japanese troops and the unwarranted bombing and strafing of the *Panay*. Ambassador Grew recognized its existence when he spoke of the deluge of letters, visitors, and telegrams received at the American Embassy, expressing shame, regrets, and apologies for the sinking of the *Panay* and the loss of American lives. It was a Japan that desired to have good relations with America, prized American popular culture, and remembered U.S. aid to Tokyo and Yokohama after the earthquake of 1923. We were understandably closer to that second Japan. We came into contact with it daily and understood its thinking much better than the aggressive and contentious logic of the Japanese leaders at the center of power.

I remember staying in line with hundreds of Japanese to see *Captains Courageous* and *Gone with the Wind,* and listening to the latest American records at Kikuya, the conveniently located coffee shop and bakery on Moto-machi patronized after school by the older St.Joseph's College students. Mama's and Papa's experience with the Japanese public was similar to mine. They, too, encountered situations exemplifying pro-American feelings and a deep aversion to war. In her contacts with women, Mama often heard Japanese housewives whose sons had been conscripted into the army or navy confiding in whispers how they felt about the futility of war. Papa's Japanese friends openly told him that they could not understand how friendly Japanese-American relations had gone astray to satisfy the power-hungry military clique.

Pro-war hysteria notwithstanding, life in Japan continued to be safe, predictable and surprisingly unfettered, despite the stormy clouds on the political horizon. Most foreigners in the Tokyo-Yokohama area tended to disregard the warning signs. Even Ambassador Grew did not think that Japanese-American relations were in a state of crisis or he would not have taken a five months furlough in 1939. Unlike Europe where personal freedom was rapidly losing ground at the hands of the newly established dictatorships, Japan was still a free country. Except for military installations such as Yokosuka, there were no travel restrictions for foreigners. Nor was there any excessive surveillance such as one found in Nazi Germany or the Soviet Union. Even in the more remote regions where local Japanese officials and residents rarely saw foreigners, we were treated kindly and with respect. Putting it in a nutshell, there were no strong and convincing reasons for concern in 1939. Life in Japan was still very good.

For our family thinking about leaving Japan was out of the question. Papa's case against the Japanese government was still in litigation. Mama's dormitory venture was commencing to be profitable. By 1939, she had nine boarders and, with some minor house alterations, a potential for three more. The Russian School in Tokyo was expanding to accommodate newly arriving families from China, and Papa was asked to become its principal in 1940. Our studies at St. Joseph's were proceeding according to schedule, and both Papa and Mama were entirely satisfied with the quality of our education and our progress. Even if we wanted to relocate to the United States, we probably could not have managed it anyway as we did not have enough in savings to finance such a move.

Our new abode in Sagiyama was about two miles away from Honmoku, and I often bicycled there on weekends and holidays. I had not yet dissociated myself completely from the community where we lived longer than anywhere else. During the summer of 1938, Nick and I spent most of our time in Honmoku at the Hachioji Swimming Club, swimming, fishing, and playing cards or mahjong in the modest but comfortable club house run by Mrs. Graham, a kindly English lady in her fifties who had been living in Japan since World War I. That summer I read Tolstoy's *War and Peace* in the original Russian and also Dickens' *Tale of Two Cities*. But the big event that summer was our climb of the 12,388 foot Mt. Fuji, Japan's highest mountain.

We really did not plan to climb Mt. Fuji, but after consultation with some Japanese hikers who were camping near us on the shore of Lake Kawaguchi, we decided to join their climbing group. From the road-head located at approximately 3,500 feet, we started for the top at 6:00 PM, climbing steadily on a zigzag path between lava blocks strewn over the mountain slope. The plan was to reach the top at daybreak to see the early morning sun as it rose over the Kanto plain. The Kawaguchi route is relatively easy, but long and dogged, hot and sweaty during the day, and quite nippy in the cool of the night. There were hundreds of people on the winding path the day Nick and I climbed Mt. Fuji – some walking alone, others in groups, and some sitting on chairs lashed to the backs of hardy mountain carriers who made their living toting tourists to the top. A Japanese proverb says that every Japanese should climb *Fujisan* (Mt. Fuji), but only fools climb it more than once. I was one of those fools. I climbed it two more times – in 1941, with a St. Joseph's classmate, guiding a party of tourists via the Gotemba route and, again in 1946 via the same route, with four young American officers of the U.S. Army of Occupation.

We reached the crater and the stone summit hut just a few minutes before sunrise. It was beginning to lighten up, but the western sky was still dark. In the dim shadow of the hut stood a Shinto shrine with the traditional *tori* (temple gate) and a stone tablet with beautifully inscribed ideographs. Inside the hut there was hot green tea and a post box where one could drop a post card to prove that he or she had reached the top. In an atrociously dismal setting of sand, rock, and snow soiled by the dirty boots of climbers, at a short distance from the hut, were rough walls of lava blocks – probably erected for protection against the wind. Beyond, in the early light of the rising sun, was the whole expanse of central Honshu all the way to the Pacific Ocean to the southeast and the snow-covered peaks of the Japan Alps to the north and north-west. It was an experience I have never forgotten. We were on top of the world in a state of intense exhilaration and brotherly bliss. A Japanese climber asked Nick how old he was, and when he told him that he was a few months shy of fourteen, he shook his head in disbelief, uttered the customary Japanese *saa* to express amazement, and said in all seriousness that he was probably the youngest to make the climb, certainly the youngest *gaijin* (foreigner). We sat for at least an hour watching the huge ball rising higher and higher, and then we started our descent, this time over the much shorter but steeper Yoshida route, a long and tedious glissade over what seemed like miles and miles of sand and crushed volcanic rock. By the time we staggered into our campsite, our aging hiking boots were scraped and scarred beyond recognition.

The rest of Nineteen Thirty-Eight flew by with fleeting haste. The war in China produced an economic crisis resulting primarily from the government's inability to deal with the ballooning trade deficit due to reduced exports and vastly increased imports of raw materials needed for the war effort. War casualties were also growing beyond expectations. Processions of grieving relatives marching through the streets of Tokyo and Yokohama carrying urns with ashes of fallen soldiers and sailors were becoming a common occurrence. The Japanese army occupied Canton (Guang-zhou) and Hankow (Wuhan), but beyond those large cities it was moving inland at a snail's pace against impressive Chinese resistance. In fact, it was not unusual to read in the local press that towns that had been occupied some time ago were again being fought over. The Japanese attempt to set up a friendly Chinese government in Nanking was also floundering. Japan had obviously overextended its resources and now needed time and considerable political acumen to improve its relations with the United States and Great Britain in order to settle the mess in China. Both Hachiro Arita and Admiral Kichisaburo Nomura, foreign ministers during 1939 and the first half of 1940 made genuine efforts to improve Japanese-American and Japanese-British relations. The eighteen months between January 1939 and July 1940 were a much needed interlude when political passions in Japan waned and diplomacy made a concerted effort to find a compromise on the China question. Years later, writing about the rise of militarism in Japan, Edwin Reischauer called this period a "Diplomatic Pause."[19]

The lessening of tension could be perceived in the rhetoric of both Japan and the United States, in the official diplomatic exchanges between Washington and Tokyo, and in the desiderata that each nation put forward in an attempt to clarify their positions on China. We could even see the change in attitudes ourselves. In

April 1939, the U.S.S. *Astoria* arrived in Japan bearing the ashes of Japan's Ambassador to the United States Viscount Makoto Saito. The transfer of the ashes at the pier in Yokohama was a carefully orchestrated ceremony organized jointly by the Japanese Foreign Office and the staff of the American Embassy in Tokyo. Flags were at half mast. The guard of honor was composed of both American and Japanese sailors. The procession included Japan's foreign minister and American Ambassador Joseph C. Grew. To the tune of Chopin's funeral march, it moved slowly through the people-lined streets of Yokohama with the urn containing Viscount Saitos's ashes to a funeral train specially dispatched for the occasion. It was a solemn and impressive event carried out by the two nations with great precision and sense of decorum. Watching the procession, the foreign community of Yokohama interpreted the event as a gesture of continuing Japanese-American friendship that dispelled any suspicion of growing dissent. Most Japanese also assumed that a new leaf had been turned in Japanese-American diplomacy and that the United States was finally acquiescing to the idea of a new order established in China by the Japanese. Another local event that seemed to demonstrate improved Japanese-American relations was the eightieth anniversary of the landing of Commodore Perry and the opening of Japan to American trade, celebrated for some reason in 1939 rather than 1938. It was a gala affair with congratulatory speeches, foreign and Japanese dignitaries, and a historic pageant depicting the landing and signing of the treaty. Many of the taller boys from St. Joseph's, dressed in U.S. naval uniforms of the period, participated in the pageant playing the role of American sailors and marines. I did not take part in the extravaganza because in 1939 I was still one of the smaller boys in my class.

Two very different occurrences that determined my future interest in outdoor sports took place in the late spring and early summer of 1939. During the first week of May, I went sailing in the Bay of Tokyo with a classmate from St. Joseph's. It was a warm day, the bay was calm, and we were complaining that there was not enough wind. About five miles out of the Yokohama Yacht Club and three or four miles from shore, the weather changed suddenly in the afternoon and before we were able to lower the mainsail we were hit with the full force of a rain-soaking squall from the southeast. As anyone who has sailed in Tokyo Bay knows, squalls from the southeast are often of taifun ferocity and extremely hazardous for small sailing craft. The boat capsized and we found ourselves suddenly in ice cold water, desperately trying to disengage ourselves from the sail that had ballooned out in the water. For the next two hours that seemed like eternity we hung onto the capsized boat, hoping someone would pick us up. Our first potential rescuer was a Japanese fishing boat returning after a day of fishing. The fishermen offered to take us on board but refused to take our sailboat in tow. I did not feel that we could abandon a boat that belonged to our sea scout troop, and I declined the offer. It took another full hour before we sighted a Blue Funnel Line freighter on its way to the Yokohama harbor. Someone at the Yacht Club where we moored our boat must have signaled the ship that we were out in the bay and needed assistance. The ship cut its engines and lowered a life boat with four strong English sailors speaking rapid-fire cockney that we found difficult to understand. With their help we succeeded in righting the sailboat and lashing it to the ship's cable thrown overboard. It was a close call. I will never forget the sudden surge of security that I felt when we finally reached the ship's deck, given some dry clothes, and sent down to the boiler room with huge mugs of steaming hot grog. It could have been a lot worse – we were on the verge of hypothermia when the Blue Funnel Line freighter pulled us out of the bay

The other experience was more pleasant and personally rewarding. In July, after several weeks of planning, Nathaniel Dundas, our scoutmaster, Alex Volkoff, a graduate student from the University of Vancouver who was visiting his aunt and uncle in Yokohama, and I spent a week hiking and climbing in the *Kita Arpsu* (Northern Japan Alps) out of the small hamlet of Kamikochi. We first climbed the easily accessible Yake and then the much more distant and difficult Hotaka. The sun was just beginning to come up as we roped up for the final push to the summit of Hotaka, across some formidable rock formations we did not notice from our bivouac on a snow field during the previous night. It was my first real climb – Fuji was a walk-up – and I was terribly excited when we reached the top. Below us, in a diffused glow of the shining sun hung a gentle mist that covered the deep canyon we traversed the previous day. Sixty years later, my wife and I visited Kamikochi. Mt. Hotaka looked as beautiful as when I first saw it in 1939, but Kamikochi had become much more touristy and congested with outdoor enthusiasts from nearby Matsumoto.

The climb of Mt. Hotaka crystallized in my memory as one of the most trenchant experiences of my youth. It was not just climbing that made it so memorable. It was also the comradery and the discussions on the state of the world. In March Hitler had annexed the Czech provinces of Bohemia and Moravia and, in April, Mussolini had occupied Albania. Over a campfire we played out the various scenarios of the Nazi assault in Europe. Who was next, Poland, France, England, Yugoslavia, and what effect would the European imbroglio have on Japan's relations with the United States and the Soviet Union. Dundas was terribly pessimistic about the future. He was sure a new world war was to break out and that England and Russia would again take the brunt of the German onslaught. That fall he returned to England to rejoin his regiment. I have been told by mutual friends that he was killed in North Africa during Montgomery's victorious dash to Tobruk. I lost track of Alex – he returned to Canada and for all I know may still be alive today.

The two experiences that summer defined my outdoor interests for the rest of my life. I still enjoy an occasional dunking in warm water – Hawaii or the Mexican Riviera – but the shock and memory of spending three-and-one-half hours in cold water have never completely faded away. It's not death by drowning that I am afraid of. The risk of death in serious mountaineering is at least as extensive as it is in water sports. It's the cold water that I dislike and try to avoid as much as possible. It reminds me too much of that day in the Bay of Tokyo when the water was intensely cold and there was no possibility of getting out of it short of abandoning our sailboat. The war put an end to sailing and I never picked it up after the war. The Kamikochi experience, on the other hand, had just the opposite effect. I got hooked on the mountains in Kamikochi and have climbed and trekked all over the world since then, often disregarding the obvious risks of mountaineering and the anxiety my climbing excursions must have caused my wife and family.

That summer I also began to mature intellectually. Physically, I was still one of the smaller boys in my class – I did not gain my full height until my senior year – but intellectually, I was growing by leaps and bounds. I read a lot, held long discussions with Papa and Mama on a variety of subjects that interested me, and indulged in daydreams and fantasies about the future. The previous year I volunteered to work as student librarian, and my reading expanded impressively. For a small school, St. Joseph's had an excellent library, and I soaked up during my two years as student librarian most of Sir Walter Scott and Raphael Sabatini, a fair number of H. Rider Haggard's and Alexander Dumas' novels. My appetite for history was genuine. It came from Papa who challenged me regularly to read as much history as I could find in our school library. I was also beginning to disagree with some of my more doctrinaire and conformist Catholic brothers who taught history and literature, especially on questions of freedom and the role played by history in the life of nations. I can't fault the school's general policy of freedom of religion. The Marinist brothers are a teaching order; as much as possible, they tried to avoid proselytization as a matter of policy. During my eight years at the college I can recall only two conversions to Catholicism. But not all brothers followed this policy uniformly. Some were more militantly Roman Catholic than others, less analytical in their approach to Catholicism's transgressions throughout history, and more uncompromising on questions of philosophy. I had the bad luck of having two such teachers in my junior and senior years. Despite the very laudatory remarks on my St. Joseph's transcript by the school's principal, Brother William Ambrose, that I was a "model of diligence and scholastic attainment," I received in my junior year my only Cs in high school – one in literature and the other history, fields of study in which I had a genuine interest. I received them because I refused to bow to the religious fervor and prejudices of Father Ulrich who taught history. Besides, I don't think Brother Kessler, a doctrinaire Texan and our senior year class advisor, liked my reading Guy de Maupassant and Dostoevsky whose works he found in my desk by accident. He raised an uproar about it by referring me to the principal on the grounds I had been bringing books to school that were on the Index, and was thus clouding the minds of my unspoiled Catholic classmates by exposing them to authors who were proscribed by the Catholic Church.

My childhood was on the whole a sunny one, but I found my last two years in high school somewhat stymieing. As I think about it now, it was probably the result of my mounting skepticism of established religions and the growing political insecurity brought about by the rise of militarism in Japan. The fact that the hormones were finally running wild also did not help. I felt suspended between the past and the future, unwilling to compromise the independence in thinking that I had internalized over the years with the orthodoxy of my Catholic teachers and the fierce propaganda of the Japanese military that lead Japan to a calamitous war. And yet, I knew that I had to suppress my reactions and rebuttals, knowing that the consequences could be unpleasant and even distressing if the confrontation got out of hand. The one thing that compensated for the inner conflict was that I finally put on some weight in 1940 and made the first string of our soccer team. I also found out that I enjoyed track, and was actually quite good at running long distances, having succeeded in doing the mile in less than five minutes, an accomplishment of considerable consequence for a high-school student in the 1940s. The physical exertion and the discipline of daily practice helped to alleviate the anxiety I suffered as a result of the conflicts that complicated my life in early adulthood.

V

The "Diplomatic Pause" that Ambassador Reischauer wrote about did not last long. Japanese-American relations suddenly worsened in early 1940 when the United States made it clear to Japan that it wanted Japan out of China and that it was not going to make compromises on its China stance. Japan reacted by hardening its China policy. It saw its position in China as legitimate, arguing resolutely that it also had a right to spheres of influence that produced strategic raw materials just as the other imperial powers did. Living in Japan, cut off from European and American public opinion, it was extremely difficult to assess what was actually going on in Japanese-American relations during the spring of 1940. The *Japan Times and Advertizer* was not much help as it trumpeted mostly the official position of the Japanese Foreign Affairs Ministry. American magazines that Papa had access to through friends in Japan's foreign community – *Life, Time, Foreign Affairs* – arrived too late to give a realistic picture of the deliberations taking place in Washington and Tokyo. We now know, of course, from documents released after World War II that the Japanese military were not sitting idly in 1940. It was during that year that the Japanese civil government suffered a lasting defeat at the hands of the military who completely monopolized all branches of the government, turning what was at one time a constitutional monarchy into a ruthless totalitarian state dreaming of not only victories in China but also in all of southeastern Asia.

Our family also suffered a defeat that spring. On April 30 1940, the Appeals Court delivered its verdict on Papa's claim for the return of the gold. It was the same as in 1936. An entry in father's diary sadly reported: "In mid-summer, crisis on all fronts, not enough money for living expenses, the case collapsed on April 30." More as a nuisance than a credible attempt at litigation, Papa filed another appeal with Japan's highest court, but the case never moved ahead. Stripped of any other options, under pressure from the Japanese government to put an end to the claim, and swayed by feelings of responsibility to the family, Papa simply gave up. In July 1940 he agreed to withdraw the claim in exchange of a promise by the Japanese government to pay the accrued expenses of the suit. In the summer of 1941, Japan honored its promise and paid 30,000 yen to his lawyers.

Hitler did not stop with just Austria and Czechoslovakia. On August 23, 1939, Germany signed the Nazi-Soviet Non-Aggression Pact, allowing Hitler to attack Poland without worrying about the reaction of the Soviet Union, and a week later German panzers crossed the German-Polish border. On September 3, England and France declared war on Germany in support of the guarantees they gave to Poland in the event of a German invasion. The Poles were no match for the crack Nazi divisions and the fighting lasted less than four weeks. The "phony war" that followed the invasion of Poland lasted seven months. On May 5, 1940, Hitler sent his tank divisions across the Netherlands and Belgium into the plains of northern France, bypassing the fortified Maginot Line on which the French placed all their bets. Paris was occupied and France surrendered on June 21. The remains of the Allied armies were evacuated to England from Dunkirk while Hitler waited for Britain to sue for peace. The Japanese watched the German blitzkrieg with a certain amount of envy for the awe-inspiring success of the German armies. The rapid progress of the German divisions through the Benelux countries and northern France received daily billings in the Japanese press. I remember a long conversation with Papa about what was happening in Europe. He was pessimistic and was certain that the Japanese military planners are not going to overlook the German experience. "If the Germans can do it," he said, "the Japanese probably think they can do it too."

He was right in his analysis. The success of the German blitzkrieg threw Japanese-American relations into a tailspin. In July 1940, under pressure from the military, the pro-American Prime Minister Yonai was replaced by Prince Konoe. On the assumption that Germany was bound to win the war in Europe, Konoe agreed to a four-pronged policy approved by the Japanese General Staff: (1) strengthen relations with Germany and Italy, (2) seek a non-aggression pact with the Soviet Union to avoid fighting on two fronts, (3) incorporate the Asian colonies of Great Britain, France and the Netherlands into a new East Asia order under Japanese control, and (4) reject American interference in China, but avoid any direct conflict with the United States while Japan prepares for its push south.

The new policy determined the events that followed. Responding to German overtures for closer cooperation, on September 27, Japan signed the Tripartite Alliance with Germany and Italy negotiated by the pro-German Foreign Minister Yosuke Matsuoka. The Neutrality Pact with the Soviet Union had to wait until April 1941, but it too was also signed according to plan. The Japanese-Soviet Neutrality Pact surprised everyone. In 1941, Papa was president of the Society of White Russian Émigrés in Japan. I remember how concerned he was about the Soviet-Japanese rapprochement. He feared that it would adversely affect the White Russian community, but it turned out to be nothing more than insurance for both nations against having to fight a war on two fronts. The agreement negotiated in 1925 by former Russian Envoy to Japan D. I. Abrikossow with the Japanese Foreign Office regarding the White Russian community in Japan remained intact.

After long and complicated negotiations with the French authorities in Indo-China for Japanese military bases along the Chinese border, Japanese troops entered Indo-China in July 1941. Tokyo claimed that the move was only temporary, but the obvious result was that the Japanese army was now within striking distance of the Malay Peninsula and the Dutch East Indies. Having signed the Neutrality Pact with the Soviet Union, Tokyo had decided that it was now safe to proceed south even if this meant war with the United States and Great Britain. In an attempt to force the Japanese to reconsider its expansionist move southward, the United States froze all Japanese assets in America on July 25 and, on August 1, imposed a total embargo on scrap iron, oil, and aviation gasoline. To the foreign residents of Yokohama and Tokyo who had been following the dramatic events of 1940 and 1941, Japanese-American relations never looked darker. Rumors about a possible Japanese attack on Singapore and Hawaii did not help. Almost everyone now believed that war was inevitable.

It was in this climate of apprehension about the future that I graduated from St. Joseph's College on July 5, 1941. Out of the twenty-six Juniors who entered their Senior year in 1940 only eleven graduated in 1941. The others – citizens of the United States, Great Britain, Australia, Portugal, and Japan – dropped out because of the tense political situation in Japan. The foreign students returned to Singapore, Hong Kong and their native countries, while the Japanese transferred to Japanese institutions of learning because their parents were made to feel by the government that it was no longer patriotic to attend a foreign school. At the commencement exercise, our visiting speaker was the governor of Kanagawa Prefecture. Speaking in English, he thanked the brothers for their dedication to teaching, reviewed the exigencies of the political climate, admitted that we were stepping out into a very fickle and hostile world, and urged us to rise to the challenge of working toward the preservation of peace. It was the best one could say at a time when Japanese-American relations were crushing on the sharp rocks of political competition for the control of East Asia.

Throughout the first half of 1941, our family talked about going to America, but lacking sufficient funds and U.S. immigration visas that were almost impossible to obtain due to the high level of immigrants from Europe and East Asia, we remained in Japan. Anxious to attend the University of California in Berkeley, I sent an application for the Fall 1941 semester and was waiting for my high school transcript from St. Joseph's College, which for some unknown reason was not completed until July 27 – at least, that is the date on which it was signed – too late for the University's Admission Office to process it and get back to me with an acceptance. By mid-summer communicating with the United States was a hopeless endeavor. Japanese-American economic relations had been severed, and the last commercial passenger liner had left Yokohama for San Francisco in mid-August. In retrospect, it was providential that the transcript was somehow misplaced or overlooked. It would have been a terrible mistake for me to depart for the United States that summer and leave the rest of the family behind to contend with nearly four years of misery and war.

Instead, I went to work for the F & K Engineering Company in Omori, a suburb of Tokyo on the Tokyo-Yokohama electric train line. I had seen an advertisement in the *Japan Times and Advertizer* for a production clerk who spoke English, answered the ad, and was interviewed by Mr. Foster, the "F" of the F & K Engineering Company himself. My job consisted of monitoring the production of turret lathe machine parts against a work schedule based on a pre-determined plan of production. It was easy work, but sometimes nerve-racking because very soon I discovered that my weekly reports of lagging production were a source of contention between the production department and our easily angered boss. The engineers made excuses or claimed that my weekly reports were inaccurate. I had to learn to stand up and defend myself, a lesson that has served me well throughout my entire life. With time I learned to enjoy my work, despite the unavoidable confrontations with the production department. The commute from Yokohama was tolerable and I was earning 105 yen per month, more money than I had ever seen, a much-appreciated addition to the family's monthly cash flow.

In the meantime, Japanese-American relations were moving with lightning speed toward a complete break down. The freezing of Japanese assets in America and the oil embargo did not go over well with the Japanese military leadership. The army considered the American action an insult to Japan's honor and its emperor, and demanded direct military action against the United States. In a dramatic and final attempt to reach an understanding with the United States, Prime Minister Konoe appealed to President Roosevelt and asked for an emergency meeting in Honolulu. The Japanese public welcomed the summit conference, but nothing positive came out of the offer. On the advice of the State Department, Roosevelt declined the invitation, stating that nothing would come out of the meetings unless the two governments first resolved the individual issues on which Japan and the United States remained apart. Stymied by the American rebuttal and under tremendous pressure from the military who called for either a resolution of the political impasse on conditions that were acceptable to the army or the commencement of war against the United States, Konoe resigned on October 16 and was replaced by General Hideki Tojo, the irascible and pro-war Defense Minister in Konoe's cabinet inclined to theatrics and extravagant rhetoric. Two different explanations of the change in government were voiced by the old-time foreign residents. Some felt that this was a sensible resolution of a festering problem. Tojo was the only man in Japan, they said, who was capable of holding the army hotheads from starting a war. In his capacity as premier he would have to act in the interest of Japan, they argued – not the army – to initiate a more balanced policy vis-à-vis the United States. Others saw in Tojo's appointment the final stage of preparation for an all-out war.

The view that Tojo might succeed in neutralizing the military extremists suddenly gained precedence in the press when it became known that Japan was sending to Washington former Ambassador to Germany Kurusu aboard a Pan-American clipper specially dispatched to Hong Kong for his flight across the Pacific. He was to assist Retired Admiral Nomura, Japan's Ambassador to the United States, in negotiating a Japanese-American political settlement. It seemed like a good try to most foreign expatriates living in Japan, but it did not work. Neither Kurusu nor Nomura were able to convince Secretary of State Cordell Hull that Japan was serious about trying to resolve the impasse. Looking for an answer in the Japanese press why negotiations in Washington were not producing results was a hopeless pastime for those who still had hopes for peace. The *Japan Times and Advertizer* accused Cordell Hull of stalling, and declared that "it was now up to America to keep the peace." It was becoming clear to everyone living in Japan – our family included – that time was obviously running out. On November 26, Hull finally handed Nomura and Kurusu a ten-point draft proposal for adjusting the Japanese-American differences in the Far East. The Japanese press did not go into the details of the proposal, but left a general impression that, for all practical purposes, the proposal was an ultimatum that Japan could not accept. Some long-time foreign residents still hoped for a resolution, but the dye had already been cast. In the early morning of December 7 (December 8 in Tokyo) Japanese planes from an armada steaming toward Hawaii from Etorofu in the southern Kuril Islands mounted a surprise attack on Pearl Harbor. The war that everyone dreaded and said would not happen was suddenly on.

3
FOREIGNER IN WARTIME JAPAN

War! That mad game the world so loves to play.
Jonathan Swift

I

I found out about the commencement of hostilities at the Sakuragi-cho railway station in Yokohama, on my way to work at about 7:45 AM on December 8, Tokyo time. It was Monday, I had been to a party the night before and was running late. The railway station was jammed with early morning commuters as usual, but there was something different that morning about the large waiting hall. At the gate I was stopped by a military policeman in civilian attire who asked to see my travel papers which were only recently issued to all foreigners residing in Japan. This was the first time that this happened, and I was understandably disturbed. The station's public address system was playing martial music and I remember saying to myself, is this it, has war been declared. But there was no concrete proof to confirm my conjecture. The policeman fanned me through without saying anything. I found out that my speculation was correct only at work. The entire factory – workers and staff – were ordered to assemble in the factory yard at 9:00 AM to the sound of the radio playing the Japanese naval march over the public address system. Japan was at war the radio spokesman announced. The U.S. fleet in Pearl Harbor was destroyed and Japanese units were landing in Hong Kong and the Philippines. Japanese workers raised their arms and a loud "banzai" roared through the factory yard. The foreigners were too stunned to say or do anything. After a few minutes of awkward silence, we filed out of the yard to our individual offices too overwhelmed by the news to perform productively during the rest of day.

The bombing of Pearl Harbor was, of course, a despicable and nefarious action for which Japan had to be held accountable. Like the attack on the Russian stronghold at Port Arthur in 1905, it was carried out surreptitiously and without a prior declaration of war. It caused massive destruction and loss of life. It was also an act of unmitigated folly based on the mistaken premise that Japan had to protect its flank from the threat of United States naval action if it went ahead and seized the Dutch Indies and its raw materials. It also completely overlooked that the attack on Pearl Harbor would put an end to the U.S. isolationist sentiment and unite the American nation with its vastly superior economic potential for an all out encounter in the Pacific.

How the attack was planned and debated in the top Japanese military circles did not come out until much later. Relevant documents and transcripts of critical conversations became available only after the war. It was also not until 1946 that it became possible to arrange interviews with senior Japanese army and navy officers who participated in the planning of the attack. Without additional findings to piece together the crucial data an impartial conclusion was not possible. I don't believe anyone – not even informed journalists and diplomats – had a clear idea in 1941 of how the two countries drifted into war during those critical weeks of November 1941. I certainly did not, nor did my parents who followed closely the escalating tension between the United States and Japan after the declaration of the oil embargo.

Japan's intrusion into China, her occupation of French Indo-China after the collapse of France in 1940, and her unwillingness to find an acceptable *modus vivendi* with the United States and Great Britain in East Asia clearly served as an underlying cause of war. So did the secret discussions and reckless maneuvering of the Japanese military extremists who sought to build an Asian empire with Japan at its helm. But as I think about it now, after reading numerous studies of Japanese-American relations before the bombing of Pearl Harbor, I find I cannot blame Japan alone. The United States also must shoulder some responsibility for the commencement of hostilities in December 1941. Whether or not a summit meeting which the Japanese asked for in October 1941 between President Roosevelt and Prime Minister Konoe could have averted the war remains problematic, but it should have taken place in the interest of both nations. It's entirely possible that diplomacy at that high level could have clarified the conflicting positions that in the end led to the breakout of war.

The oil embargo and the freezing of Japanese assets in America was a mistake of vast proportions. Instead of forcing Japan to negotiate a compromise in China, it unified Japanese public opinion and made the Japanese military leaders even more bellicose and determined to confront the colonial powers in East Asia. The embargo disregarded the notion of "face and honor" that are so important to the Japanese psyche. It also put an end to all further Japanese deliberations on the subject of where and how Japan should move next. After the embargo it became absolutely clear to the Japanese leadership – military and civilian – that the next move had to be south, toward the Dutch East Indies and their oil fields, not north to eastern Siberia, as some army generals still envisioned. Cordell Hull's cavalier and patronizing attitude and the mistaken view of his foremost expert on Asia, Dr. Stanley Hornbeck, that the Japanese envoys in Washington were being disingenuous in the efforts to reach a settlement and were there merely to make it look like Japan was seeking a peaceful solution, was a serious error in judgment. So was the mistaken belief that Japan would not go to war over the embargo. Prince Konoe was genuinely interested in meeting President Roosevelt and felt certain that he could work out a face-saving settlement acceptable to the Japanese military, especially the navy that continued to have doubts about war with the United States. The same kind of poor judgment on the part of the State Department also applied to the last thirty days before the start of the war. Ambassador Kurusu was sent to Washington to find a peaceful solution to the impasse. It has now been established beyond any degree of doubt that he went to Washington on the direct order of the Emperor who told Prime Minister Tojo to "go back to blank paper,[20] to save the peace," and only if negotiations failed, to put in action the attack strategy that the military planners had mapped out for Pearl Harbor.

Under tremendous pressure to satisfy the wishes of the Emperor, Kurusu and Nomura submitted two proposals to Secretary Hull. The second and more compliant offer proposed a face-saving expedient of withdrawing from Indo-China and reducing the number of troops in north China in exchange for the lifting of the oil embargo and the unfreezing of Japanese assets in the United States. The Japanese proposals remained unanswered for two weeks while Chiang Kai-shek and Churchill lobbied President Roosevelt to take a hard line on the North China question, and Dr. Hornbeck, a recognized Japan basher, pressured Secretary of State Hull to decline the Japanese proposal. In the end, convinced that the Japanese envoys could not be trusted,

President Roosevelt refused to consider the Japanese offer. Instead, on November 26, Cordell Hull handed Nomura and Kurusu a note that demanded among other things the signing by Japan of a multilateral non-aggression treaty with the United States, Britain, the Soviet Union, the Netherlands, and Thailand; the withdrawal of all Japanese troops from China, Manchuria and Indo-China; the recognition of Chiang Kai-shek's Chongqing government as the only rightful government of China; and the abrogation of the Tripartite Alliance with Germany and Italy. It was obvious from the note that the United States had consulted with Churchill and Chian Kai-shek and was not acting independently.

According to the State Department, the note was meant to be a draft proposal representing the U.S. maximum position subject to further discussion, but the Japanese took it as an intended insult and ultimatum, triggering on November 30 a previously arrived decision to attack Pearl Harbor if the peace negotiations failed.

My opinion may be influenced by my long residence in Japan and my sympathy for the suffering Japanese people during nearly four years of devastating war. But I am not the only one who believes that the Japanese-American confrontation could have been avoided and the war confined to the European theater. There are others who feel strongly that the Japanese-American conflict could have been side-stepped if our State Department had been less prejudiced toward the Japanese, better informed about Japanese culture, more flexible, and less self-righteous in our dealings with Japan. Ambassador Grew pleaded with the State Department to schedule the Konoe-Roosevelt meeting before time ran out. In his dispatches to Washington he warned Secretary Hull that the Japanese were "capable of sudden surprise action" and under severe pressure were bound to develop "a national psychology of desperation" that would lead them "to risk all."[21] In the end, Ambassador Grew's counsel was ignored and Japan and the United States went to war as a result of what Barbara Tuchman called "culture ignorance."[22] Both Japan and the United States miscalculated because they did not take into consideration the psychological and cultural impact of their decisions on the behavior of the adversary.

And war it was, nearly four years of it, with huge losses of life on both sides. In the Japanese case, it was also hundreds of thousands of civilian casualties. It also caused massive devastation in the islands of the South Pacific, the Philippines and Japan itself. I was against the war on principle. It did not make any sense to me, and I don't think it made much sense to responsible Japanese leaders and certainly to most Americans before the bombing of Pearl Harbor. In addition to the purely ethical considerations against the war, I also had selfish and personal reasons. I was nineteen when it broke out, at that pivotal and difficult age when young men try to chart their careers and make plans for the future. I had planned to immigrate to the United States, go to college, embark on an interesting and productive career and, after years of stateless wandering, become an American citizen. All of those youthful dreams blew out of the window in one ominous gust on December 7. Instead, I found myself marooned in a political and cultural vacuum trying to make the best of a situation that turned ugly as the war dragged on. To say that I was angry was an understatement. My only hope was that the war would not last long.

The overall control and surveillance of all foreign nationals living in Japan was the responsibility of the Foreign Section of the *Tokkotai* ("Thought" Police), but the day-to-day supervision was left to the local police who on the whole exercised considerable discretion in dealing with foreigners. The outbreak of war did not change the pre-war system. It merely codified its policy, pigeonholing the various national groups on the basis of their country's posture on the war. As stateless White Russians we were not interned. Officially, we were classified and registered as "non-belligerent foreign nationals" with the right to move freely in the Tokyo-Yokohama area. Beyond it, permission had to be requested in advance, and was customarily granted without too much of a bureaucratic rigmarole. Other stateless foreign nationals – Jewish refugees from Nazi-occupied Europe and Eastern Europeans displaced by the Nazi-Soviet Non-Aggression Pact – were treated in the same way as the White Russians. Tokyo authorities continued to treat Jewish refugees decently despite pressure from Gestapo Colonel Joseph Meissinger of the German Embassy to toughen the relatively benign Japanese attitude toward the Jews. American, British and Dutch citizens were automatically interned if they were between the ages of eighteen and sixty. In accordance with Japanese reverence for age, the local police were allowed to decide on their own how to treat those who were older than sixty. The same policy applied to individuals and families of mixed foreign and Japanese blood. Some were treated in much the same way as those who were age sixty and over, others were placed under local house arrest, and some were actually interned. Citizens of Japan's allies – Germans, Italians and Vichy French – continued to live as before without any formal restrictions, although Richard Sorge's arrest in October 1941 and subsequent indictment as a Soviet spy[23] greatly increased the surveillance of many German and White Russian nationals living in Japan, especially those who were old residents and had no affiliation with any of the recognized organizations. In general, I believe it can be safely said that the Japanese handling of foreign nationals living in Japan – belligerents and non-belligerents – was on the whole considerably more responsible than our treatment of Japanese Americans living in California. There were, of course, individual cases of arrest, interrogation, and harassment, but they were more an exception than the rule, especially during the first year of the war.

The physical aspects of life did not change much during the first year of the war. Except for petrol, rationing was not introduced until the second half of 1942, and applied only to such high demand items as sugar, cooking oil, textiles, and cigarettes. On the whole, during the first eighteen months of the war, we managed to get everything we needed. I remember Easter of 1942 with its usual abundance of traditional foods. Mama had prepared a ham and a veal roast, baked four or five *kulichi* (Russia's version of Italian *paniatone*), and prepared *paskha*, the traditional Easter cheese cake. We had on our holiday table not only vodka, but also French wine. What was missing was news on what was happening in the rest of the world. The English-language *Japan Times and Examiner,* considered by most foreigners in Japan to be the mouthpiece of the Foreign Affairs Ministry, changed its name to *Nippon Times* and now blatantly trumpeted the official *Domei News Service* line about Japanese victories in Hong Kong, Malaya, Singapore and the Philippines, and Japan's "compassionate" participation in the construction of the Greater East Asia Co-prosperity Sphere. The lack of news from the Russian theater of the war was particularly hard on Papa. He had been following the details of the German advance into Russia on a daily basis through November 1941 and was finding it very frustrating in not being able to determine if the Germans had broken through the Pskov-Leningrad line of defense where he grew up and where as far as he knew his brothers and sisters still lived.

In general, the most disturbing and psychologically upsetting aspect of life in Japan in 1942 and the first half of 1943 was not food shortages or reduced living conditions, but the abrupt and irreversible shortage of reliable information and the sudden shattering of the social fabric that made up the expatriate culture which had become part of our life in Japan. Gone were back copies of the *Christian Science Monitor, Life Magazine, The National Geographic* which allowed us to keep up with what was taking place abroad. Gone were American films and latest popular melodies. The Yokohama Country and Athletic Club was closed down and Honmoku became "off limits" because of its proximity to the harbor and the shipping lanes of Tokyo Bay. The departure of American and British citizens before the breakout of the war and the internment of those who remained thinned out the population of Yokohama's foreign community, and created a social vacuum that was deeply felt by those who remained in Japan. The American brothers at St. Joseph's College were dispatched to the Order's summer retreat in Yamakita, placed under house arrest and eventually repatriated on the exchange ship *Gripsholm* with members of the U.S. Diplomatic Corps, the press, and the remaining American missionaries and businessmen. Opportunities for informal discussion on politics and exchange of information and gossip that made a good part of the expatriate society's daily experience also came to an end. One had to learn to live a new life in self-embraced solitude within the confines of one's immediate family and the national group to which he or she belonged.

I was in some respects more fortunate than most White Russians. My work at F & K Engineering, renamed Nichidoku Engineering(Japan-German Engineering Company) in January 1942, gave me a certain amount of direct exposure to other nationals of the expatriate community. Willy Foster, President and sole owner of Nichidoku, was a very unique and atypical specimen of the expatriate community. A mechanical engineer, originally from the Black Forest region of southern Germany, Foster first left his native land for the USSR during the heyday of the Soviet-German cooperation in early 1920s after the Genoa Conference. In the Soviet Union he worked on several industrial projects, but apparently ran into some difficulties with the Russian authorities. Just what those difficulties were no one in Japan knew for certain; he was very careful in disclosing his experience in the Soviet Union. He did not return to Germany – he did not like what the Nazis were doing to it, he would often comment – and instead came to Japan in the early 1930s where he opened a motorcycle repair shop. Through hard work, a fair amount of bluff and intimidation, by the time I came to work for him in 1941, he owned a machine tool factory that employed nearly four hundred workers building high speed turret lathes of the latest German design for the Japanese navy. He was by all counts one of the most successful foreign entrepreneurs among a bevy of other business expatriates in pre-war Japan. He owned three houses, two late model cars, a wine and whisky cellar that would make the most affluent connoisseur envious, and enough petrol stored in fifty-gallon drums in one of his warehouses to last the entire war. It seemed like everything he touched turned to gold.

The factory work force was exclusively Japanese, but the office and engineering staffs consisted mostly of foreign nationals, and almost all of the internal business was conducted in English, the *lingua franca* of the Far East. I don't think Foster ever fully trusted the Japanese. His chief engineer, Ernest Quastler, was an Austrian Jew who had fled Austria after the Anschluss with Germany. His chief-of-staff was a Czech refugee. The Chief Accountant was a German who left Europe in the 1920s and married a striking Eurasian woman living in Japan, violating thereby the racial code of Nazi Germany. The head of Cost Accounting was Henry Fernandez, a St. Joseph's graduate originally from Macao. There were at least five other St. Joseph's graduates in the office – White Russians, Eurasians -- and a Croatian who came to Japan after working in the USSR. Foster ruled this motley crew of expatriates with an iron hand, softened occasionally by bouts of jovial drinking and friendly conversation after work. In contrast to his extraordinary success in business, his personal life was in a sorrowful state. His only son had committed suicide, allegedly after a violent argument with his father, and his German wife had divorced him after she found out he had an affair with his Japanese secretary by whom he had a little girl. For all his bombast and exterior audacity he was, I believe, a lonely and troubled man – a workaholic who found it difficult to separate his private and business lives. To ease his loneliness and at the same time cultivate a more congenial relationship with his expatriate colleagues, he often invited us to his house for a drink after work. The married members of the staff often declined, knowing that the drinking could last for hours, but the bachelors – and there were at least six or seven of us – usually accepted, often staying on until the last electric train home.

I appreciated these drinking sessions, even though I never learned to enjoy hard liquor. Most of the time, I cheated by sipping my drink slowly while most of the others downed theirs. The drinking sessions were a welcome diversion from the daily grind of an otherwise fragmented life made monotonous and pedestrian by the war. We usually sat in Foster's comfortable living room at a large round coffee table with a bottle of Japanese Suntory whisky or, if he wanted to make a special occasion, with a bottle of Johnnie Walker that he produced out of nowhere with the showmanship of a magician to surprise us all. It was not unusual for our group to kill two bottles before it was time to go home. We talked about everything, literature, music – Foster was fond of Brahms and Beethoven and often played selections on his gramophone – history, politics and, of course, the war. It was an honest adult conversation carried on freely without any fear that there was amongst us a stool pigeon who could report our discussions to the *Tokkotai* police or the Gestapo agents at the German Embassy. Foster was extremely pessimistic about the war in the Pacific and was not afraid to say openly that the Japanese had "bitten off more than they were able to handle." His view on the war in Europe was equally bleak. He did not think that Germany, despite its industrial and technological vitality, would in the long run stand up to the combined power of Russia and the United States. ""Hitler is a psychopath," he would say after a few drinks, "a maniac who is dragging Germany into a deep abyss." As I look back and think about our drinking sessions, I believe they served a distinct therapeutic purpose at a time when it was both difficult and dangerous to talk freely about the war. Foster used them to "dump his bucket," to unload his frustrations and relieve himself of strong feelings of hostility he had against the German community in Japan that considered him a pariah because he did not fit the profile of the typical card-carrying Nazi.

In contrast to the emotional tensions that the war forced on our family, our financial situation actually improved in 1942. St. Joseph's College did not close immediately but continued to function with an expanded faculty of French Alsatians who came from other Japanese schools to replace the American teachers interned in December 1941. To conserve its resources, it closed down its boarding school department, but stayed open as a school through the spring semester of 1943, before it was finally closed down permanently and its huge campus taken over by the Japanese army. The closing of the boarding facility at St. Joseph's was an unexpected boon to Mama. Our boarding house expanded overnight to twelve students, making the whole operation a lot more profitable than in previous years. In 1940, Papa accepted the position of principal in the Tokyo Russian School and now had a regular income. By the spring of 1942 I was earning 140 yen per month. With three sources of income our family cash flow improved dramatically and for the first time that I could remember we were actually beginning to save. In the meantime, the Japanese conquest in the Pacific rolled farther and farther beyond the Japanese homeland with lightning speed. By mid-April, all of the Malay Peninsula, Thailand, most of the Dutch East Indies, Singapore, and Bataan had fallen. The battleships *Prince of Wales* and *Repulse*, the pride of the British Far East Fleet, had been sunk in the Gulf of Siam. Japanese newspapers and news reels glorified the military with a naive confidence that made them look almost infantile to a more mature eye. Everyday life in Tokyo and

Yokohama continued as if war had never been declared. There were no conspicuous food shortages in the first half of 1942, trains moved on schedule with typical Japanese precision, and the Japanese public basked in the beaming sunlight of initial victories. To the majority of Japanese, the war seemed remote, faraway, and incapable of touching their homeland.

But the war was not that far away. On April 18, 1942, Colonel James H. Doolittle, in command of a squadron of sixteen modified B-25s, roared off the deck of the *USS Hornet* and took a direct course for Tokyo. The Nichidoku factory and office were working even though it was Saturday. At about 12:25 PM I walked out of my office to get some fresh air after a bag lunch. I was immediately struck by the roar of overhead airplane engines, looked up and saw two American bombers flying at approximately eleven o'clock from where I stood. The workers who were enjoying the noon break outside the factory thought at first that they were Japanese planes, the tail end of an air raid drill conducted that same morning. They were not Japanese, however, but large twin–engine American bombers with clearly defined US markings visible through the black puffs of antiaircraft smoke on their tails. After releasing their bombs, they swept westward without any apparent opposition from Japanese fighters in the air. It was a strange sensation to see American bombers flying freely so close to the ground. The Japanese press called the Doolittle raiders "demons who carried out an inhuman and indiscriminate bombing attack on the sly," and claimed that nine enemy planes had crashed on Honshu, Japan's largest island. The Japanese claim was obviously a deception; even if only one plane had been brought down, the papers would have been full of exuberant pictures featuring the wreck and American prisoners or dead. No such pictures surfaced after the raid. Much later, when eight American airmen were captured in Japanese-occupied China and brought to Tokyo for trial, the Japanese press outdid itself with harrowing photographs of the airmen and contemptible stories of the raid. It was only after the war that we learned from official American sources that three men were killed in a crash landing in China, a crew of five landed safely in Vladivostok, and the rest, including Doolittle, touched ground in China and made it though Japanese lines to Chungquing. Only one crew was captured by the Japanese.

As far as physical damage was concerned, the raid was a failure, but psychologically it was a towering success for the United States. It caused the Japanese high command to recognize that the homeland was not impregnable, forcing it to reassign four air fighter groups to

Japan proper from overseas bases where they were in high demand. After the war, we also learned that the Doolittle raid accelerated Japan's poorly conceived plan to invade Midway in order to lure the remnants of the U.S. fleet out of Pearl Harbor. The Midway operation turned out to be a huge disaster for the Japanese navy, turning the tide of the war in the Pacific in favor of the United States.

That evening, we met as usual in Foster's living room for drinks and discussion of the day's happening. Foster came out of his office too late to see the American planes, and wanted to know if they had turbo-jet engines instead of propellers. He said he knew that German engineers were experimenting with turbo-jet engines and he was certain the Americans were doing the same. The planes were propeller-driven, however, and could not have made the long flight from Midway to stage the air raid and hope to escape safely by way of the Chinese mainland. It was obvious they must have been launched from an aircraft carrier that had steamed into Japanese waters, but no one believed it was possible to catapult a twin-engine bomber from the deck of a pitching aircraft carrier in heavy sea. In the end after much debate and a fair amount of whisky, we concluded wrongly that the Doolittle raiders must have come from a forward base somewhere between Sian and Hankow in unoccupied China still controlled by Chiang Kai-shek.

The Doolittle raid disturbed the military planners but did not really register with the Japanese public. The first months of the war brought such imposing victories and grandiose dreams for the establishment of the Greater East Asia Co-Prosperity Sphere that the entire nation, caught up in the mood of triumphant conquest, seemed mesmerized by the war propaganda and the forward momentum of the army and navy. The newspapers were full of patriotic rhetoric and the radio played day and night, to the drumbeat of marching soldiers, *Umi Yukaba* (Across the Ocean), Japan's most uplifting martial tune. It was not until the defeats at Midway and Guadalcanal that the setbacks slowly and cumulatively began to seep through to the general public. But even they did not slow down the nation's fervor. It was the economic situation, the rise in food prices in the spring of 1943 and the disappearance of new clothing styles and fuel, that caused people to realize that the war was not going quite as well as the propaganda mill proclaimed each day. The price of rice doubled and flour became three times more expensive than it was before the war. A black market for spirits, higher quality cigarettes, and cooking oil – non existent until then – suddenly began to show its ugly head. The National General Mobilization Law overruled the public's clamor for more efficient food distribution. The government imposed controls on virtually every aspect of national life, including literature, education, the press, and even the workings of non-government organizations. Japanese ideologues and propagandists literally fell over one another coining phrases, patriotic slogans, and nationalistic rhetoric in support of the imposed controls. Admiral Yamamoto's reservation that Japan could "fight ferociously for six months or a year, but there was no assurance for the second or third year of battle" was coming to roost. The country was slowly losing the battle that Yamamoto spoke about and drowning under a flood of military fascist directives that pulled it down into a bottomless economic abyss.

Our lives were also affected by the economic and political changes. In anticipation of even greater food shortages, in the spring of 1943, we plowed our garden down and planted potatoes and carrots which we harvested in the fall. St. Joseph's College, run now exclusively by the French Alsatian brothers, closed its doors in June 1943 with a graduating class that included my brother Nick. With the shutting down of St. Joseph's Mama's dormitory venture also came to a close. On the positive side, in May 1943, I received a promotion. To the surprise and consternation of many of my colleagues, Foster appointed me Head of the Operational Tool Department at Nichidoku, a position that brought me in touch with the growing Japanese industrial shortages since it was my responsibility to find replacements for operational tools no longer available in the open market. Life became tougher in 1943, but it was still tolerable. In February, I spent four days skiing in the mountains of Nagano prefecture and during the summer even managed to take a week off to climb in the southern Japan Alps. With an Austrian associate from the office and a distant member of the Japanese imperial family we summited the almost perpendicular conical face of Jizogatake, one of the more difficult climbs in the southern Japan Alps.

The full impact of the war on people's lives came in the spring of 1944. That spring, the procurement of food supplies became an all-consuming obsession. Long lines formed every day at markets offering even the least desirable commodities. For all practical purposes, the Japanese economy was now operating on a barter basis. Unless one had something to offer in exchange for beef, chicken, eggs,and cream, one had to be prepared to be without them. We, too, were drawn into the barter economy, not because we wanted to, but because there was no other alternative. We started to produce ersatz whisky and crude soap – two commodities that became almost non-existent during the last eighteen months of the war. My job was to scour neighborhood pharmacies for tinctures, alcohol-based old wives' remedies, and sodium and potassium salts. To avoid suspicion, I never purchased more than one kind of tincture or alcohol-based medication from a pharmacy that was on my buying list. Brother Mike, a tinkerer, who already then was exhibiting an interest in the sciences, rigged up a distilling apparatus to purify the medications and a large metal container to manufacture the soap. We diluted the distilled alcohol with water, colored it with tea, added a pinch of salt and sugar and a few drops of vanilla syrup, bottled it, and offered it as whisky. It would have been easier to manufacture ersatz vodka, but the Japanese did not have a taste for vodka before the war. We cut the crude-looking soap into hand-sized slabs which we packaged in colored paper. Brother Nick's assignment was the most critical and dangerous. He had to find safe and trustworthy farmers and underground food distributors who were interested in exchanging food for our whisky creation and home-made soap. It was a risky business, but it did put fresh eggs, cream, and an occasional cut of meat or foul on our dinner table.

II

In the spring of 1944 we moved from Yokohama to a smaller house in Omori, a suburb of Tokyo on the Tokyo-Yokohama Electric Line. The short-term advantage of the move was that it cut Papa's long commute to the Russian School in Ochanomizu by at least an hour and made my walk to the factory less than ten minutes. With the end of the war coming closer and the likelihood of a major air raid over Yokohama now a distinct possibility after the American victory in the Mariana Islands, we wanted to bring the family closer together in an area that was less vulnerable to bombing from the air. The move turned out to be providential. Our Yokohama house in Sagiyama was completely destroyed in an air raid that almost obliterated Yokohama in the spring of 1945. When I came to look for it after the war, all I could find was the foundation and a burned out tree skeleton that was at one time a majestic poplar whose leaves I had to rake every fall as a teenager.

That spring I also came face to face with another predicament. I cannot remember exactly if it was in March or April, but it was sometime during early spring that Willy Foster was arrested. I arrived at the factory one morning to find it swarming with police. The office was cordoned off from the factory, and the staff was being interrogated by a detail of rather unsavory looking plainclothesmen. Foster had been taken by the police in the early hours of the morning before the office and the factory opened. No explanation for the arrest was offered, leaving all of us in the office in a state of complete shock. Some thought his arrest may have had something to do with the Sorge espionage case that was being tried that spring in the Tokyo Criminal Court. Willy Foster knew Sorge and like Sorge also spent a number of years in the Soviet Union, but I don't believe Foster had anything to do with the Soviet spy ring. Transcripts of the Sorge trial that became public after the war did not show any connections between Sorge and Foster. Others were of the opinion that his arrest had something to do with the black market. Foster often bought and sold critical materials on the black market in violation of government regulations, and openly bragged that he bought petrol, liquor, and building materials through his underground contacts. His black market transactions may have had an indirect connection, but the more obvious reason for the arrest, I believe, was the factory. The Japanese had been trying to take over the operation of his factory for some time in order to move it from Tokyo to a safer location in the countryside. The high-speed turret lathes that Nichidoku manufactured were essential to naval shipbuilding. Foster dragged his feet and refused to cooperate. Unsuccessful in expropriating the factory voluntarily, the Japanese probably turned to the German Embassy for assistance, and the Gestapo gave the Japanese police the go ahead signal to arrest him on fabricated charges that satisfied the existing sabotage laws. The Gestapo had been trying to intimidate and embarrass Foster since the beginning of the war.

The bureaucratic wheels of the Japanese government moved slowly but methodically. It took several months for it to decide on a course of action. Foster had apparently refused to give up the factory under any conditions and told his captors that if they wanted it they would have to requisition it. He was undoubtedly looking ahead toward the end of the war and reassurance that he would then be properly compensated for property that had been seized by the Japanese navy. Short of any other alternative, the Japanese expropriated the factory and, in mid-June, Chief Engineer Ernest Quastler and I were summoned to Osaka to execute the necessary papers acknowledging the transfer of the factory to a Japanese firm selected by the navy. I remember arriving in Osaka on the night train and being entertained in true Japanese fashion with geishas and sake at a fancy restaurant frequented by the Japanese elite. In a ceremony of perverse legality, Quastler and I signed the transfer papers on the next day. What it amounted to was that two foreign representatives of an unjustly arrested German national, one an Austrian Jew and the other, a twenty-two year old stateless White Russian, signed the factory away to help the Japanese fight the war. The whole thing smelled to high heaven of pre-meditated coercion and cheap burlesque. Because Foster's personal accouterments were commingled with those of the factory and office, I was appointed as his representative to inventory his personal possessions and take responsibility for them while his case was being considered by the court. The factory was finally moved in late summer to the Osaka-Kobe area, and all of us in the office became unemployed.

In the meantime, the Japanese losses in the Pacific brought down the Tojo cabinet. Tojo resigned and a new prime minister, General Kuniaki Koiso, the governor of Korea, took over the helm. The *Nippon Times* intimated that there might be some policy changes, but the new government continued to devote all existing resources to the war as before. By the fall of 1944 – even before the air raids started – the economy and Japanese society, in general, were almost in a complete state of shock and disarray. Much of Japan's shipping capacity had been destroyed in the battles for the Solomons, Kwajalein and the Marianas, and shipment of grain and food from the occupied countries of the Greater East Asia Co-Prosperity Sphere were no longer reaching the Japanese homeland. Fertilizer production was down, and the 1944 domestic grain harvest came in short of even the most pessimistic expectations. In the countryside, people could still depend on food from family plots cultivated privately without the knowledge of the government, but in the large cities agricultural produce became a rarity. Better restaurants, geisha houses, bars and beer halls were ordered closed. Many smaller restaurants were converted to soup kitchens that served a putrid looking gruel consisting of rice, tofu, and seaweed. In anticipation of air raids, children of parents working in vital industries were evacuated and lodged in rural schools where they suffered terribly from poor living conditions and shortages of food. Those who could afford it or had friends and relatives in the countryside fled Tokyo by the thousands. Waiting rooms at the Ueno and Shinjiku railway stations – Tokyo's principal terminals for travel inland – were jammed to their limits with people, baggage, futons and cooking utensils, waiting for departing trains going north and west. Almost every family in Tokyo had or knew someone who had been killed or injured in China and the Pacific. Our neighbors in Omori, a professor at Rikyu University in Tokyo and his wife, had two of their sons in the Pacific from whom they had not heard, and now they were getting ready to send their youngest also to serve. It was heart-breaking to see them struggling to find some degree of sense between the futility of their family situation and the patriotic justification for the continuance of the war. The whole fabric of civilized living was torn apart by a war that should never have been started in the first place. Even the propaganda machine was beginning to flounder. Due to shortages of paper, newspapers stopped putting out evening editions and morning editions shrank in size.

The war had been going on for almost three years now, and our family had survived it reasonably well. Like many other so called "non-belligerent foreigners" we probably should have moved out of the metropolitan area to avoid the inevitable bombing raids, but that took money and we never had enough. Omori, a predominantly residential suburb of Tokyo, seemed safe to us and we hoped it would remain so until the end of the war. We did take some precautions, however; in November we excavated an air raid shelter in our backyard, stocked it with water, canned foods, matches, candles and blankets, and also moved into it all of our family photograph albums, prized books, memorabilia, and the most loved *objets d'art*. In September, the Tokyo Russian School closed, and Papa also became unemployed. Except for an occasional excursion for food to Tokyo and the countryside, we remained now in virtual self-confinement in suburban Omori and its immediate surroundings.

Everyday life now became a tiresome routine of foraging for food and waiting for the end of the war. To pass time, I immersed myself in a reading and self-study program in the humanities. Over the years, Papa and Mama had accumulated an excellent collection of Russian classics. As we moved, other possessions were often abandoned, but somehow books escaped that fate. They traveled with them and they grew in number through their years in exile. Papa was an inveterate intellectual who loved books – not just a military professional waiting on the sidelines to renew a career arrested by the Civil War. In his spare time he would scour second-hand bookstores in the Kanda district of Tokyo for works on philosophy and the social sciences, bringing home his newly acquired possessions with a joyful announcement on how lucky he was to find them at a bargain price. He loved poetry; he wrote it himself and could recite from memory: Pushkin, Lermontov, Blok, Maximilian Voloshin, and when asked how life was in Russia before the Revolution, he would often quote excerpts from Nekrasov's satirical epic *Who Lives Happily in Russia?* to make his point. Mama's taste in literature was less focused. She usually read whatever was available, preferring contemporary novels and the poetry of the Russian émigrés. She excluded Tsvetaeva, however, whom she considered a psychologically blemished turncoat who returned to Soviet Russia unable to contain her nostalgia for her cultural homeland.[24] That fall and winter, I read, in the original Russian, Dostoevsky's *Brothers Karamazov, The Idiot,* and *The Demons,* all three works dealing, in one way or another, with the central theme of intellectual torment over faith in an age of reason, not exactly the most relaxing reading material at a time of war. I also read Tolstoy's *Anna Karenina* and *Resurrection,* and poured over some of Papa's Kanda bargains: Aldous Huxley's *Brave New World,* Arthur K Rogers' a Student's History of Philosophy, the Greek plays in English translation, and Henry George's *Progress and Poverty,* a shocking expose of the sins of industrialization during the last decade of the 19th century. For some reason, George's book – especially the photographs – have stayed with me my entire life. To this day, I can close my eyes and recall in minute detail the ghastly pictures of emaciated children working in squalid sweatshops and dark and grimy mines.

In the absence of other diversions Papa embarked on a course of philosophical inquiry along the lines of what later became known as the "Great Books" program. I joined him and we often spent entire evenings examining philosophical precepts that we literally had to sift out of our library collection. Mama occasionally also participated in our discussions, even though she usually prefaced her remarks by saying that she had no time for "idle philosophizing," a qualification that was entirely factual, considering that she really had very little spare time because she was almost always preoccupied with the impossible task of keeping the family fed and clothed. Nick was only casually interested in our discussions. In the fall of 1943, he started studying Japanese at the International Department of Waseda University and was totally absorbed in his language study. Mike listened, but said little – at age sixteen, he was more interested in applied science, not in abstract theorizing on ethics, politics, and social issues. In retrospect, as I look back to those bleak days and nights shut off from the outside world by a black curtain rigged to keep indoor lights out in case of an air raid, I am convinced they were far more important to my intellectual development than formal education. They laid the groundwork for my interest in history and sharpened my understanding of moral values. I got a great deal out of our discussions and debates, obtained a better understanding of my parents' intellectual stature, and acquired a fondness for poetry that has stood me well during my entire life. Our poetry readings and the thoughtful exchanges of opinion on literary and philosophical topics were like a breath of fresh air in an otherwise stifling climate of social and intellectual immobility brought by the narrow confines of the war.

If I remember correctly, the air raids started in November. At first, they were directed almost exclusively against industrial targets, rarely touching residential areas in Tokyo and its surroundings. South of Omori, the industrial cities of Kamata and Kawasaki were bombed methodically with high explosive ordnance for several weeks. They were night raids that usually commenced at about ten o'clock. The drone of the planes flying at high altitude, the unremitting firing of the anti-aircraft batteries, and the sound of exploding bombs blended together into a thunderous uproar that swept the night air like a powerful hurricane. It was a horrifying experience marked by an intense feeling of anxiety and sudden palpitations of the heart. The ground shook, the sky was aglow in bright red and yellow from hundreds of explosions and the flooding beams of constantly shifting search lights. But like everything else, it was something one could get accustomed to given sufficient time as long as the bombing remained distant. After a few weeks, I learned to sleep through most air raids, despite Mama's frantic calls to get up and evacuate the house.

Papa, for the first time in mufti, at his desk at the
Chinese Eastern Railroad, Mukden, 1924.

Mama, at home, Mukden 1924

Nick and I, in our studio backyard, Mukden, 1927

Playing tennis, Mukden 1926

Nick and I playing soldiers, Mukden, 1928

Papa's photo studio, Mukden 1927

Nick, Mike and I, Shanghai, 1931

Mama and friends in our front parlor, Yokohama, 1934

Mama and friends in front of our Honmoku house, Yokohama, Japan 1934

Nick and I on our first day at St. Joseph's College, Yokohama, 1933

Papa and the three of us in our front parlor, Yokohama, 1934

As a Sea Scout in the front yard of our Honmoku house, Yokohama, 1935

Graduating from St. Joseph's Yokohama, July 1941

Р О С П И С К А

Дана сія росписка Японской Военной Миссіей на ст. Маньчжурія Начальни-
ку Снабженій дальне Восточной Арміи Генеральнаго Штаба Генералъ Маіору
Павлу Петровичу П е т р о в у въ томъ, что Японской Военной Миссіей на ст.
Маньчжурія принято на храненіе двадцать /20/ ящиковъ съ золотой монетой и
два ящика съ золотомъ въ слиткахъ.

Ящики съ монетой за №№ 3091, 3039, 3001, 3015, 4207, 3353, 3333, 3883,
4937, 3989, 5479, 3019, 4091, 3293, 3363, 3577, 3183, 3249, 2975, и 3831.

Ящики со слитками за №№ 15 и 23.

Всѣ ящики опечатаны сургучной печатью " Управленіе Начальника Снабженій
Дальне Восточной Арміи " и пломбой " Ялуторовскъ Казначейство".

Вышеозначенные ящики съ золотой монетой и золотыми слитками составляютъ
собственность Дальне Восточной Арміи и никакому отчужденію по чьимъ-бы то
нибыло заявленіямъ не подлежатъ.

Обязуюсь по первому требованію Генеральнаго Штаба Генералъ Маіора Петрова или по его довѣренности выдать все принятое на храненіе.

Что подписными и приложеніемъ печати свидѣтельствуемъ. Ноября 22 дня
1920 года Ст, Маньчжурія.

*В случаѣ смерти Ген. Петрова золото
надлежитъ выдать Генералу Вержбицкому
а послѣ него Генераламъ Лучкову и
Бангерскому*

2

*Начальникъ Японской
Военной Миссіи
Полковникъ Исоме*

Receipt given to Major General Paul Petroff, Chief of Supply of the Far Eastern Army by Colonel Isome of the Japanese Military Mission at Station Manchuria on November 22, 1920 for the safe-keeping of Twenty (20) boxes of gold coin and Two (2) boxes of gold bullion. The receipt unequivocally states that they are to be returned to Major General Petroff at his first request.

Receipt given to Major General Paul Petroff, Chief of Supply of the Far Eastern Army by Colonel Isome of the Japanese Military Mission at Station Manchuria on November 22, 1920 for the safekeeping of Twenty (20) boxes of gold coin and Two (2) boxes of gold bullion. The receipt unequivocally states that they are to be returned to Major General Petroff at his first request.

Willy foster and I in front of his house, Omori, 1943

Climbing in the Japan Alps, near the summit of Jizogatake, 1943

In Red Cross army uniform, Tokyo 1946

Nick, one of our Red Cross colleagues and I, in front
of the Imperial Palace, Tokyo, 1947

Central Yokohama:
Bombing Assessment, taken by 7th AF Combat Camera Unit

The strategic bombing of selected industrial targets continued through February 1945. During the night of March 9, the American Air Force changed its strategy. Flying at altitudes of 5,000 to 10,000 feet, three hundred B-29s led by Pathfinders attacked Tokyo's residential and business sections with napalm cluster bombs. The air raid started at about 10:30 PM and went all night. Fanned by ground drafts and high winds, the fires leaped from one block to another burning the small wooden Japanese houses in a matter of minutes in an inferno that swept the residential and business quarters, including Asakusa, the historic entertainment quarters of Tokyo. Some died terrible deaths by asphyxiation, others burned to death, while others were crushed by collapsing timbers. According to official Japanese estimates, the death toll that night was more than 100,000 – more than in the atomic blast over Hiroshima.[25] The bombing was confined primarily to Tokyo, and Omori suffered only minor damage from planes that had strayed from the targeted area. Our house was untouched and the fires in the neighborhood were put out by morning. More napalm bombing followed in the next five weeks; the air raid of April 13 was especially hard on Omori. Our house again escaped damage but, whipped up by winds and spreading fires, a large part of western Omori burned to the ground. The inferno lasted through most of the night, this time coming within five hundred feet of our house. We were vulnerable, but around 3:00 AM the winds subsided and the fire changed direction. We were extremely lucky – our house could have easily burned to the ground. A frightening aspect of napalm bombing was the floating debris from the cluster missiles that split apart in the air and came floating down to earth. One small piece of such floating debris hit Mama on her right shoulder, but she was wearing a heavy overcoat and fortunately suffered only a nasty bruise.

The fire bombing of Japanese cities was devastating. In Tokyo, the palace, the central business district, the major railway terminals survived the carpet bombing, but everything else burned down to the ground. The power grid and the transportation network were also damaged. But the heaviest harm was suffered by the civilian population. In addition to hundreds of thousands who died, there were also at least as many who survived but lost their homes, their jobs, and their meager supply of food. It's hard to understand why the Japanese people did not rise to demand an end to the war. Instead, they remained outwardly calm and resigned to the burden of their deplorable condition, digging out of the remaining ruins and searching for food. On several occasions, Nick and I helped Omori's maintenance crews and volunteers from the neighborhood associations to brace up damaged overpasses with sand bags and clear the streets of the smoldering debris. We didn't have to do that, but the devastation and the risk of resulting damage were so great that we felt we had to help. Our reaction was almost spontaneous; we did not feel we could remain bystanders when our neighbors were risking their lives. Whenever that happened, a delegation of the neighborhood's elders always called on Papa and Mama to thank them for "allowing their sons" to participate.

The war was clearly coming to an end. I don't think the urban population could continue taking the punishment for more than another four or five months. On April 15 we were informed by our local police in Omori that all "non-belligerent foreigners" in the Tokyo-Yokohama area were to proceed to Karuizawa in Nagano Prefecture, including all Germans who were now reclassified also as "non-belligerent foreigners" because the war in Europe was drawing to an end. Apparently, the

Ministry of Foreign Affairs had decided that the time had come to evacuate all foreigners from the Tokyo metropolitan Area. I don't know what prompted this action, a sudden spasm of compassion for their plight after the terrible March and April raids, fear that there might be incidents of retaliation by Japanese ultra-nationalists, or the purely pragmatic consideration that it will be easier for the Japanese police to keep an eye on all foreigners if they are concentrated in one location. Whatever it was, we were informed to pack immediately, taking only the most essential belongings, and prepare for departure on the next day for Karuizawa by a special train that had been commandeered out of Ueno station in Tokyo. The essentials did not include books, photographs, china, works of art, and we left them behind in the air raid shelter, covering it with an extra foot of earth for additional protection. This was done with the approval of the local police who promised to watch over our pitiful hoard. It's gratifying to note that not a single item was stolen when the family returned to Tokyo and opened the shelter after the war.

Leaving for Karuizawa also meant saying goodbye to the old Japanese lady who had been Mama's loyal helper since 1938. We called her *Obasan* (Grandmother). She had been absolutely indispensable to Mama during the student boarding house phase of our life in Yokohama, and was in all respects part of the family, sharing our wartime experiences, our grief and joys, and our daily struggle to stay alive. During the last years of the war, she even offered to help us financially out of savings she had accumulated during nearly seven years of service to the family. It was a tearful parting for all of us. She was an exceptional human being and we hated to leave her behind so that she could return to her ancestral village in central Japan.

Papa, Mama, Nick and Mike left as ordered. I remained in Omori for another two weeks under beefed up surveillance because the local police did not know what to do with someone who was an officially appointed guardian of Willy Foster's property. I did not feel comfortable leaving Omori without written assurance that someone in authority would take over from me the custody of Foster's property. The predicament was really quite comical. I did not have a Japanese national as an alternate guardian, and the local police did not feel that they had permission to take responsibility for property belonging to someone arrested by the *Tokotai*. It was a classic case of conflicting jurisdictions, and it took the local police nearly two weeks to secure permission from the Foreign Department of the *Tokotai* to release me and take the responsibility themselves. While the brouhaha lasted, I remained in Foster's partially burned out Omori house an innocent victim of Japanese bureaucracy, in what seemed like total isolation experiencing two more bombing raids without suffering any harm.

I arrived in Karuizawa on May 1. Spring was just beginning to break out in the mountains and the air was full of the sweet scent of apple blossoms and the freshly running resin of the pine trees. After the groveling misery, devastation, and the stench of the still smoldering rubber and refuse in burned-out Tokyo, green and flowering Karuizawa looked like something out of an imaginary world. The White Russian contingent was housed in a cluster of pre-World War I hotels that had seen better days, about a mile from the center of town in a sparsely growing pine forest through which on a clear day one could see Mt. Asama. I did not experience any problems in locating my family; they had been anxiously waiting for my arrival and were glad to see me looking well. Mama had imagined all sorts of dire scenarios and burst into tears when I hugged her and she saw that I was unharmed. The hotel room assigned to our family was approximately 12x15 feet with a small balcony looking out at the pine forest and Mt. Asama. It had no beds – we slept on futons --. a wooden table, three dilapidated chairs and a *hibachi* made out of pottery clay completed our utilitarian furnishings. Later, we built two additional chairs out of old wooden crates that Nick snatched up in the center of town. As the weather warmed up, Nick and I moved to the outside balcony where we slept at night. The hotel had a large tiled Japanese public bath that was fired up once a week. The cold water system kept breaking down; in June, under Papa's direction, we rebuilt the monstrosity, using old metal clamps and piping that we surreptitiously lifted from an unoccupied building in the vicinity.

Each week we received a ration of two ounces of rice and four cheap "Golden Bat" cigarettes per day per person, a weekly allotment of half a liter of cooking oil for the entire family, and a straw bag of charcoal to fire up the *hibachi* on which Mama cooked. Papa and Nick did not smoke; I stopped smoking, and Mike was too young to receive a ration. Mama, who started smoking during World War I, received half of our family's ration; the rest became our exchange currency for flour, sweet potatoes, and green vegetables with the farmers of the Karuizawa plateau. I brought with me from Omori two bottles of Suntory whisky, six tins of corn beef, a pound of Lipton tea, and a two pound bag of sugar which I took from Foster's kitchen pantry. I did not think he would mind; besides, I rationalized the piracy as compensation for the extra two weeks that I had to spend in Omori guarding his personal property. In the following four months, the tea and sugar became our only source of luxury, and the whiskey and corn beef, a means of exchange for fruit and protein. In Karuizawa, we had gotten down to the lowest possible level of subsistence. Every bit of extra food we could find made a tremendous difference to our scanty and unappetizing diet.

There was very little surveillance in Karuizawa. The chief police officer of the Russian contingent was a military police reserve sergeant in his early fifties with some knowledge of Russian. We were technically neither prisoners nor detainees, and were free to do whatever we wanted as long as we stayed within the confines of the Karuizawa countryside. All that our police chief was concerned about was that no one skipped out of the camp, an endeavor that was quite inconceivable because Karuizawa is a high mountain plateau surrounded on all sides by mountains and small villages where a Caucasian would be immediately recognized. To show his authority and make sure everyone in the camp was accounted for properly, our police chief staged a weekly "nose count" that was straight out of a B-class movie. Every Monday at about 10:00 AM, he would walk into the hotel lobby jammed with men, women and children, ceremoniously sit down at a small table behind which two of his assistants – also military policemen – stood at attention against a wall on which hung the photograph of the emperor. He would then unbutton his tunic regardless of whether it was warm or cool that day, place his revolver on the table, and in a raspy voice begin to call the names from a list attached to a clip board. The ceremony would last about half an hour. He would then stand up, rebutton his tunic, replace the revolver in the holster and, in a voice that was now even hoarser, growl *spasibo* (thank you, in Russian) and solemnly walk out of the lobby. The ceremony was not without occasional incidents that could easily turn into a major confrontation. By most standards of Japanese camp practice our experience was mostly innocuous, despite the obvious annoyance of having to turn up every Monday morning to satisfy the wishes of our camp commander. We did have one incident, however, that could have turned ugly. Our camp commander insisted that all those present bare their heads for the nose count, because, as he meticulously explained at the outset of the confinement, we were in the presence of the Emperor whose picture hung on the wall behind his desk. There was no open protest to that dictate. Most people understood that, for all its banality, it did not make sense to argue with the man who had power to make things very difficult for the entire camp. One Monday morning, however, a young woman – the belle of the camp – came into the hotel lobby wearing a kerchief over her head. Our fearless commander bristled, stood up and, in a voice that had been probably nettled by a night of heavy drinking, ordered her to take the kerchief down. She refused, insisting that in Russia women cover their heads even in church. He became almost apoplectic, started shouting obscenities in Japanese and, in a theatrical outburst of consummate authority, ordered his assistants to take the kerchief off by force. The mood in the hall turned explosive. Some of the younger men moved forward to protect the damsel in distress, but before the assistants could reach her, an older man offered a compromise. Speaking fluent Japanese, he apologized for the "unfortunate incident" and explained to the sergeant that the woman was too young to understand the "gravity of the situation." He said he would like to talk to her and was sure she would comply with his "directive." At his request, the young woman took the kerchief off, and the unfortunate incident came to a harmonious close. There was a backlash to it, however. Even though the incident ended without any adverse repercussions, our intrepid camp commander disappeared from the scene. With the exception of the weekly "nose count," he became totally unavailable, compelling us to deal with the camp administration through his two assistants who were also often hard to find. In the calculus of power and authority, so important to the Japanese psyche, he had lost face and was no longer willing to deal with us on a one to one basis.

The internal organization of the White Russian compound was therefore left to its residents. Sanitation, clean-up, maintenance, bathroom schedules, and the resolution of conflicts became the responsibility of a council that elected Papa as its head. As the most senior member of the camp community he had to preside over four hundred often difficult and hostile residents housed in adjoining hotels allocated to the Russian group. On the whole, the camp ran smoothly, but it was not without disciplinary problems that poor Papa had to handle every day. Most of them dealt with sanitation, raucous drinking after lights out, conflicts between neighbors, and even a few fist fights. The biggest problem had to do with the public bath. Everyone wanted to use it first, before the hot water ran out and the tiled Japanese bath turned cold. The women demanded that they have a full day to themselves, the men wanted to use it only in the evening; in the end, a complicated schedule of bath hours had to be worked out to allow everyone at least one bath every two weeks. Group living can be a complex and exhausting endeavor, even in the best of times. Tempers flare, people say things they later regret, and conflicts develop because people have different ethical standards and different ways of reacting to pressure. In Karuizawa, as spring turned to summer, all of the above imperfections came to the forefront as people became more anxious and angry about the harsh conditions of their everyday life. The constant search for food and struggle for existence turned the artificially created condition of group living into a free-for-all ready to explode. Like a stack of hay ready to burst into flames at the touch of a match, the Russian contingent in Karuizawa was primed for an unavoidable firestorm.

Fortunately, outside events came to the rescue. By the first week of August, rumors of Japan's surrender were freely circulating in Karuizawa, undoubtedly the result of leaks from the Swedish and Swiss legations that had moved to Karuizawa and were privy to Japanese attempts at negotiations that started in July. We now know that as early as July 8, the Emperor made it clear to his close advisors his desire to end the war. In July, Japan asked Moscow to assist her with peace negotiations, but Stalin and Molotov never replied. They did not want to take a firm position before the Potsdam Conference; nor did they want to end the war in the Pacific before they were ready to enter it themselves. The Japanese also tried to negotiate through unofficial channels seeking help from Switzerland and Sweden, but nothing concrete developed out of this. On July 26, after the success of the atomic bomb testing had been confirmed, President Truman announced the contents of the Potstdam Declaration that called for Japan's unconditional surrender. In the meantime, the stakes were raised even higher. On August 6 and 9, the United States dropped atomic bombs on Hiroshima and Nagasaki, and on August 9, the Red Army crossed the border into Mongolia and Manchuria, advancing rapidly toward China proper. Defeated in the Pacific, threatened in China, Korea and the Kurile islands and devastated in its homeland by unrelenting bombing, Japan now had no choice but to accept the terms of the Potsdam Declaration. Breaking with long-established tradition and in opposition to the more militant generals and admirals who wanted to continue the fight on Japanese soil, the Emperor decreed that it was time "to endure the unendurable" and accept the terms of unconditional surrender. Several more days were spent in heated debate in Tokyo on a clause in the proposed surrender document that would promise the continuation of the imperial system of government, but the Allies held tight on the question of unconditional surrender. They refused to give any firm assurance that the imperial system would be allowed to remain, and stipulated that the final shape of the Japanese government would be determined by the freely expressed wishes of the Japanese people, intimating, that they would not oppose the retention of the Emperor if the Japanese people sanctioned the continuation of the imperial system.

In Karuizawa, we had no knowledge of what was going on in Tokyo and the Allied capitals, although we knew that there were negotiations going on. We did find out through the Swiss Legation that the Soviet Union had entered the war in August and that huge new bombs were dropped in southern Japan, but we were not aware of the true nature of those weapons. For us, the first fourteen days of August were days of nail-biting suspense peppered with the hope that the war would end soon. Our attitudes and morale hung precipitously on every piece of news that came out of the Swiss and Swedish Legations. It was a great relief, therefore, when we were informed on August 15 that Japan had agreed to accept the unconditional surrender demanded by the United States and the Allies.

Speaking at noon over the national radio, Emperor Hirohito proclaimed that he was accepting the joint declaration of the four powers, United States, Britain, China, and the Soviet Union. The broadcast was subject to a great deal of atmospheric disturbance and the Emperor's language was extremely perplexing. The Emperor spoke in the ancient court language that even most Japanese found difficult to understand. The broadcast was actually a recording transcribed on the previous day by radio technicians sent to the Imperial Palace by the Japan Broadcasting Corporation. Left in the safeguard of the Imperial Chamberlain the recording almost did not make the scheduled radio program when young officers of the Military Affairs Bureau occupied the palace in an attempt to stop the broadcast.[26]

The jubilation that grasped the compound was genuine and lasted through the entire day. The camp's two alcoholics got drunk on hair tonic and had to be revived by having their stomachs pumped. Our camp commandant and his two assistants disappeared after the broadcast never to be seen again. The resident poet dreamt up a limerick, something about "no more bombs, no more cheap cigarettes, and no more military police." By popular request, the day's working detail fired up the boiler for the public bathroom three days before the usual schedule, no longer concerned if the firewood would last until the end of the month. People relaxed, adversaries started talking again to each other, someone came up with a portable gramophone, and we danced that night to celebrate the end of the war. It was not until the next morning that people began to worry about what was in stall for them now that the war had ended. How do we get out of Karuizawa, how do we approach the occupying Americans, and myriads of other practical questions suddenly loomed on everyone's mind. I will never forget August 15, 1945. It was as if the skies had suddenly opened up after a long period of storms and consistently bad weather. I had no idea what I would do tomorrow or during the oncoming months, but I knew that in the long run I had been suddenly liberated, unchained, and free to do what I wanted, desert Japan forever and finally reach America. I was ecstatic about what tomorrow would bring.

Leaving Karuizawa and going to Tokyo immediately did not seem to be an acceptable option. In Karuizawa we had a roof over our heads, enough food stored for emergencies, and freedom to move, if we wanted to leave. It was by no means clear what we could expect in the Tokyo-Yokohama area after months of bombing and destruction. We decided to wait until more precise information became available about living and working conditions there. In any event, we did not want to return to Yokohama before it was fully secured by American troops. In late August, Karuizawa was beautiful, the apple trees were bursting with fruit, wild flowers were everywhere, in mountain meadows and along the neglected pathways leading to town. Staying a few weeks longer in Karuizawa seemed almost like taking a family vacation that all of us needed but never could take during the war. Papa, especially, needed a rest. The war had been hard on him, both physically and emotionally. He had grown paler and thinner and was suffering from a peptic ulcer activated by unhealthy war-time diet. He was depressed. He blamed himself for the sorrow and the pain he had caused the family by not realizing earlier – long before the war started – that his law suit against the Japanese government was bound to end in failure and he should have instead moved the family out of Japan to a safer and more permanent locale. Throughout the entire war he had also been troubled by what was happening in his native Russia. He was certain the German occupation was a tragedy of massive proportion for the people of western Russia and Ukraine. If there was anything positive about the wartime experience it was that the war and its associated misery had somehow erased Papa's and Mama's distressing estrangement regenerated their love and respect for each other and brought them closer together again. In fact, we all needed a rest, a time-off to consider our options before we ventured out to rebuild our lives. We took long walks, went swimming, relaxed in the hot summer sun. In the evenings, we talked a lot, about our war experience, the vicissitudes of our twisting and unpredictable lives in China and Japan, about what we thought the future would bring us and what, collectively and individually, we actually wanted out of life. I was terribly excited about the possibility of finally realizing my hopes for a continuing education and settling permanently somewhere in the United States. Two weeks flew by with great swiftness. Before we knew it, it was time to move on.

III

On September 2, after much hugging and kissing, Nick and I took the morning train to Tokyo. U.S. Army troops began landing as early as August 27, and the formal surrender ceremony was scheduled for the day we left. Hitched to our train that originated in Nagano were three rail cars with Australian prisoners of war on their way to Tokyo for processing and eventual return home. They had been POWs working in the Nagano mines since the fall of Singapore and they were in no mood to be reined in. They looked exhausted and under-nourished, but there was an undaunted spirit of comradery and *joie de vivre* that transcended their physical condition. As the train stopped at intermediate stations, they broke out of their rail cars and, chanting *Marching Matilda*, smashed everything standing on the platform to smithereens. The extraordinary aspect of this occurrence was not the conduct of the Australians – they had been POWs much too long – but the behavior of the Japanese station masters and their crews. Standing on the platform at attention, they took it all in with complete detachment, never uttering a word.

At Ueno station in Tokyo we came face to face with the process of Japan's military demobilization. Thousands of mustered out servicemen loaded to the hilt with bags of rice, futons, blankets, army boots, tools, and huge bundles with what looked like excess uniforms were sitting or lying on the floor of the large station hall waiting to board trains to take them home. They had obviously taken possession of army property and were now bootlegging it home. One poor fellow had a huge long-bedded Japanese typewriter strapped to his back. Some looked like they may have been waiting for several days; others had obviously just arrived and were still trying to find a place where they could sit down and take off their loads. There were so many of them and the floor space was so compactly crowded that it was physically impossible to move. The air smelled of sweat and pungent leather. The large waiting hall seemed incredibly silent considering how many demobilized soldiers were sprawled on the floor. Except for an occasional cough and whisper, the tired and cheerless men of the Imperial Japanese Army looked as if they had been temporarily paralyzed. I remember saying to Nick: "what we see here today is a defeated army patiently waiting to be disbanded."

On our way from Ueno station to Yokohama we passed block after block of burned out buildings and abandoned lorries. I had traveled from Omori to Tokyo at the end of April, and the devastation looked enormous already then. Now it was total. With the exception of the Imperial Palace, Tokyo's Central Railway Station and the Marunouchi business center, there was nothing standing between Shimbashi and Kamata. Across the Tama River, Kawasaki was a ghost town leveled to the ground. Most of Yokohama was also destroyed. Except for the Bluff and the business section along the harbor, one could see block after block of solitary chimneys, ruined foundations, downed electric and telephone poles, and an occasional burned out safe with its metal doors wide open and scarred by fire. But the most frightening thing about Yokohama was that it looked like it had been completely abandoned; there was absolutely nothing alive and moving until we reached the main boulevard of the city's business section, not even a lonely tramp or a stray dog. Convinced by war propaganda that they would be victimized by the victorious troops of the U.S. Army of Occupation, the Japanese had deserted the entire city. Near the harbor, we saw our first American GIs and spotted a military policeman directing traffic who took us for American internees and told us to report to the American Red Cross.

The Red Cross facility was a large warehouse stacked to the ceiling with Red Cross supplies, some only recently landed and others apparently delivered during the war by the Swiss Red Cross for American POWs and internees, but never distributed by the Japanese. In the warehouse we met Field Director Roger K. Leathers who was head of the American Red Cross contingent attached to the XI Corps of the U.S. Eight Army. He, too, mistook us for Americans and, when we explained who we were, asked us if we spoke Japanese. When we said yes, he told us that he could use us to help him find Japanese laborers to unload and store supplies from a ship that was tied up at a nearby wharf. It was almost dinner time and when we told him that we had not eaten since early breakfast, he called in a young private who escorted us to the mess tent a few blocks away. There, we were issued mess kits and told to join the chow line. It's hard to forget that first American meal, an *ambarass du richesse* by our wartime standards, meat loaf with gravy, mashed potatoes, green peas, fresh bread rolls, canned peaches, and all the coffee you could drink. That evening we were also provided with portable cots, blankets, towels, toilet articles, cigarettes, a clean set of khakis, socks and shoes, and told to report at 8:00 AM next morning. The shoes were an especially critical item as ours were barely holding together. I recall Nick saying to me "how lucky can one get, within a few hours we accomplished everything we wanted and even more."

Overnight, we had become employees of the American Red Cross with all of the related privileges that came with the job. Two or three days later, Nick was assigned to the Red Cross office attached to the First Cavalry Division that was deployed inland, and I moved to the ARC main office in Yokohama attached to the Headquarters of the XI Corps. Roger Leathers discovered that I had office experience and put me in charge of his correspondence with parents who had not heard from their soldier sons for some time and wanted the American Red Cross to locate their units and report home on their well-being. We also acted as intermediaries between the army and parents requesting early discharges for their soldier sons. Leathers had excellent rapport with the colonel in charge of personnel at Corps headquarters and we generally succeeded in securing early discharges on grounds that they were needed at home to help run the family business or farm. At first, Leathers supervised my work closely, but when he learned that I could write well and used good judgment, he left me pretty much alone to run the entire department. At the height of the "search and vouch for early discharge" activity, we were responding to hundreds of inquiries each week.

Roger Leathers was an outstanding no-nonsense all-business executive. He made his decisions quickly, was a good delegator and, I believe, loved what he was doing. Unsophisticated, direct and outgoing, he had a personal touch that made people like him immediately. I am profoundly grateful to him for his on-the-spot decision to hire Nick and me. Someone less decisive could have easily hesitated and made our search for a job much more difficult. He had been with the Army as a Red Cross Director since the Solomons, had witnessed the fighting in the Philippines, and was anxious to return to his native Rhode Island where, if I remember correctly, he owned and managed an insurance agency. His only obsession was that he wanted to acquire a samurai sword and see the insides of a Geisha House before leaving for home. We got him a sword – they were a dime a dozen during the early weeks of the occupation – but it was a little more difficult to find an authentic Geisha House in the rubble of burned-out Yokohama or Tokyo. I suggested Atami on the Izu peninsula, a prime attraction of vacationing Japanese businessmen, untouched by bombing and miles away from areas occupied by the U.S. forces. Whether or not he followed through I never found out. He knew that my parents were still in Karuizawa and that I wanted to make a trip there as soon as possible. Again, he made a quick decision. "Go ahead," he said "just don't do it alone, take someone with you for protection, we don't want to get in trouble with headquarters."

I found a friendly sergeant who was interested in seeing more of Japan than just the bombed out streets of Yokohama. We made the trip official by securing written orders for an inspection junket inland, checked out a jeep from the XI Corp motor pool and, two weeks into my job on a weekend, left for Karuizawa. That early in the occupation, US. Army units were still deployed primarily in the cities along the shores of the Pacific Ocean. We got through the check points without difficulty, and sailed through Kumagaya, Takasaki, and other smaller towns without any problems. Ours was probably the first U.S. vehicle seen by local denizens as we drove through the countryside of central Japan. Some stood in silence, others waved and, when we stopped for direction, crowds of little kids surrounded our jeep. We came prepared with candy bars and chewing gum, and we passed them out graciously to the children. We arrived in Karuizawa in the afternoon and almost immediately found Mike and then Papa and Mama. They had been waiting to hear from Nick and me, and when I described what we accomplished in Yokohama, they simply could not believe our good fortune. We brought with us a large can of smoked ham, canned fruit, flour, sugar, powdered milk, powdered eggs, beer, coffee, candy bars and, of course, several cartons of Lucky Strikes for Mama. That evening we had our first decent family dinner and gratefully acknowledged our thanks to the U.S. Army of Occupation.

A few weeks later, Papa, Mama and Mike moved to Yokohama where they first stayed with friends who owned a house on the Bluff that miraculously survived the bombing. Seeing that the American GIs were behaving as gentlemen, the Japanese also started to return. The first troops that landed were veterans of intense fighting in the steamy jungles of the Pacific islands. Like the defeated Japanese, they too were tired of war and had a deep sense of compassion for the dispossessed and starving people with whom they now had to live side by side. It was not at all unusual during the early months of the occupation to see a tough-looking American soldier sharing his rations with a bunch of hungry street urchins. The excesses of the occupation came with the raw replacements who never saw combat, not with the seasoned fighters of the Pacific campaign.

In general, the occupation was in all respects benevolent, enlightened, and breathtaking in its execution from its first day. That may sound too laudatory and insufficiently analytical, but I am dealing in my memoir with the big picture, not the minutia of Japan's gradual transformation from a bitter enemy to our most responsible ally in Asia. General Douglas MacArthur's decision to retain the Emperor – albeit, in a less sovereign capacity than previously – was critical to the success of the occupation from day one. MacArthur understood the deep-seated thousand year-old reciprocal relationship of the people to their emperor and his to them. Their obligation was to obey the emperor unconditionally, and his to assure order and calm. That is exactly what took place during those first weeks of the occupation. With but a few exceptions, the people of Japan obeyed their emperor, relieved that they would not have to face the prospect of hand-to-hand combat on home ground. He, on the other hand, did everything in his power to reduce the chances of continued hostility after the Japanese surrender had been announced. On his orders, members of the imperial family were dispatched overseas to persuade Japanese forces to lay down their arms peacefully. Contrary to established tradition, he also placed the initial responsibility for cooperation with General MacArthur's headquarters on his own shoulders by appointing a member of the Imperial family, Prince Higashikuni, prime minister of the first post-war cabinet.

General MacArthur's long and distinguished service to the nation was not without shortcomings, especially during the last years of his military career. He can be criticized for his theatrical and imperial behavior, his politically risky decision to move beyond the 38th parallel in Korea, his insubordination and arrogance vis-à-vis President Truman, but his determination to retain the Japanese imperial system for the benefit of a smooth and calm transformation of Japan was not a mistake. By not putting Emperor Hirohito on trial and winning his confidence, he pulled off one of the greatest achievements in military history at no cost to his country or its people, and he did it in the face of considerable opposition. The hard-liners in Washington, the China lobby, prominent members of his own staff, and even a fair number of Japanese liberals tried to obstruct his decision to treat the Emperor leniently. A story that was making the rounds during the first two weeks of the occupation is especially instructive about how MacArthur felt. According to it, on the night before the surrender ceremony on the battleship *Missouri,* he told his staff that they were sitting in an enemy country with a handful of troops, surrounded by nineteen fully armed Japanese divisions and millions of fanatics. "One false move," he said, "and the Alamo would look like a Sunday-school picnic." But there was no false move. MacArthur's decision not to prosecute the Emperor and instead secure his support for the occupation removed the risk of a Japanese "Alamo.".

A corollary of MacArthur's "emperor decision," supported fully by President Truman, was his stand against multinational occupation and against direct U.S. governance of Japan. With President Truman's blessing, he refused to divide Japan into zones of occupation as it was done in Germany, avoiding many sensitive problems that sprang up between the United States and the Soviet Union as the Cold War tensions came to the forefront. The early plan for direct military control, put together in Washington, was scrapped in favor of a more enlightened policy of indirect control through a Japanese civilian administration that was entrusted to govern Japan. In practice, there were, of course, numerous exceptions to the policy of indirect control. General MacArthur was deified by the Japanese, and his directives were carried out often as emergency measures, later ratified by government ordinances and legislation voted in the Diet. Regardless of where reform was initiated, the net result was almost always the same. Democratization followed demilitarization, as Japan slowly recovered from the humiliation of defeat.

There was something paradoxical and contradictory about General MacArthur's benevolent dictate. Despite his inborn conservatism and antagonism to liberal programs at home in America, he was astonishingly receptive to the recommendations of young New Dealers who were on his staff at General Headquarters. Under their supervision, the Japanese government granted women the right to vote, passed a whole series of laws protecting the rights of workers, overhauled the entire educational system, reformed the incongruous legal structure, passed new laws to restrict absentee land ownership, and broke up the *zaibatsu* by ordering the dissolution of the holding companies and cartels. As I look back to the early period from September 1945 to April 1947, all of which I witnessed personally, I can't but feel that the reforms were accomplished with superb precision and little resistance, largely because the Japanese bureaucracy and the newly empowered post-war elite were made to feel that they participated in the reforms themselves. There were, of course, some cases of defiance and even comedy. Old text books that were considered too militaristic were replaced with new material, but before enough of the new books were printed, elementary and middle school students had to use old books with the most offensive militaristic passages blacked out. Parents told preposterous stories how their children tried to uncover the expunged passages by placing the banned material behind an electric light or dousing it with a secret formula that was supposed to dissolve the black ink. There were fist fights in the Diet between the land-owning members of parliament and the liberals representing the tenant farmers, but the most intense confrontation took place between the *zaibatsu* and the GHQ. Shocked by the severity of the U.S. policy of decartelization and confident that money can talk even during an occupation, Mitsui and Mitsubishi went directly to General MacArthur complaining that they had suffered during the war and were now being repressed again, this time by the U.S. military officers. They did not get anywhere with their entreaties and, together with Sumitomo and Yasuda holding companies, were promptly dissolved, only to reconstitute themselves again some years later into even more powerful industrial and financial giants By almost every appraisal at the time of the occupation, the democratization and reform programs were highly successful. The press – both American and Japanese – recognized this every day. However, it was not unusual to hear negative comments on occasion, especially from members of the Japanese intelligentsia. I can recall one conversation with a friend of mine, a young Japanese professor of Waseda University, who said to me that he thought the American specialists in MacArthur's headquarters were conducting social experiments that they would never dare to initiate at home.

IV

The American Red Cross can also take a bow. It did an outstanding job in making life easier for the returning POWs and Allied internees. From its bulging warehouses, it handed out clean clothing, footwear, toilet articles, extra food, chocolate bars and cigarettes. Within the first two weeks, it also opened canteens that served coffee and doughnuts to thousands of enlisted men each day. October saw the arrival of the American Red Cross women, attractive and energetic "Red Cross girls," who helped the men open Red Cross entertainment centers for the homesick GIs waiting to be sent home. In late October, we also had a changing of the guard. Roger Leathers was finally allowed to return home and, in his place, Otis Brown came as our new Field Director.

Otis was a very different kind of American from Roger Leathers. In his early fifties, born and raised on the east side of Manhattan, he attended Columbia University, had worked at one time for a large New York foundation, and had a high regard for music and theater. He was apparently unable to secure a commission- probably due to age or a medical impairment – and signed up with the American Red Cross. Like Willy Foster, he also liked his whisky, and it was not unusual to find him after working hours with a bottle of Bourbon listening to Tchaikovsky's *Swan Lake* or *Symphony Pathetic*. Despite our age differences and positions on the American Red Cross employment ladder, Otis Brown and I became good friends. I think he was genuinely captivated by my unusual Russian background. He had a fair knowledge of Russian classical literature and history, had read a number of books on the Russian revolution, knew who Kerensky and Kolchak were and, I believe, truly enjoyed exchanging views on the subject of the Russian revolution and Russian civil war with someone who was the son of an authentic participant.

We often got together, sometimes for a drink, or to enjoy a cup of coffee. There was no limit to what we talked about. He was interested in how and why our family came to Japan, how we were treated during the war, what we thought of Japanese art and culture, and what we thought of the occupation. I introduced him to Papa and Mama, and he also met some of our Japanese friends. Sometime in late December, over a cup of coffee, he said to me in all seriousness: "You know you're wasting your time working for the American Red Cross." I really did not know how to take this comment and at first thought that there was something he did not like about my work. But he followed through with a comment I did not expect. He said: "with your knowledge of Russian and Japanese and understanding of Japanese culture and politics, you should be working for our intelligence service, not the American Red Cross. That was the last thing in the world I expected him to say. I was not sure whether this was just a random comment, or I was being recruited to work for G-2. I put our discussion out of my mind, but within a few days I had a call from GHQ over the safe military phone line. The speaker was someone who knew Otis at Columbia and had heard about me from him. He was interested in meeting me to discuss a possible connection, and we arranged a clandestine rendezvous at one of Tokyo's many parks.

GHQ had good reason to worry about what was taking place on the political playing field of Japan. The Japanese Communist Party made phenomenal advances during the first four months of the occupation.

Released from prison in early September, long time communist leaders, Sanzo Nosaka, Kyuichi Tokuda, and Yoshio Shiga immediately went to work on rebuilding the Japanese Communist Party that had been brutally crushed in the 1930s by the Thought Police. Disillusioned by the defeat and disheartened by post-war economic conditions, thousands of young people joined the Communist Party in Tokyo and other large cities of occupied Japan. The communist newspaper *Akabata* (Red Banner) appeared again on city streets, and Marx's *Communist Manifesto* and *Das Kapital* and Lenin's *State and Revolution* sold in thousands of hastily printed copies in urban bookstores throughout Japan. In November, the Party began infiltrating the labor unions and university student councils, triggering labor and student strikes in the larger cities of Japan. The Soviet Military Mission in Tokyo had also grown from a small group that came with General Derevyanko to sign the surrender agreement on the *Missouri* to a substantial contingent that was housed in the Marunouchi 22 Building in central Tokyo. One did not have to be an intelligence expert to see that the domestic political situation could become ugly if concrete steps were not taken to contain the growth of communism in Japan. Major General Charles Willoughby, a stern and intractable anti-communist was absolutely paranoid about what was taking place in Japan. The Cold War had not started yet, but the early indications of a more intense competition with the Soviet Union were already discernable. It was obvious that GHQ's interest in me had something to do with the growth of communism in Japan.

I don't recall the name of my first contact with the Counter Intelligence Corps. He was a man in his late forties or early fifties, well educated, urbane and fully acquainted with the domestic political situation in occupied Japan. Even if I had remembered his name it was probably fictitious, as this was generally the case in many of my other contacts with agents of the Counter Intelligence Corps. He reviewed the domestic situation along lines with which I was already familiar and told me that General Willoughby was concerned about three specific aspects of communist activity in Japan. He was troubled by the possibility the Soviet Union could gain control over the Japanese Orthodox Church and its nearly two-hundred Orthodox religious communities scattered throughout Japan, a concern that was entirely reasonable, considering that the Japanese Orthodox Church, in the last months of the war, had lost its religious leader, an ethnic Russian, Metropolitan Sergius of Japan. It seemed entirely possible that the Soviet Union would try to replace him with a Moscow bishop and a team of Orthodox clerics who were actually KGB agents. He was also distressed by the lack of solid information reaching the Counter Intelligence Department at General Headquarters on the Japanese Communist Party and what he called the "comings and goings" of the Soviet Military Mission in Tokyo. To counteract those deficiencies, Headquarters wanted to increase the surveillance of the Japanese Orthodox Church, the Soviet Military Mission, and the Japanese Communist Party. We talked for about an hour; he was interested in my background, why our family came to Japan, and how we survived the bombing and nearly four years of war. It was obvious he was sizing me up, and I was not surprised to hear from him on parting that somebody of my own age from Counter Intelligence would call me to work out the details on how we would go about structuring our relationship and obtaining the objectives he had outlined. I told him I would have to think about it. For obvious reasons, I had some doubts. I was afraid of the clandestine nature of the relationship, of what some of our White Russian friends would say if it they ever found out I was working as an underground intelligence contact, and I also had a certain amount of anxiety about how such a relationship would affect my primary objective of emigrating to the United States. Would the U.S. Army intelligence drop me cold in the event of a serious mishap or would they provide support? I had read enough spy novels to know that in the "cloak and dagger" business of intelligence gathering, it's not unusual for headquarters to wash their hands and disavow a relationship with an underground agent to protect their presumptively legitimate standing. But the proposition sounded exciting, clearly more interesting than answering inquiries from anxious American parents looking for their estranged sons. Besides, I recognized the growing communist challenge, and was not averse to being involved in an operation whose objective was to halt the spread of Soviet influence in Japan.

A few days later I received another phone call, this time from Hyland Stewart III, a G-2 operative who was three or four years older than I. I reviewed my concerns and he assured me that the proposed relationship had the very top backing of G-2, and that he would make sure personally that we would maintain the optimum of secrecy. To maximize security, we agreed to meet in different places and at different times and avoid the use of the telephone unless there was an absolute emergency that called for urgent action. At his suggestion I moved out of the government quarters in central Tokyo assigned to civilian employees of the U.S. army to the Ikebukuro district in northwestern Tokyo where I rented an apartment that became at the same time my living quarters and a safe house where I could interview and debrief Japanese nationals without having to worry about being discovered by other American occupation personnel and the press. For cover, my jeep had ARC markings, and if anyone asked what I was doing I was to say I was still working for American Red Cross. As I look back at the arrangement, I have to chuckle about the extreme secrecy, but it was apparently the way all undercover agents and their handlers operated in the murky waters of counter-intelligence. In March 1946, Papa and Mama moved to a house in Dennen-chofu in the southern outskirts of Tokyo, and I joined them using the Ikebukuro apartment primarily as a safe house and a place to bed down if I got stuck in central Tokyo late at night. It was easier that way to keep my cover and move freely without worrying about creating accidentally a faux pas that could be embarrassing to General Headquarters and the U.S. government.

My assignment was to assess the mood and intentions of the lay council of the Orthodox Church of Japan, more specifically, to try to discover what steps it was taking to appoint a new prelate for the Orthodox Church of Japan. It was also to find out as much as possible about the inner organization of the Japanese Communist Party and to keep an eye on the officers and enlisted men of the Soviet Military Mission, especially their contacts with White Russians residing in Japan. To make sure that what I uncovered was passed on to G-2 without interruptions, Stewart and I met weekly at predetermined locations selected in advance. If there was nothing new to report, I generally advised him using very circumspect language over the telephone that I was unable to keep the appointment. The idea was to hold our meetings to the minimum in order to reduce the chances of being recognized.

The fate of the Orthodox Church of Japan was resolved to everyone's satisfaction in the fall of 1946, with some unexpected help from a U.S. Army colonel in the GHQ. After nearly a whole year of discussion the lay council and the Japanese clergy decided to invite a bishop of the Orthodox Church of America instead of someone from Moscow. The catalyst for that decision was Colonel Boris Pash, Chief of the Foreign Liaison Section on General MacArthur's staff. A Russian-American born in San Francisco, Pash was the son of Metropolitan Theophilus, Prelate of the Russian Orthodox Church of America. A swash-buckling soldier who among many other distinctions had fought with the Whites against the Bolsheviks in the Crimea and commanded the U.S. War Department Scientific Task Force in Europe during World War II, Pash convinced the Japanese to accept one of his father's bishops to take the post of Archbishop of Japan. It was one of those rare accidents of history. Without Colonel Pash and his connection to the Orthodox Church of America through his father it would have been very difficult to orchestrate the affiliation of the Japanese church to the Russian Orthodox Church of America. I have been told that General Derevyanko, head of the Soviet Military Mission in Tokyo, was furious when he found out that an American had been appointed Archbishop of the Orthodox Church of Japan. He had been trying to convince the Japanese to seek help from Moscow since the start of the occupation, and now a resolute senior U.S. Army officer, with a most direct connection to the Russian Orthodox Church of America, had somehow succeeded in foiling the Soviet attempt to establish a KGB network in Japan under the mantle of the Moscow-directed Orthodox Church. Bishop Benjamin of Pittsburgh arrived in Tokyo in January 1947, dismissing General Willioughby's concern about Soviet penetration of the Orthodox Church of Japan. Other than report periodically on the progress of the deliberations of the lay council and clergy I had very little to do with the final outcome.

The other two assignments proved to be more difficult. My connections with Japanese academics were helpful in evaluating what was taking place in the Japanese Communist Party, but they were never reliable enough to formulate policy on how to deal with the growing Communist threat. There were undoubtedly other sources of information on the Japanese Communist Party besides me, but they were apparently inadequate and failed to give an accurate picture of the Party's work. General Willoughby was tempted to use more repressive measures to stem the tide of communist penetration in the unions and the student councils, but U.S. policy of democratic reform made any such attempt to restrict political participation from the top out of the question. It was not until the winter of 1946-1947 when we finally succeeded in penetrating the Communist Party in Tokyo that it became possible to secure more accurate and timely information about impending strikes and demonstrations. A son of one of Papa's former attorneys who joined the Party was extremely helpful in obtaining advance information on Communist-initiated demonstrations in central Tokyo. I was told that General Willoughby was ecstatic when he heard that we succeeded in infiltrating the Communist Party. He despised all demonstrations that took place in front of the Palace or Dai-Ichi Building that housed General MacArthur's headquarters in Tokyo. To him they were a symbol of GHQ's inability to control public opinion and a sure symptom of worse things to come. The fact that we were now able to secure advance information about Communist-planned demonstrations did not eliminate them, but it did help G-2 and the Japanese police to prepare for them and develop appropriate strategies to reduce their significance for the press.

The surveillance of the Soviet Military Mission turned out to be even more difficult than that of the Communist Party. The wily Russians did not hire Japanese help, and infiltration of the Soviet Embassy and Marunouchi 22 Building was simply not in the cards. A young Russian sergeant whom I picked up on the road in Yokohama did provide some elementary information, but when I tried to recruit him as a permanent contact, panicked and I never saw him again. I did succeed in placing a friendly Japanese clerk in the hotel where most of the transient Soviet officers were billeted, but this tactic was not fool-proof as it was impossible to maintain a twenty four hour watch. In the end, a team of U.S. signal corpsmen succeeded in installing a continuously operating surveillance camera outside the entrance to the Marunouchi 22 Building which gave G-2 accurate information on who was entering and exiting the building. But it, too, had its limitations. It was not always possible to identify everyone for whom there was an existing photograph.

Time flew by rapidly. Before I knew it, we celebrated the coming of 1947, a new year that brought us to America and a new and more stable and rewarding life. St. Joseph's College reopened its doors in 1946, and Mike graduated in the summer of 1947. In late 1946, the United States opened its consulate in Yokohama, and we applied for immigrant visas to America that were granted to Nick and me on the Chinese quota almost immediately, because we were adults and were born in China.

Papa, Mama, and Mike, who was still a minor, had to wait for a vacancy in the Russian quota which was oversubscribed because of the tremendous number of Russians who were trying to immigrate to the United States from western Europe and Shanghai. Nick and I had saved enough American dollars to pay for the passage of the entire family and have some extra money – if I remember correctly around $500 each – to start our lives in San Francisco. Papa and Mama had many friends and Civil War comrades in California who immigrated to the United States in the early 1920s after the revolution and civil war. There was some concern about how soon Papa's, Mama's and Mike's visas would come through, but Joseph Swing, Vice Consul in Yokohama, assured us that their visas had high priority and would be approved as soon as there was an opening.

Nick and I could have waited for the rest of the family, but it was time to move on. We had been innocent bystanders during the war too long. To begin a new life it made sense for us to go ahead and get settled in San Francisco as soon as possible. Also, I never had complete faith in the security of my relationship with Army intelligence. I don't believe there was ever any physical danger, but maintaining my cover was often a chore. I was glad to put an end to it as soon as possible. On April 19, 1947, under clear skies and in unusually warm weather, Nick and I left Yokohama aboard the U.S.S. Meigs, a troopship that had been only recently returned to the American President Lines. Papa, Mama, and Mike came to the dock to give us their blessing, bid us *bon voyage*, and wave goodbye. Slowly, we moved out of the harbor, past Honmoku and Hachioji where we first encountered Japan, past the naval base at Yokosuka, and out of the Bay of Tokyo into the great expanse of the Pacific Ocean. I was both glad and sad to leave Japan behind. For nearly fourteen years Japan had been our foster country. Living there wasn't always easy – especially during the war – but it was an experience hard to replicate. I was leaving behind a Japan that I had learned to respect and admire, not the Japan of military fanatics, but that other Japan about which Lafcadio Hearn and Ambassador Grew wrote with such affection and regard.

Aboard, we had to rectify an embarrassing situation that became a favorite family story in years to come. Believing that Nickita, Nick's full Christian name, was feminine, the ship's steward placed him in the women's section of the ship. Nick thought it was kind of fun to spend the next two weeks in the company of women, but propriety and travel regulations prevailed. After a check of his travel documents and some reshuffling of passengers, the abashed steward moved him to the men's section of the ship. The thirteen day passage was uneventful. We read a lot, played chess – Nick usually winning, he was a whizz at both chess and bridge – and just loitered aboard in the warm sun as we approached the Hawaiian Islands. The ship was full of Russian and German Jewish immigrants from Shanghai. Many of them spoke little English, and Nick and I became their pro bono translators of documents that they needed to begin life in the United States. On April 25, we crossed the 180th meridian and on April 26 arrived in Honolulu. There, we had our first real non-military American breakfast – fresh ham and eggs, good coffee, and all the milk we could drink, a delicacy that we did not have before as all army breakfasts featured powdered eggs and powdered milk. The ship remained at anchor for twenty-four hours in Honolulu. We rented a jeep and circled the island of Oahu, ending our Hawaiian experience in style with a drink at the Royal Hawaiian Hotel bar

On May 1, with the setting sun behind us, we sighted San Francisco, Marin Headlands, Seacliff and, before we knew it, the Golden Gage Bridge. I remember standing on deck with the red setting sun behind me on the horizon watching the beautiful panorama of the San Francisco Bay unveiling as we slid under the bridge. We were extremely lucky. The air was clear, the skies a shade of brilliant blue. There were no ominous clouds or gale-force winds blowing from the ocean. Nor was the city in fog, which for San Francisco, was unusual for the time of the year. It took some time for the tug boats to guide our ship through the harbor to the pier where we docked at about 11:00 PM. It was too late to disembark and we spent a sleepless night aboard ship thinking about what awaited us the next day.

4

PERMANENT RESIDENT
IN U.S.

America, another name for opportunity.
Ralph Waldo Emerson

I

We woke up to a glorious day on May 2 to begin our new life in America. We were conveniently cleared by the Immigration and Naturalization Service aboard ship in Honolulu, and it was now only a matter of getting through customs which hardly took any time at all. As we stepped off the gang plank we were met by General Puchkoff, Papa's War College classmate and Civil War comrade in Siberia. After customary introductions, small talk and polite questions about Papa's and Mama's health and our wartime experience, we took a taxi to the home of Colonel Efimoff, the last commander of the famed Izhevsk Worker Brigade that the Red Army never succeeded in routing during the Civil War. The Efimoffs, also old friends of Papa and Mama, had a room ready for us in their flat on Lake Street, in a very nice section of San Francisco.

In contrast to the dreadful destruction of Tokyo and Yokohama, San Francisco looked like a spotless fairyland. Clean, manicured, and glistening in the morning sun, a far cry from the dust, desolation, and grime of the bombed out sections of the Tokyo-Yokohama area, it cried out to be embraced and explored. We began walking its streets and riding the clanging cable cars and trolleys that same day. We wanted to soak up San Francisco's world- acclaimed history and familiarize ourselves with its more prominent landmarks and geography. At first glance, everything looked so different from what we had been accustomed to in the Orient, so sanitary, cared for and well preserved.

Even the less prosperous neighborhoods frequented by alcoholics south of Market Street appeared relatively clean in comparison to the shanty towns that had sprung up in the bombed out districts of Yokohama and Tokyo. We were also overwhelmed by the living conditions of ordinary people, the profusion of privately owned automobiles, the abundance and variety of foodstuffs, and the quality of the appliances in people's homes. Kitchens sparkled, electric ranges and washing machines looked spotless, showers worked flawlessly. After years of low water pressure during the war and the occupation, showering now became a satisfying daily ritual of personal gratification. Food markets were stocked with luscious-looking fresh fruit and vegetables, all kinds of appetizing canned foods, and an assortment of beautifully displayed fish, fowl and meats. To top it off, almost everyone we talked to seemed to own their own home. Middle class America projected a convincing picture of super abundance and consumer-oriented technology that one read about but did not believe possible.

But at a personal and more intimate level, San Francisco and its inhabitants did not seem to be too different from what we were accustomed to in Japan. We felt very much at home in the new surroundings, notwithstanding the novelty of the material abundance. We spoke the same language without an accent, read the same magazines, and watched the same motion pictures as our new American friends. In some respects, we were even better informed and had a finer and more penetrating understanding of American history and politics. Years of acculturation in Yokohama's expatriate community and a year and nine months in the service of U.S. Occupation Forces prepared us exceptionally well for life in the United States. We were legally immigrants but, culturally, we were already Americans -- pseudo-Americans may be a more appropriate description --- but American enough to be taken for natives by people we had never met before. In 1947, the San Francisco Bay Area was bursting at the seams with returning servicemen -- many of them newcomers to California -- and we easily blended with them into the post-war demographic swell. We did make a few mistakes in our early weeks in San Francisco, but on the whole they were of little consequence. One - a ludicrous blunder -- deserves mentioning because it was so outlandish that I still laugh about it today. Shopping for suits to replace our GI khakis to augment our civilian wardrobes and trying to buy them as cheaply as possible, we made the mistake of falling for a bargain that turned out to be a regrettable faux pas. At a rather grubby-looking surplus store on Market Street, beyond the more fashionable retail district, we each bought what turned out to be flashy zoot suits, double-breasted with excessively broad shoulders, baggy pants that narrowed at the ankles, and a body outline that made us look like tough-looking Chicago gangsters. If I remember correctly we paid only forty dollars for the two suits, but it was money that we could have used to better advantage, and I don't think we wore those suits more than a few times. They were museum pieces from the prohibition era, not something that well-dressed young men wore on Montgomery Street in the financial district of the city.

One of the first things we did upon arrival was to visit Berkeley. As I remember, it was an unusually warm day. The campus was teeming with students -- pretty girls in bright colored skirts and athletic-looking young men, many still in their GI khakis. On Sproul Plaza facing the Administration Building a large crowd was listening to a speaker castigating U.S. policy on Central America. In front of the majestic Campanile, students in a variety of configurations and poses, were relaxing on the grass, some reading, some conversing, and some quietly sunning themselves in resigned solitude. Sather Gate, the magnificent Campanile, the abundance of greenery and the size and mixture of Grecian and modern architecture looked spellbinding in the hot and sizzling sun.

Armed with letters of recommendation from prominent military and civilian leaders of the Army of Occupation, we spent the whole day exploring the possibilities of becoming students at the Berkeley campus. To our dismay we soon found out that tuition for out-of-state students at the University of California in Berkeley was beyond our very modest means. A very nice middle-aged lady in the Admissions Office, after hearing our story, told us that it would make better sense in our situation to wait a year to qualify for California resident status and the low tuition that came with it. Instead, she suggested we enroll in the Summer school which was very reasonable by comparison to the regular Spring and Fall sessions, take extension courses for credit during the 1947-1948 scholastic year, and start the 1948 Fall semester having completed perhaps as many units as it was possible in regular session. Her advice made consummate sense. The one thousand dollars Nick and I brought with us to the United States were dwindling rapidly. It was painfully clear to both of us that we had to start looking for some kind of meaningful work. We checked out the university employment office, and I landed a part-time job with Montgomery Ward, moving kitchen appliances in and out of their Berkeley warehouse. An admissions adviser helped me wade through the university catalogue, evaluated my St. Joseph's College transcript and steered me to the courses I had to take for an undergraduate degree in Economics. Three weeks later I moved to Berkeley and enrolled in the First Summer Session. Nick decided to look for a more permanent white collar job in San Francisco and defer his admission decision until a year later.

I thoroughly enjoyed those early months in Berkeley. The academic work load did not seem overly heavy. I managed to complete thirteen units in four required undergraduate courses that summer, earning a B+ average. I also signed up through the University's Extension Division for two three-unit courses in History of Philosophy that I completed with straight As and a gratifying comment that I had a "very comprehensive" knowledge of the subject and should perhaps consider philosophy as a major. What the professor did not know was that I had done a lot of reading in philosophy during the war years, making what appeared to many a difficult and obscure subject an effortless exercise requiring very little supplementary study. The work at Montgomery Ward was strenuous and physically taxing, but just the sort of thing I needed to balance the rigorous regimen of my study program. It was in harmony with the old Roman adage of *men sana in corpore sano;* at least, that is how I reconciled the two in my mind. Each week, I managed to squeeze roughly thirty hours of work into my daily schedule which, at $1.10 per hour, allowed me to keep body and soul together on a tight and unpretentious budget.

Papa, Mama and Mike arrived in late August. One had to be a magician in 1947 to find decent lodging in San Francisco. Property owners demanded exorbitant rents, outrageous deposits, and on top of that what was euphemistically known as "key money," a one-time cash reward to the owner for agreeing to rent the apartment and deliver the keys. I must have followed up hundreds of leads before I ran into a Russian-American who had served under Papa during the Russian Civil War. He emigrated to the United States in the 1920s, and was willing to lease the upstairs of a town house he owned in a very nice area of the Sunset District. The flat had to be furnished, and Papa's credentials again came to the rescue. The benefactor turned out to be Boxer's Furniture Store on Fillmore Street owned by a veteran of the Russian Civil War who was well-known in San Francisco's Russian and Jewish communities for extending credit to arriving immigrants

We were now again together as a family, this time in a comfortable newly painted three-bedroom town house on 21st Avenue, less than a block from the Golden Gate Park. Papa needed medical attention, and in October underwent a surgical operation for a bleeding ulcer. Mama started an intensive reading program in American literature and history. Nick landed a permanent job with the Southern Pacific which he parlayed in 1948 into a junior executive position in their Traffic Control Division. Mike took a job with Crown Zellerbach Company, signed up for two required University of California Extension courses, and in the fall of 1948, upon attainment of California resident status, was admitted as a full-time student in the Physics Department. Because it was easier to find part-time work in San Francisco I moved to 21st Avenue and continued with my studies in the Extension Division, working at a variety of non important and mostly menial jobs that gave me the freedom of carrying a fairly heavy study load. By the fall of 1948, together with the credits I received for work at St. Joseph College and the courses completed in four Summer sessions in 1947 and 1948, and the University's extension program, I was just a few units short of attaining Upper Division status as a full-time student in economics in the School of Letters and Sciences.

Our first year in America was a hodgepodge of experiences within the framework of San Francisco's large Russian community. Many of Papa's and Mama's old friends and Civil War comrades had settled in San Francisco and it was not surprising that their initial months in California were consumed in reestablishing old relationships and closely-knit ties that came about as a result of the Civil War and the early years of life in exile. For them the first months in San Francisco were a series of lunches and dinners and a formal reception hosted by the Russian Veterans' Association. For us it was a generous interregnum during which we sized up the offspring of our parents' friends, and formed new social relationships. The grown-up children of Papa's and Mama's friends -- in most cases, born in California -- welcomed us with open arms. They treated us as long lost brothers and made every effort possible to include us in all their plans. We attended dances and meetings of their various organizations, participated in outdoor outings and patronized the same haunts and drinking establishments. The "El Portal" on Lincoln and Eighth Avenue was the favorite watering hole for the young Russian-American crowd. In the fall of that first year, Nick and I joined the Russian Soccer Society and played in the San Francisco Soccer League for "Mars," made up almost exclusively of young Russian-Americans. It was fun while it lasted, but there was something always missing in that experience. As I look back and think about it now, I believe there were good reasons why we never succeeded to fit in. Although about the same age, we were much older in terms of life's experience. We had witnessed the war at a very personal level, had to learn how to survive and make a living, and also had other interests besides sports. We were adults, in the full sense of that word, and were consciously ready to get on with our lives. They, on the other hand, were still overgrown kids trying to prolong the remaining traces of their youth. We were also raised under very different conditions. We grew up in the expatriate culture of Yokohama's international community with a minimum of ethnic Russian influence. They, on the other hand, were raised as second generation Americans in a predominantly Russian immigrant enclave with all of the cultural aspects the community imposed on them. They were the product of the slow and sometimes harsh process of acculturation that was part of the American immigrant experience from one generation to another. We never were part of that process; nor did we want to enlist in it. This did not mean that we were not proud of our Russian heritage or were somehow trying to camouflage our Russian roots. We did not anglicize our Russian names as many immigrants did. On the contrary, we accepted our Russian heritage unconditionally and, throughout our ensuing lives, exposed it openly without any attempt at subterfuge. I recall one rather amusing incident that was a subtle reminder of my Russian roots. Checking into the Boston Statler in the early fifties. I was asked by a rather arty-looking hotel clerk who must have noticed my distinctly Russian appellation on the registration blank if I was with the ballet. "No," I said, "but thank you for the compliment." He had obviously mistaken me for one of the young Russian dancers who made up a good part of the New York Ballet Company.

What we did not want to do during our first years in America was to get mired down in the immigrant milieu of San Francisco's Russian town. We wanted to get beyond it as soon as possible and look for the broader and richer pastures of authentic American life. It actually happened very innocently and without any backlash for Papa and Mama or repercussions for us. In May of 1948, Papa joined the faculty of the Russian Department at the Defense Institute of Languages in Monterey, and shortly thereafter he and Mama left for Monterey. My brothers and I also left San Francisco to go our separate ways. In the fall of 1948 Nick was transferred to southern California and a year later was recruited by Kaiser Engineers to take charge of the traffic department at the Hanford Atomic Works in eastern Washington. Kaiser Engineers, the primary contractor on the Hanford atomic project, needed someone who knew the "ins and outs" of the US railroad system and could coordinate the logistics of transporting building materials at the lowest possible cost from the far-flung industrial centers of America to the high desert of eastern Washington. Edgar Kaiser, the son of the founder, personally interviewed Nick, liked him, and offered him the job. Mike and I moved to the East Bay, first to a decrepit old Victorian town house on Adeline Street about a mile from the campus, and then to a more comfortable apartment in Oakland, near Lake Merrit from which we commuted to the University through 1949. In 1950, I moved to New York and Mike to the International House on Piedmont Avenue, Berkeley's fashionable fraternity row.

Nick's recruitment by Kaiser Engineers deserves a comment because it illustrates how different our world of today is from the unfettered and innocent world of 1949. Kaiser's top management appointed Nick traffic manager of a highly sensitive construction project without even asking him if he were an American citizen. It was only after he arrived at the construction site that the officer in charge of security raised the question of citizenship, loyalty and security risk. Edgar Kaiser stuck by his decision, and the U.S. Atomic Energy Commission was compelled to approve the appointment, after a comprehensive security check. What was most remarkable about this unexpected fumble was not the obvious need for a security check. Clearly, a high level of security has to be maintained in government projects of high sensitivity. Inconceivable today, was the failure on the part of the Kaiser people to ask Nick if he were an American citizen. In 2008, when we worry if airport security guards are citizens, and require applicants for positions with only minimal sensitivities to complete pages of personal and family history, Nick would never have been hired to work on a comparable project. In 1949, the Cold War was still in a state of unconcerned infancy. We had not yet lived through the McCarthy era, the Cuba crisis, the long and terrible war in Viet Nam, and the hysteria of our confrontation with the "Evil Empire," Fear and suspicion had not yet penetrated America's national consciousness. In 1949, America was still an open and innocent society untouched by the chicanery of ideology, geopolitics, and the pressures of domestic political strife.

Both Nick and Mike had clearly defined objectives and strategies for what they wanted out of life. Nick stayed with the Kaiser Companies, moving up the Kaiser executive ladder through numerous foreign assignments to become by the time of his retirement director of Kaiser Cement's largest foreign subsidiary. In 1957, while on assignment to India, he met and married the daughter of the former Italian governor of Eritrea and, after countless projects in South America and Asia, took over the presidency of Kaiser Cement's largest foreign subsidiary in Southeast Asia. Part of the American multi-national business community, Nick and his wife put on thousands of miles each year traveling a circuit that took them to Italy -- where their only daughter married a young Italian stock broker banker -- London, Jakarta, Washington, D.C. and Oakland, Kaiser's corporate headquarters in California. Mike also stayed focused on what he wished to achieve. In 1954, he earned a doctorate in physics that led him to a lifetime career in research and fame in the field of infra-red physics. Shortly after earning his Ph.D. in Berkeley, he married a young doctoral candidate of Russian extraction. They moved to southern California, raised two daughters -- one a physician and the other a professor at the University of Washington -- and settled down to a life of plenty and a regimen of continued learning within the tightly-knit fellowship of their professional societies.

My path to fulfillment did not follow the same straight and predetermined line. For a number of reasons I found it more difficult to follow a straight course. It was not the new environment or the demands that it placed on me. I was thoroughly prepared for the new experience and was thrilled to have finally reached the land of my youthful dreams. It was something deeper, more complex, more intertwined with the years of misdirection and boredom that I endured during the war and the occupation in Japan. Nick and Mike were unseasoned youths when the war started. I was an adult with grown-up ambitions that were never given a chance to materialize. When I graduated from St. Joseph's I was strongly drawn toward a career in geology, something that I could combine with my interest in travel, mountaineering and life outdoors. The war had somehow dampened this attraction and I opted for a more practical career goal in finance only to find out later that I really did not care for it.

There was also, I believe, a personality determinant that separated me from my two brothers. In the context of Isaiah Berlin's famous treatise on Tolstoy, "The Hedgehog and the Fox," they were hedgehogs and I was a fox. "The fox knows many things, but the hedgehog knows one big thing," the Greek poet Archilochus wrote in antiquity. Based on that citation, Berlin wrote a penetrating essay arguing that Tolstoy was by nature a fox who thought he was a hedgehog. I, too, at times believed I was a hedgehog, but deep down in the bowels of my personality make-up I knew I was always an incontrovertible fox. From early childhood, Nick and Mike were drawn toward clearly defined career aspirations, and their hobbies and interests were attuned to those goals. Nick wanted to be a businessman -- he collected and bought and sold stamps and coins, sold old newspapers, during the war traded with Japanese farmers, and had an inherent understanding of the value of money. Business was his "one big thing" and he was very good at it throughout his life. Mike's interest was in science and engineering. As a child, he took old-fashioned clocks apart to find out how they worked and put them back together. He played with erector sets and chemicals, read books on astronomy and spent hours inventing helpful household gadgets. He went to college knowing exactly what he wanted to do as an adult, earned a doctorate in physics, and ended up his career in science with a number of significant patents in the field of infra-red physics. Science was his "one big thing" and he, too was exceptionally good at it.

Unlike my brothers, I was never able to find one dominating interest to guide me. I was easily distracted by a variety of diversions that seduced and sidetracked me from the pursuit of "one big thing" that Berlin wrote about. Early exposure to management, history, philosophy, politics, travel, and mountaineering prompted me to think about "many things" rather than one. I cannot say that I did not pursue them with fervor, but never with enough intensity to make them my "one big thing" in life. The war probably also had something to do with my lack of focus. In the six years between my graduation from St. Joseph's and my arrival in the United States I was, by necessity, exposed to "many things" which I had to master in order to help the family survive the war and its immediate aftermath. On arrival in the United States, I wanted to learn more about what was to become my chosen country. I began reading the American writers of the Twenties and the Depression -- Sinclair Lewis, Dreiser, Steinbeck, Faulkner, Dos Passos. I was carried away by Ansel Adams' majestic photographs of the American landscape, especially the High Sierra which I found irresistible, and by the devastatingly realistic pictures of Dorothea Lange and Horace Bristol featuring the hardships of family life in California's Central Valley during the Depression. I read the *New Yorker, the Atlantic*, and *The New York Times*. I had a strong desire to find out for myself what America was all about. I wanted to internalize its essential values and ideas and visit its historical sites and places of interest -- New England, New York, the prairie, Hannibal, Missouri where Mark Twain created the Tom Sawyer and Huckleberry Finn personae, see for myself the vast sweep of Texas, the Civil War battlefields, Appalachia and the deep South. There was almost no limit to what I wanted to see.

In the summer of 1949 I was nearly twenty-seven, bored with the whole process of American higher education, especially with what seemed to me the tiresome upper division courses in economics.

The economics taught during the early post-war period was still predominantly Keynesian. Friederich A. Hayek's *The Road to Serfdom* had not yet had enough time to alter the basic principles of prevailing economic theory. In the economic entrepreneurial explosion that followed the war, Keynsian thinking was becoming largely irrelevant and out of date. Along with many other students in economics I was questioning whether or not it was worthwhile to change majors or continue working towards an economics degree. I was also just plain tired of grubbing and leading the life of a poverty-stricken student I wanted to do something more exciting, something that would allow me to become more independent, experience what I had been reading about, and start enjoying life. During the previous summer I had worked part-time for a San Francisco garment manufacturer as a kind of a many-faceted assistant, helping the sales promotion manager write advertizing copy and public relations releases, meeting arriving buyers at the airport and the railroad station, assisting the in-house salesman with the display of the fashion line, and doing all sorts of odd jobs. I had met the owners -- Leon and Nathalie Nicoli -- socially, and I called them about a summer job. Leon Nicoli was a Russian World War I air force pilot who had served with the Russian Expeditionary Force in France. Nathalie Nicoli, nee Anichkov, came from an old Russian aristocratic family, remembered to this day for the Anichkov palace and bridge over the Neva River in St. Petersburg. They had emigrated to the United States soon after the Revolution, opened a small factory making women's blouses, prospered during World War II and, by the time I met them, were sole owners of several corporations that manufactured a full line of women's up-scale fashions. They had tried to recruit me in the spring of 1948 when I worked for them on a temporary basis, but I decided to return to college.

A year later, thinking that I had nothing to lose and could always go back to finish college, I accepted and became sales promotion manager in training with a company car and a salary that allowed me to spruce up my modest wardrobe and move to a much nicer townhouse in Oakland. The Nicolis wanted me to become familiar with all aspects of their production and distribution, and I spent the first month traveling through northern California with one of their salesmen who was to "indoctrinate" me into the secrets of selling the Nicoli line. Later that summer and early fall, I traveled alone through the smaller towns of California and southern Oregon that we missed on our joint hop through the larger cities.

I liked what I was doing. That fall I spent several weeks in production, shipping, and the planning of the spring 1950 fashion line, "learning the business," as Mr. Nicoli called it with a certain amount of over-extended seriousness that I found sometimes too paternalistic. I did not sever completely my connection to the University. I signed up for two evening extension courses that qualified as electives and spent most of my weekends with student friends in Berkeley. In many ways, I was enjoying the best of both worlds. That fall the big issue on the campus was the "Loyalty Oath" and the bitter controversy that it sparked among the faculty. The real problem, of course, was the question of free speech and academic freedom in an environment that was slowly yielding to the exigencies of the Cold War. The informal student group that I belonged to consisted of students in Russian studies and the humanities. It was a bright group that had been meeting together since the spring of 1948. A reserve captain who had seen fighting in Europe and I were its oldest members. Over beer and cheese and bologna sandwiches we debated endlessly the pros and cons of President Truman's uncompromising stand against Communism and the effect that it was bound to have on the right to speak freely. We were also concerned about the future of peace in what was becoming a sharply divided world.

At the office, there was also a lively debate going on about how it was best to adapt to the new conditions of doing business in the more competitive climate after the war. The Nicoli companies had prospered tremendously in the years from 1940 to 1948, but the business climate was changing. During the war years and their immediate aftermath it was largely a sellers' market. Store buyers of ready-to-wear scrounged for finished goods wherever they could find them, placing little emphasis on style, price and delivery terms. Sales were really allocations based on the record of past purchases and friendly relations formed as a result of granted favors and under-the-counter payoffs. Now the shoe was on the other foot. The larger accounts in the East -- department stores and women's specialty outlets -- no longer wanted to make the long trip to California two or three times each year to review the spring, cruise and fall lines of California manufacturers. The Nicoli companies had a permanent office and showroom in Los Angeles; to maintain previous levels of sales and production it was now absolutely essential to have one also in New York, the ready-to-wear capital of the United States.

Mr. and Mrs. Nicoli tried to find an established New York ready-to-wear broker willing to represent their lines on a non-competing basis, but that was not as easy as it first seemed. In the end, they decided to bite the bullet and open their own office and showroom, a substantial investment without any guarantee of an immediate return. They toyed around with all sorts of propositions, and finally -- I believe in desperation -- asked me to head the project. I was to relocate to New York in January 1950, find space in one of the newer and more fashionable buildings around Times Square, furnish it, hire a staff, and establish connections with the New York buying offices and the fashion press. The plan also called for a grand tour of the larger eastern cities to meet store buyers and merchandise managers of our existing clients and, wherever possible, open new accounts -- a big order for a twenty-seven year-old neophyte only recently initiated into the money-making mysteries of what was generally referred to as the "rag business." The plan was to have everything ready for a gala opening in May when ready-to-wear buyers begin placing orders for the fall season. I was both elated and terrified --elated because I saw in this assignment an opportunity to become part of that exciting and glamorous life in Manhattan, and terrified because I was not sure I could pull it off. I think the Nicolis had more confidence in my ability to accomplish the assignment than I had myself, and if they didn't, they certainly did not show any uncertainty. I told them that I preferred to drive over the year-end holidays when there was not much happening anyway. It was easier for me to transport my personal belongings that way and I needed a car in New York anyway. I also wanted to see the countryside, the cities and the nation's historic places between San Francisco and New York. It was something I wanted to do since our arrival in America, and now an ideal opportunity presented itself.

II

In mid-December I put my furniture in storage, canceled my lease and, on December 23rd, embarked on an adventure which -- as I look back now -- was one of the highlights of my young adult years. I spent the Holidays with Papa and Mama. They had just bought a small house in Seaside, a new suburb of Monterey. I don't think I have ever seen them as happy as I found them that Christmas. Papa's work at the Language Institute was going better than he had anticipated. Together with a Soviet Air Force general who had defected, he was authoring a Russian dictionary of military terminology and restarting his old hobby of photography. Mama was puttering in the garden, getting it ready for spring planting. She had joined the faculty wive's auxiliary association and was organizing teas, dances and ethnic cultural activities for the officers and enlisted men who were students at the Language Institute. For the first time in their lives outside Russia, they had found permanence and security in one of the most beautiful areas of northern California. Like newly-weds who had just settled in their first house, they could not wait to tell me how wonderful it was living on the Monterey peninsula.

I stayed through the twenty-eighth. That year snow came early to the High Sierra and the Rockies, and I decided to take the longer but safer southern route, the historic Route 66 through northern Arizona, New Mexico, the Texas Panhandle and Oklahoma, that served as the avenue of hope and promise for tens of thousands of dispossessed farmers and families who came to California from the ruined farms of the Midwest during the drought and dust storms of the Thirties. I had hoped to see the Grand Canyon, but the cut-off at Flagstaff was closed because of heavy snow, and I had to settle for the Petrified Forest in Arizona and the main street of Gallup, New Mexico, through which Route 66 ran as it still does today. Gallup was my first exposure to Native Americans and their arts and way of life. What I saw there I didn't like. With its shabby motels and greasy spoon restaurants sporting Western sounding names and garish neon signs, tired-looking buildings, outdoor stalls featuring Indian blankets, rugs, Kachina dolls, Zuni and Navajo jewelry, and miscellaneous tourist paraphernalia, Gallup looked like an abandoned Hollywood film site in the middle of nowhere, uninviting, bleak, and forlorn . Repeating the same trip fifty years later, Gallup appeared much the same to me, except that the rundown motels and dreary restaurants were now replaced by national chains, and the cafes and shacks by modern buildings with extravagant window displays of tourist curios and Indian crafts. On the outskirts of Gallup, Native Americans continued to live in the same depressed and despoiled conditions I first saw fifty years earlier on my way to New York.

I reached Tulsa, Oklahoma on the thirty-first of December and spent New Year's Eve at a downtown hotel, fraternizing with a group of rednecks from the Oklahoma oil fields. Oklahoma was dry, and we drank coca cola spiked with spirits out of an unfamiliar whisky bottle that one of the men had obtained from the bellman, no doubt paying an exorbitant price. We talked about football, local and national politics, new car models that were coming on the market, and, of course, about women and Hollywood. They were pleasantly outgoing and, except for politics, it was a most cordial and friendly gathering accented by an exchange of opinions occasionally stained by Southern prejudices. Most of them were Southern Democrats from Texas who had voted for Truman in 1948 but were now unhappy with the President for his stand on civil rights. Prompted by the need to maintain black morale in the armed forces and the challenge from the left during the presidential election, Truman issued in the face of Congressional obstruction an executive order in July 1949, calling for the end of segregation in the armed forces. The desegregation process was slow to get off the ground, but many in the South were convinced that it was only the beginning of more radical reforms to come. I can't recall exactly what was said that evening in Tulsa, but it was something very close to "If we don't watch out, the damn niggers will soon be running the country." I was appalled, but, as a newcomer, did not feel I had a right to question their obvious bias. It was my first direct encounter with American racial prejudice repeated over and over again in the years to come. I tried to downplay it by saying to myself that the anti-black feelings of my evening companions in Tulsa reflected their working class bias, but soon found out that racial prejudice in America was much more pervasive, transcending all classes and professions, especially in the South..

From St. Louis I took a detour up the Mississippi river to Hannibal, Missouri, and from there to Springfield, Illinois. Having grown up reading Mark Twain, I wanted to see for myself the land where Tom Sawyer and Huckleberry Finn lived and played. It was a cold sunny day, and the Mississippi looked beautiful even though its banks looked naked, shorn of the abundant foliage about which Twain wrote. I also wanted to see Springfield where Lincoln had lawyered and where he got his political start. I found it extremely interesting, full of older brick commercial buildings, stately government structures, an imposing Civil War monument, tree-lined streets denuded by winter, and large turn-of-the-century houses and mansions in the center of town. I stopped to visit Lincoln's home and the obelisk-shaped Lincoln Tomb State Memorial in Oak Ridge cemetery. Springfield looked very different from anything I had seen so far. It looked older, more durable, with a kind of a provincial American elegance that was missing in the cities and towns of California. From Springfield, I drove with but a short stop in St. Louis, Missouri through Indiana, Ohio, the Pennsylvania Turnpike and New Jersey, arriving in Manhattan through the Holland tunnel at sundown on the next day.

If my recollection is right, it was a Saturday. I say that because the streets of Manhattan were relatively empty Somewhere around 57th

Street on Seventh Avenue I stopped a pedestrian to find out how it was best to get across town to Long Island and Jackson Heights where I had an apartment waiting for me. I got absolutely nowhere with my query. I stopped two or three other pedestrians and the result was always the same: "Don't know where it is," telling me something about New Yorkers who either did not like giving directions or simply did not know the layout of their city beyond the immediate neighborhood where they lived. Finally, a friendly elderly owner of a smoke shop where I stopped to buy a map of New York City, explained to me in great detail and with a degree of fatherly indulgence, how I could reach 86th Street in Queens. I told him that I had just driven in from California only a few minutes ago and was trying to find out what was the best way to reach Jackson Heights. He must have thought I was a little crazy, driving all the way from California without knowing where my ultimate destination was. I am almost certain that on arriving home that evening he probably told his wife that there was this crazy kid from California who arrived in New York and didn't even know how to get to where he was going.

My destination on 86th Street in Jackson Heights, a quiet neighborhood of brick-covered homes, tree-lined streets and faultless middle-class fastidiousness, looked inviting even at the height of winter. In the fifty plus years since I first saw it, the neighborhood has changed, and is now a rundown backwater populated mostly by the Columbian drug crowd. The owner of the apartment with whom I corresponded turned out to be not a Frenchman as I originally thought but a Russian guard officer who had added the obligatory "de" to his name to publicize his aristocratic roots. Mr. Nicoli had met Monsieur de Mejeve somewhere in his travels, and had given me his name when I agreed to move to New York. De Mejeve and his Austrian wife had converted part of their four bedroom house and basement into living quarters for themselves and two separate studio apartments which they rented out to "deserving" bachelors, as Mrs. De Mejeve explained to me. Mine turned out to be downstairs in the basement -- not exactly what I was expecting -- but it was nicely furnished, had a walk-in shower, and an outside door directly into a very pleasant garden in the back of the house. The de Mejeves welcomed me like arriving royalty; they were delighted, they said, to have a general's son as a tenant. Going to bed that first night on Long Island, I remember saying to myself that for some ill-fated reason I had again wound up in immigrant surroundings from which I had tried so hard to distance myself. But the connection turned out to be not as bad as I thought. It

155

actually opened a window into a world of new experiences that I never thought would come my way.

During the next two or three weeks -- I don't remember exactly how long it took to find a suitable office and showroom -- I followed up numerous leads in the vicinity of Times Square. My idea was to find space that required a minimum of renovation so that we could start displaying our lines as soon as possible. I lucked out beyond my wildest dreams. I subleased a beautiful showroom on the 10th floor of 1440 Broadway, in the very heart of the garment district. The office and showroom were only recently redecorated and carpeted in a light shade of French blue-grey that I knew Mrs. Nicoli would appreciate. The runway was not very long, but long enough for models to sashay out through an archway decorated on the sides in white and gold. Mrs. Nicoli flew out to New York for a few days in mid-February to help me with the purchase of showroom furniture. I think she was afraid that, left to my own devices, I would buy furniture that was too modern for her taste. One of our lines sold under the "Mode de Paris" label, and she wanted our furnishings to project a French look. We found exactly what she wanted, decorating the showroom in the Louis XV style, not very different from our other showrooms in San Francisco and Los Angeles. We took in a musical one evening – it was Cole Porter's *Kiss Me Kate,* if I remember correctly – and even managed to have dinner with Rouben Mamoulian, world-renowned director of *Oklahoma,* whom Mrs. Nicoli knew from her days in the twenties when she tried to break into film in Hollywood.

That spring I worked harder than anytime in my life. I had to find permanent salesmen for New England and the entire seaboard from New York to Washington, D.C. I had to contract three or four models for our May opening, and make the rounds of scores of buying offices to let them know that we were opening a New York showroom. I also had to visit the editors of the principal fashion magazines and prepare invitations and news releases for the gala opening in May. After the Easter holidays in April, I made a two week swing of the major stores on the eastern seaboard: Filene's in Boston, Wannamaker's in Philadelphia, Hutzler's and Hoschel-Kohn in Baltimore, Garfinkel's and Woodward and Lothrop in Washington, and Thalheimer's in Richmond. I had hoped to spend some free time to explore those cities, but except for Washington -- and even that was very perfunctory -- I had to stick to a tight schedule that left little time for doing what I always wanted to achieve. A more thorough visit had to be put off to another time. The Nicolis arrived in New York in mid-May. The gala opening and the market week that followed went well; there were no serious slip-ups or unexpected emergencies. The Nicolis were satisfied with the level of activity, even though in cold dollars and cents, orders for the fall line could have been better. I arranged luncheons for Mrs. Nicoli at the St. Regis with the editors of *Vogue* , *Harper's Bazar, Town and Country,* and *Women's Wear Daily.* The editor from *Vogue* canceled out at the last minute, but the others did attend, making Mrs. Nicoli deliriously happy. The reviews were passably enthusiastic but not raving. On the whole, I believe we did rather well, considering that it was our first showing in New York.

During this highly saturated period of activity I had very little time for any personal life. If my memory serves me right, I managed to squeeze in two visits to the opera -- in 1950, the Metropolitan was still at the old Opera House near our showroom on Broadway -- and one Sunday matinee at Carnegie Hall. Dmitri Metropolis was conducting Berlioz's *Symphonie Fantastique* and, if I recall correctly, Respighi's *Pines of Rome.* It was the first time I heard Metropolis conducting. The performance was sharp, well-defined and highly impressionistic. I walked out of the hall spellbound by the sound of Metropolis' interpretation of Berlioz's polyphonic masterpiece. The theater district was a stone's throw from our showroom, and I sometimes took in a show after a long day in the office. Arthur Miller's *Death of a Salesman* was still playing and I was so taken by it that I had to see it twice. Working in sales I had a great admiration for Miller's grasp of the drama of Willy Loman's life as an aging salesman, a life that was "riding on a smile and a shoeshine," and in a broader sense a "dream" that Arthur Miller perceived coming "with the territory." Miller brilliantly dissected the dream's promise and its destructive side, something I never forgot as sales manager and sales executive counseling salesmen on how to keep their eyes on the heavens and the feet on the ground. I would have liked to have more time to pursue my own interests, but they had to wait; I was too preoccupied with trying to make our New York venture a success.

This did not mean that it was all business and no time for an occasional distraction. As time went on, the distractions multiplied, particularly during the hot summer months. One of the sources of the distractions, was the other tenant at the de Mejeve establishment. Baron Vladimir (Volodya, to his friends and associates) von Freygang was a Rick Blaine type of character straight out of the film *Casablanca* played by Humphrey Bogard. In fact, he even looked a little like Bogard. A scion of a prominent Russian Baltic-German family, Volodya had served as a cadet in the White Army of General Denikin, wound up in Paris in the early Twenties, and, after nearly ten years of assorted fun and games, became the sole owner of *Sheherezad,* the Russian restaurant and night club in Paris that was very popular in the Thirties and early Forties. After the war, he first immigrated to Argentina with a sufficient stash of money that allowed him to be financially independent. I suspect he had to leave Paris because *Sheherezad* was a favorite watering spot of the German officer corps during the war, and Volodya, with his well-recognized German name, was probably looked upon with suspicion by the new French government after the war. From Buenos Aires he made his way to New York, where he settled down to play the role of an eligible bachelor and man about town. Nearly fifty, athletic -- he could still do hand-stands to show his prowess -- good looking with exquisite manners, and a spellbinding fluency as a raconteur, Volodya knew nearly everyone of importance in New York's exclusive colony of high-living Russian aristocrats and their many-faceted American sponsors.

It did not take long for us to get acquainted. As a general's son, I fit his prototype of an eligible bachelor acceptable to the crowd in which he moved; I also had a late model automobile that he did not have. Through him I met Prince Gurelli, a Russian guard officer of Georgian ancestry, married to Helena Rubinstein, the doyenne of American cosmetics, and the Cassini brothers, grandsons of Count Arturo Paul Nicolas de Cassini, Russia's Ambassador Extraordinary to the United States during Theodore Roosevelt's administration. Oleg Cassini, an American couturier, later became Jacqueline Kennedy's fashion designer, and Igor, was society and gossip columnist writing for the Hearst papers under the name of Cholly Knickerbocker. I also met Serge Obolensky, one of Barbara Hutton's former husbands, and a whole collection of New York jet-setters, alumni of the New York City Ballet, and ardent American Russophiles who ran together and knew all kinds of people in the right places. Through Volodya I could count on periodic offers to spend a weekend in the Hamptons on Long Island, invitations to receptions in Manhattan and occasional free tickets to the opera and the theater. Among many engaging episodes of this stage of my life, I recall one particularly. The Gurellis had a penthouse in Manhattan on Park Avenue and, each year, hosted a gala reception after the midnight Russian Orthodox Easter service on Saturday night. It was a black tie affair, elegantly catered, with a traditional Russian Easter buffet featuring meats, fowl, elaborate *zakouskas* (Russian hors d-oeuvres), *kulich* (tall Russian Easter bread that tastes like panitone), and, of course, *Paskha* (pyramid-shaped cheese cake with currents and marzipan). Friends and business associates considered it a sign of social acceptance to be seen at the Gurellis in the early hours of Easter Sunday. Somehow, Volodya managed to have us both invited -- he and Prince Gurelli played bridge together and had known each other since time immemorial when they were poverty-stricken exiles in Paris. We stayed too long, had more to drink than it was probably prudent, and had no way of getting back to Jackson Heights without spending several uncomfortable hours on a subway bench, waiting for the first train on Sunday morning . The hosts took pity and put us up in the guest wing of their very spacious penthouse. I fell asleep almost immediately without giving any thought to where I was. When I awoke in the morning, still somewhat dazed by the night's overindulgence, I could not for the love of me understand where I had spent the night. The room in which I awoke had been decorated by a wild decorator with a penchant for Surrealism, projecting a preposterous mood for the unreal. The ceiling featured a large dream-like juxtaposition of unnatural and incongruous objects in bright blue, green, black and magenta on an undulating background of refrigerator white. The fantastic overhead decoration was not the kind of thing one expected to wake up to, and it took four or five minutes to recover my bearings and separate reality from the surrealist fantasy that seemed to hang precipitously over my head. To this day, I cannot look at the art of Rene Magritte, Man Ray, and Salvadore Dali without thinking about that Russian Easter Sunday morning in New York.

Conversation at receptions and visits to the Hamptons featured mostly small talk, gossip and casual polemic on New York's preoccupation with modernist art and New York City politics. Some people asked about my experience in war-time Japan, about Hiroshima and the atomic bomb. I had put the war years behind and usually tried to avoid the subject by saying that they were not as bad as most people thought. As to Hiroshima, I usually got away from further discussions by saying truthfully that I did not visit it after the war and therefore did not have the opportunity of experiencing personally the horror caused by the atomic bomb.

Hiroshima was and remains a delicate subject for me. I believed then and I still believe today that the dropping of the atomic bombs on Hiroshima and Nagasaki was militarily unnecessary and morally unjustifiable, especially after I familiarized myself with the memoir literature pertaining to the last days of the war in the Pacific. The popular view based on President Truman's assertion that the dropping of the atomic bombs saved tens of thousands of American and Japanese lives is in my opinion a casuistic and self-serving justification brought about by the heavy U.S. losses during the Okinawa campaign. When the bombs were dropped on August 6 and 9, Japan was desperately trying to secure Soviet assistance in bringing the war to what it considered an honorable end. It was literally on its knees, hungry, physically and psychologically exhausted, and begging for an end to the war. The Japanese diplomatic code was broken, and President Truman was briefed daily on the subject of the surrender. If he wanted to hasten the surrender Truman could have softened the language of the Potsdam Declaration by assuring the Japanese leadership that the emperor would not be prosecuted, which is what took place ultimately anyway. Secretary of War Henry L. Stimson, Under Secretary of State and former ambassador to Japan Joseph Grew, and Navy Secretary James Forrestal urged the president to include such a provision to satisfy the hardliners in Japan's Supreme War Council. Instead, the President sided with Secretary of State James Byrnes and Dean Acheson who advised to drop the atomic bombs. He did this in my view for political reasons. He believed that exploding the bombs over the Japanese homeland would compel Japan to surrender before the Soviet Union could enter the war and occupy Manchuria, Korea, Sakhalin and perhaps even Hokkaido. He was also convinced that American public opinion would not look kindly at a Japanese surrender that was softened by appeasement toward the emperor. The American public was overwhelmingly against Emperor Hirohito and wanted to see him brought to trial and punished together with his generals.

Stalin must also be held accountable. At the Potsdam Conference, Truman told him that the United States had tested successfully a new kind of bomb. This was not news to Stalin as he knew from Soviet military intelligence that the United States had an atomic bomb and would probably use it as soon as it was ready to be deployed. Fearing that the Soviet Union would be excluded from a post-war political settlement in the Pacific if it did not enter the war before Japan surrendered, Stalin instructed Molotov not to respond to Japan's desperate calls for help. He did not want to see the war ended before the Red Army had successfully occupied the territories which he considered to be in the Soviet sphere of influence. It is significant that Stalin declared war on Japan and dispatched the Soviet armies across the border two days after the first bomb was dropped, weeks ahead of original plans communicated by him to the Allies.

The Japanese leadership also cannot escape responsibility for the deployment of the atomic bombs. It was the height of naïveté for them to expect the Soviet Union to come to Japan's aid in negotiating a surrender after Molotov informed the Japanese Foreign Office that Stalin was not going to renew the Neutrality Pact. Through its intelligence sources Japanese leadership was also fully aware of the massive Soviet army build-up in Outer Mongolia and the Soviet provinces on Manchuria's border. What was even more infantile and unforgiving was that the Japanese leadership chose not to respond to the U.S. ultimatum. Instead of rejecting or accepting it formally and giving Washington an indication where Japan stood on the issue of unconditional surrender, they wasted crucial days in labyrinthine and useless debates in the hope that Japan could secure better terms with respect to the preservation of the Imperial system. Even after the bombs were dropped, the Japanese military leadership waited for nearly another full week continuing the debate in the Supreme War Council before the Emperor finally intervened and ruled to accept the unconditional surrender. It is not surprising that a number of scholars have suggested that the atomic bombs were not as decisive in causing Japan's unconditional surrender as the success of the Soviet military attack.

Gibbon attributed the fall of the Roman Empire to one cause only – the triumph of barbarism and religion. Journalists and politicians have also explained the Japanese surrender in terms of one cause – the atomic bombs dropped on Hiroshima and Nagasaki. It is my opinion that a single cause explanation does not work for Japan's unconditional surrender – not that it had really worked for the fall of Rome. There was a coalition of causes that gradually tipped the Japanese leadership to accept unconditional surrender. By the summer of 1945, B-29 air raids had brought Japan's munitions factories to a point when they were no longer able to deliver what the military needed to defend the homeland. During the battle for Okinawa, the United States destroyed what was left of the Japanese navy and air force, isolating the Japanese homeland almost completely from the bases that Japan still held in the south Pacific. The economy was in a state of imminent collapse. The civilian population was beginning to experience famine, and there was even fear that there could be public disturbances. The atomic bombs dropped on Hiroshima and Nagasaki followed by the rapid progress of the Soviet army in Manchuria greatly increased the rationale for unconditional surrender, especially when Japan realized that the Red Army was planning to land not only on Sakhalin island, but probably also on the island of Hokkaido. Disregarding tradition and court protocol, the emperor took the unprecedented step of advising the cabinet that he desired to end the war. And finally, there was the ritual suicide of Army Minister General Korechika Anami, the principal military figure in Japan's Supreme War Council for the continuation of the war. It was a symbolic act of admission by the head of the army to Emperor Hirohito and the commanders in the field that the war was lost and the time had come to bite the bullet and accept unconditional surrender. The memoir literature clearly shows how those who had to make the decision gravitated from surrender to continuing the war and then back to surrender during a period of several weeks, eventually reaching the unbearable consensus that led to the Emperor's proclamation of unconditional surrender. In his recent book about the war in the Pacific, Tsuyoshi Hasegawa, Professor of History at the University of California, Santa Barbara tells us in great detail how the surrender finally came about.[27] Fluent in Japanese, Russian, and English, Hasegawa was the ideal academic historian to tackle the difficult task of sorting out the documents and memoir literature in Tokyo, Washington, and Moscow.

Hasegawa called what was taking place in the three capitals a "triangular relation," and indeed it was. Each nation tried to maximize its individual short term interests: the United States to drop the bombs in the hope that Japan will surrender before the Soviet Union entered the war; the Soviet Union to enter the war before Japan surrendered in order to expand its influence in the Far East, Japan to craft a surrender agreement that was less prejudicial to its national honor and the essence of its emperor system. They did this without giving any serious thought to the horrendous death toll and suffering from radiation of the civilian population, nor of the long term implications of the nuclear race between the United States and the Soviet Union. They also failed to give any consideration to the proliferation of nuclear capabilities, especially by terrorist networks and hostile rogue states. Nuclear proliferation today is the most serious threat to our civilization, and will continue to be so until the world agrees to prohibit the production and use of nuclear weapons, and establishes an internationally managed inspection regimen to control proliferation and the stockpiling of warheads by the nuclear powers.

So much for my painfully distilled views on the Hiroshima and Nagasaki bombs. There were also other discussions in 1950 and 1951 that treaded the murky waters of international politics. They mostly dealt with Korea and the growth of communism. On June 25, 1950, the North Korean army attacked South Korea. After pushing the North Koreans beyond the 38th parallel, General MacArthur made the mistake of advancing through North Korea to the Yalu and the Chinese border, provoking the Chinese to enter the war. The result was a difficult and bloody retreat in the midst of winter that cost heavy American casualties and hundreds of thousands Korean civilian dead. McCarthyism, which had somehow lost its initial vigor in the second half of 1950, got a new lease on life in 1951, largely as a result of the Korean War. Anxiety about a Communist take-over beyond China and Eastern Europe propelled the right wing of the Republican Party to launch a frontal attack on Truman and the Democrats. Most people I knew -- Russian-Americans as well as natives -- were Republicans, who hated Truman, disliked the social programs of the New Deal, and demanded a tougher stand against the communists. Many were convinced that President Truman was not doing enough to end the Korean War. Some even advocated the dropping of an atomic bomb. I stayed out of the debate as much as possible. To be frank, I was not sure at that time on which side of the debate I wanted to be. My staunch anti-communist upbringing predisposed me toward a strong United States position on the Soviet Union and Communism, and my thinking was much closer to the position of the Republicans than to that of the Democratic Party. However, I was also slowly coming to the conclusion that beneath the outer surface of the good life in America there were still large pockets of poverty, discrimination and injustice -- concerns that were more central to the political agenda of the Democrats Party. In the calculus of party affiliation, I was therefore slowly being drawn toward the party of Roosevelt and the agenda of the New Deal. It would take another two or three years, however, before I was able to decide which party I should join on becoming a citizen.

In December, I flew home to spend Christmas with Papa and Mama. Nick and Mike also came for the holidays and a family reunion in Monterey. I can't recall exactly, but I believe I also spent two or three weeks at the factory reviewing incoming orders from eastern customers and conferring with Mr. and Mrs. Nicoli before returning to New York. In February, I moved to an apartment in Manhattan. The von Freygang connection was becoming a bit too arduous. I was getting tired of being constantly asked to join him and his friends in their various escapades. Living in Manhattan also allowed me to maintain a better balance between the contacts I made through von Freygang and other demands of my personal and business life.

I traveled extensively in 1951. In addition to the larger cities of the eastern seaboard, I made several swings through Ohio, Indiana, Michigan and Illinois, promoting our lines of women's clothing, sometimes alone and sometimes together with our Chicago salesman. I also made two trips through the South -- the Carolinas, Georgia, Alabama, Louisiana and Tennessee. On one of these trips I accompanied Mrs. Nicoli who was making a personal appearance as part of a public relations campaign by Deering Milliken and Company, one of our major fabric suppliers. We visited not only the large cities of the South, but also the mill towns where Deering Milliken had textile mills. The Nicoli companies had an exclusive on a new and exciting Dacron-Wool blend manufactured by Milliken that we named "Visa" out of which we made women's skirts and travel ensembles. The trip was a trail-blazing success. We were treated royally by the city fathers of the mill towns. Press releases with accompanying photographs of Mrs. Nicoli and Roger Milliken standing together in front of a long line of only recently delivered high speed looms were sent out to the major newspapers of the South. Many of the store buyers whom we visited had seen the pictures in their hometown papers, making our follow-up so much easier for Mrs. Nicoli.

I must have put on 15,000 to 20,000 miles on my car in 1951. Wherever possible, I arranged my visits to such cities as Pittsburgh, Cleveland, Detroit, Atlanta, Birmingham, New Orleans, Memphis, Cincinnati so that I could spend my weekends exploring their museums, old neighborhoods, ethnic surroundings, and places of interest. I walked their main streets and their back alleys, trying to catch the local flavor and a more generalized taste of American urban life. Occasionally, I would also spend a night or two in a country town to get a feeling for small-town America. Sometimes this would come about almost accidentally when I was running short on expense money. There were no credit cards to rely on in the early 1950s; the only way one could conserve resources without bedding down in some flee-ridden dive in a big city was to stay in a smaller out-of-the-way town where food and shelter were appreciably cheaper. It was an experience I could not have duplicated. In the nearly two years since I left San Francisco I saw more of America than I had ever hoped.

Two years were slowly coming to conclusion. Our New York office was beginning to be financially profitable. We had a permanent staff in New York City and two full-time traveling salesmen covering the eastern seaboard and the states of Ohio, Indiana and Illinois. We also had permanent representation in Chicago and the cities of the

South. The Nathalie Nicoli lines were now carried in many of the more fashionable stores from Boston to Atlanta and, to a lesser extent, through a good part of the Middle West and the Mountain states. It no longer made sense for me to be based in New York City. I had seen enough of Manhattan and was ready to leave its luster and sophistication behind. It was a great adventure and a valuable experience, but I was beginning to find life in the fast lane -- both literally and figuratively -- more than I bargained for. The acquaintances that I had cultivated through business connections were just that -- acquaintances and business connections. The friends and acquaintances that I met in my personal life through Volodya I found largely superficial, egotistical and not too interested in anything that did not directly touch their own lives. I was not brought up by my democratic parents to spend the rest of my life in the pursuit of pleasure and status. I had always been somewhat of an intellectual elitist, but I never was or wanted to be a social snob. After nearly two years of personal life consigned to theater going, hanging out in New York's night clubs, small talk and social posturing in an affluent environment of fancy living in ostentatiously decorated homes with lace-collared maids serving cocktails and coffee, I was ready to give up that part of my life, return to California, and put down permanent roots.

The crucial question was how to sell the idea to Mr. and Mrs. Nicoli. The opportunity to do that came up quite unexpectedly. In October, they had again lost their sales promotion manager. He had resigned without giving them much notice, largely because Mr. Nicoli, who considered sales and distribution his responsibility, had criticized him in the presence of others once too often, an occurrence that kept repeating itself over and over again. To those who did not know Mr. Nicoli well he appeared to be a crusty and impatient employer who often said things that he regretted later. In fact, as a sales executive and employer, he was mostly all bark and very little bite, while Mrs. Nicoli, was just the opposite, sweet and accommodating on the surface, but hard as nails on the inside. Because of that, it was often difficult to work with them constructively without alienating one or the other. My strategy was to satisfy Mrs. Nicoli's concerns about the future of their companies without getting Mr. Nicoli too perturbed on details. Trying to be as diplomatic as possible, I told them that my work in New York was largely completed, that I could travel just as easily out of San Francisco to respond to emergencies in our sales territories, and that I would like to help Mr. Nicoli manage the sales organization. Mrs. Nicoli jumped at my suggestion; Mr. Nicoli was not sure that it was a good idea. He was obviously concerned that I would gradually take over from him the entire marketing and sales responsibilities for the Nicoli companies which he considered his personal and undivided domain in the business partnership with his designer wife. It took a few weeks for Mrs. Nicoli to convince her husband and work out the details before they called me to give their approval. In mid-December, I packed up my New York-acquired possessions and, this time taking the northern route through Denver, drove home to California, arriving in San Francisco in time for the Christmas holidays and an unexpected but welcome year-end bonus that allowed me to buy some expensive presents for Papa and Mama and trade in my tired Mercury for a brand new Ford.

III

I took a much-needed two week vacation, visited Papa and Mama, spent a few days skiing at Sugar Bowl, rented an up-scale apartment on the south slope of Russian Hill, and reported for work around January 10. I also hired an administrative assistant, an experienced Girl-Friday, to handle correspondence, prepare press releases, and manage everyday communication with clients and the sales force. I did an immense amount of traveling in 1952, sometimes to help our salesmen with special promotions, at others, to see what could be done to open up areas where we had very little following or no accounts at all. Except for Los Angeles where I generally traveled by auto, most of my long distance business travel was by air. Only occasionally would I take the train, and only when I could squeeze a weekend of skiing at a resort in the Rockies from which I usually traveled by rail to my next business appointment in Denver or Salt Lake City. Nineteen Fifty-Two was also a pivotal year in my personal life. That year I became an American citizen and experienced my first brush with American politics.

In August, Nick and I were summoned to take our citizenship examinations. Nick was able to do this in Seattle; I took mine at the Office of Immigration and Naturalization in San Francisco. People who had been through this previously, advised me to put on work clothes and pretend that I was an immigrant with only a limited knowledge of English, to avoid too many difficult questions by the examining magistrate. One of our family friends who took his in 1927, said that all they had asked him when he showed up in work pants and sport shirt was "who was the first president of the United

States and were there any amendments to the constitution." Mine turned out to be a little more difficult, especially when the examiner found out I spoke faultless English and had been to college. After many questions, some very simple, others more difficult, in what seemed like a final attempt to confuse me, he asked me what kind of legislative system the individual states had. Straight out of Poli Sci One, I said without any hesitation that, the state legislative system, like the federal, was bicameral except for Nebraska which was unicameral. My examiner got up from his chair, put his hands up and, with a display of obvious resignation, said "I give up, you college kids know more than you need. Congratulations and good luck!"

Walking out of the Immigration and Naturalization Office I thought about my years as a stateless resident in the Orient, and the more recent years as a bona fide immigrant and permanent resident in the United States. All of that was now behind me; what remained to make my American citizenship legitimate was now only paper work. Becoming an American is a dual process. Going through the legal naturalization mechanism is only a component of that process. Being accepted as an American by other Americans is the other part. The latter is psychologically far more meaningful and satisfying than fulfilling the legal requirements prescribed by naturalization laws. Because I spoke accent-free American English, had served with the U.S. Army of Occupation, and had culturally assimilated the American zeitgeist, no one questioned my American citizenship or asked me if I were born in another country. Unlike other immigrants, many of whom had to struggle with thick foreign accents and had to adapt to the American environment, I was spared the embarrassment and discomfort of becoming an American. The naturalization process was merely a legal step taken to affirm what I had already fully internalized. It made me a citizen not only in the eyes of other Americans but also in the eyes of international law, something that I had never been before. Papa's and Mama's travel and visa documents prepared by the American Consulate in Yokohama identified them as "former citizens of Russia." Mine, did not even extend that courtesy. I was bureaucratically listed as a "stateless person," because I was born in a foreign country and never had any legal standing in international law. Acquiring American citizenship transformed me into a citizen for the first time in my life. The swearing-in ceremony took place some months later, and the certificate of naturalization did not arrive until November, too late to register and vote in the 1952 Presidential Election. The delay did not prevent me, however, from making a connection with the San Francisco headquarters of the Republican Party.

On my return to San Francisco I met a young Republican operative from Burlingame who urged me to join the Republican Party. Like everyone else I came in contact, he too thought I was a citizen, and did everything possible to ensnare me in the election campaign activities at the local level. Mr. Nicoli also pressured me to join the Republican Party. A substantial contributor to Republican causes in the Bay Area, he was active in local party politics since the early forties, and was selected an alternate in the California delegation to the 1952 Republican National Convention. In 1952, the Republican Party still had an appreciable edge over the Democratic Party in California. Earl Warren, a moderate Republican and later Chief Justice of the Supreme Court, was governor. George Christopher, another moderate Republican with strong connections to ethnic voters, was Mayor of San Francisco. Senator Knowland, a staunch conservative and vehement anti-Communist, forcefully promoted aid to Chiang Kai-shek in Congress, and helped resettle thousands of White Russians who escaped from Shanghai and other Chinese cities in expectation of the Communist take-over in 1949. The Russian-American community, consisting mostly of the first wave of Russian immigrants who arrived in California after the Revolution and Civil War, was almost one hundred percent Republican in its party affiliation with Senator Knowland as their patron saint for his unswerving support of the immigrant cause. It was not easy for a Russian-American to be a Democrat in California in the early 1950s. Most Russian-Americans considered the few Democrats in their midst to be Communist fellow travelers who should be shunned and ostracized. I had not yet fully resolved the question of my party affiliation and I thought it made sense to see how the Republicans ran their campaign. Between business trips I had lots of spare time, and I agreed to help. Little did I know that they were planning to appoint me in charge of liaison with the Slavic Community in northern California, at least that is how my party job evolved by the time the California delegation was ready to leave for Chicago where the 1952 Republican National Convention was to take place.

I was asked to accompany the California delegation as an aid to a Mr. Jurich who was to take charge of the ethnic relations desk at the Convention. I am almost certain Mr. Nicoli had something to do with it. He was a major contributor to California Republican causes and had considerable pull in the Party organization. In 1952, it was still believed useful to sequester the state's delegation for two full days on a transcontinental train in order to reach political consensus before arriving at the Convention site. I missed the train ride, because I was out of town when it pulled out of the Oakland terminal and, instead, flew directly to Chicago the next day. At the railway terminal I joined the California contingent and, together with some eighty howling Californians, drove through the streets of Chicago in a cavalcade of open cars that had been commandeered in advance for the occasion. With red, white and blue ribbons tailing the automobiles, in straw hats with red, white and blue ribbons, with placards championing Governor Warren for President[28] we drove down State Street chanting at the top of our voices "California here I come." The noisy demonstration was a lot of fun with affable jostling, part of a Convention tradition that went back all the way to the days when California first became a state.

Despite several favorite son commitments, it was clear from the very beginning that the battle for the presidential nomination was going to be between the party's conservative forces pledged to the election of Senator Robert A. Taft as president and the more moderate and liberal wing of the Republican party that had drafted General Dwight D. Eisenhower as its standard bearer. It was also clear that neither wing was willing to risk an early ballot for the nomination before they were able to stake out their relative positions. As in 1912, when Taft's father was in a bitter struggle with Theodore Roosevelt for the Republican nomination, the 1952 race also had to run through a series of preliminary battles over convention rules and contested credentials. Because of that, the nomination segment of the convention lasted longer than expected and in the end turned out to be a close race.

At the convention hall, there was pandemonium, an orgy of noise, foot shuffling, flag waiving, and delegates milling around on the convention hall. The corridors were full of newsmen, local politicians, and just plain people who managed to obtain an entry pass for the opening session. After opening speeches and applause and the hoopla that followed them, the convention got down to business with a long and passionate debate between the two wings of the Party on the voting rights of challenged delegates. The Taft forces, hoping to enlarge their pool of committed delegates, proposed the adoption of 1948 convention rules, which would have allowed contested delegates to vote on all credential challenges except their own. The Eisenhower people countered by proposing an amendment which would seat only those contested delegates who were approved by at least a two-thirds vote of the national committee. At stake were a total of nearly seventy delegates from Georgia, Texas and Louisiana, who supported Taft.

After a prolonged and bitter contest that lasted into the next day, the more moderate forces of the Party came out victorious, increasing the momentum behind the Eisenhower candidacy.

My job was to sit in the entrance to the convention hall, answer questions that came from representatives of the various ethnic organizations and their accredited newsmen, hand out policy statements and show the changing agenda of the day. With the huge Polish and Lithuanian communities in Chicago, there was no shortage of people who stopped by my desk, mostly to inquire what kind of platform the Republican Party had adopted on the question of Communist takeover in Eastern Europe. It was tedious work without much personal satisfaction, but it was not without good public relations value. Fortunately, there were two of us and, whenever possible, I snuck into the convention hall to see what was going on. I was captivated by the mechanics of the credentials debate and its potential effect on the balloting, once it began. I had a fair idea from my reading and the Political Science courses that I had taken at UC-Berkeley how the democratic process worked in practice at party conventions, but I did not expect anything as indirect and subtle to be used in defense of a political settlement sought by competing interests. The lesson I learned in Chicago has stayed with me my entire life. Except for rare exceptions, I tend to look almost always at political alliances and enthusiastically heralded government resolutions through the sharp glasses of a skeptic who wants to know what really took place behind the scenes.

Another debate at the convention also interested me. We had temporarily closed our desk for the day and I was able to follow it almost from start to finish. It involved a non-partisan proposal to increase the number of state chairmen to the Republican national committee from states showing Republican election majorities. The primary purpose of the proposal was to reduce the growing Southern influence in the national committee of the Republican Party. The proposal passed by voice vote after a raucous discourse on the convention floor. The vote was a harbinger of the coming struggle for the soul of the Republican Party. Moderate Northern Republicans -- Lodge, Dewey, Stassen, and others of like persuasion --were concerned already in 1952 about the growing ascendancy of Southern conservatives in the Republican Party apparatus.

After numerous state caucuses and back room closed-door meetings, the convention began balloting for real. Five men were nominated for the presidency, Eisenhower receiving 595 votes to Taft's 500, nine votes short of victory. Before a second ballot could be initiated,

Minnesota switched 19 votes from favorite son Harold Stassen to General Eisenhower, giving Ike the nomination. With great fanfare the nomination was then made unanimous, Eisenhower promising in his acceptance speech to lead a "crusade against a party too long in power." Adopted by voice vote without any debate on the floor, the party platform castigated the Democrats for almost everything. Especially harsh was the foreign section written by John Foster Dulles. It blamed the Democratic Party for its appeasement of Communism, the blunders of Tehran, Yalta and Potsdam, the communist takeover in China and the war in Korea. One of my jobs was to distribute the platform document, and I had time on my hands to read it in its entirety. I found its arguments groundless and grossly overstated, catering to the far right, to Senator McCarthy, to members of the House Un-American Activities Committee, and to all those looking for subversives in Hollywood, academia, and the press.

The convention lasted nearly five full days. During the day I worked from early morning to late evening -- one day to midnight, when General MacArthur gave the key address .During most nights, I partied with other party workers, with young delegates, and with accredited journalists who seemed to hang around in search of last minute rumors and news. There were nights when roused and electrified by the events of the day, I slept only a few hours. The Republican conclave was an intense and unique experience, and I considered myself very fortunate to have participated in it. In the final analysis, however, it was an experience not without a certain amount of disappointment. Had I been allowed to vote in 1952, I would have probably voted for Eisenhower. I found Adlai Stevenson an elegant but reluctant candidate who really did not want to be president at a time of grave tensions at home and abroad. For all his polish and erudition, I did not think he could stand up to Stalin and the Republican-controlled Congress at home. I liked the Republican Party's adherence to fiscal responsibility and its inborn abhorrence of overblown bureaucracy. The belief that it is the states' obligation to control their own domestic institutions also appealed to me. So did some sections of the civil rights and labor planks, such as the section on the need to wield federal action to eliminate poll taxes and lynching, and the retention of the Taft-Hartley Act to protect labor's hard-won rights. Even the foreign affairs platform was palatable. It was the intensity of the rhetoric against Roosevelt and Truman that I found malicious and Philistine. What turned me off was not the written word of the Republican platform, but the spoken word, often let off casually and without any thought on how it would sound to others. Many of the men and women with whom I worked and partied were fine people, sons and daughters of prominent Republican leaders and politicians. Some were born with a silver spoon, others were self-made professionals, business executives and small businessmen. What I found difficult to accept was that they could quote chapter and verse of the Party platform and, in the same breath, nullify everything in it. This was especially true when they talked about labor and civil rights, for both of which they had very little regard. Labor to them was a nasty adversary, and civil rights was something that radicals and do-gooders talked about without any true understanding of the social and racial landscape that was part of the American reality. What really galled me was the attitude that "if I could make it, everyone else should also be able to do the same," without any consideration of such outside influences as education, family support, racial prejudice, and just plain good luck. It was that righteous and arrogant attitude -- so pervasive among die-in-the-wool Republicans -- that turned me off from the Republican Party.

I returned home exhilarated by the experience, but depressed by the reality of the process of selecting a presidential candidate. The selection process was a lot more conspiratorial and underhanded than I ever imagined it to be. It made me wary about getting involved again. I resolved to turn down any attempts by Mr. Nicoli or other local party operatives to recruit me for work on the election campaign. In September, I moved to an upscale apartment in San Francisco closer to work and to everything else that was part of the San Francisco scene. I was almost thirty. It was time to start thinking about the future, about getting married and having a family.

5

U.S. CITIZEN

Neither democracy nor effective representation
is possible until each participant in the group
devotes a measurable part of his life
to further- ing its existence.
Lewis Mumford

I

Nineteen Fifty-Three saw General Eisenhower become our new president; Adlai Stevenson did not stand a chance. The business establishment breathed a sigh of relief with the passing of the Truman years. For the Nicolis, 1952 was their peak business year. Despite losses in one or two of our higher priced lines, the Nicoli companies finished the year with the largest sales revenue since they started their companies in the 1930s. I welcomed the New Year with some friends in Berkeley and took a few days off from work to see Squaw Valley, the new ski resort on the east side of the Sierra Nevada near Lake Tahoe. I felt secure and satisfied with my progress in the world of business. I was also surprisingly positive about my personal life. The last five years seemed like a glorious fairy tale, but the best -- the most exciting and wonderful experience -- was still to follow.

It began over the three-day Washington's Birthday. On Sunday, February 22, 1953, I met Jane (Bunny) Amidon, my future wife, life companion, and mother of our four wonderful children. The probability of that ever happening was one in tens of millions. We came from such dissimilar backgrounds, different parts of the country, and different family histories. Call it whatever you want, fate, karma, mobility of our young people, it was a remarkable feat that I could never have anticipated. The story of our meeting is now part of the family saga, embellished and improved upon every time it is passed on to our growing brood of grandchildren. We met at what is now a defunct ski resort appropriately called Edelweiss, off U.S. Highway 50 on the California side of the Sierra Nevada. We had never been there before, nor have we ever skied there again. A friend whom I met through the Republican Party invited me to spend part of the long Washington's Birthday weekend at Strawberry at his mountain cabin. His nephew had recently arrived from Finland and he thought it would be nice if I could ski with him, but the plan did not materialize. The young Finnish lad was a cross-country skier and had no experience in Alpine skiing. I found myself skiing alone most of the time. Bunny's Washington's Birthday story was equally wrought in plans that also misfired. She had only recently arrived in California from Boston, took a job with the American Trust Company -- a California bank swallowed by Wells Fargo in the 1960s -- and came to Strawberry on an employee winter junket, only to find out that very few of her co-workers skied. The men came mostly to relax, lounge in the bar, and chase the prettier girls.

And so it was, a thirty year-old bachelor and a twenty-three year old blue-eyed brunette from Boston found themselves skiing together on the pristine slopes of the High Sierra. When asked how we met, Bunny almost always tells her friends that she "picked up this cute young guy on the chair lift" who she found out later lived only three blocks away from her in San Francisco. My story is a little different. I had spotted her earlier in the day, a statuesque, athletic-looking, graceful skier in a black and red parka masterfully cutting demanding turns through the hardpack of the downhill run. She made it look so easy. I remember saying to myself "There goes someone who has learned to ski in the icy ravines and gorges of Vermont and New Hampshire," and I was right. She was from New England, and had learned to ski there. At about 2:00 PM I heard her yell "single" in the waiting line. I responded and we slid effortlessly toward the chair that took us up the mountain. It was a glorious afternoon -- blue skies and lots of sun -- and we skied together until the lifts finally closed. But we didn't stop at that. We decided to prolong our casual meeting, and we drove together back to Strawberry for a drink and more conversation which we thoroughly enjoyed and did not wish to end. Unfortunately, I could not stay for the last day of the long holiday. I had to leave the next day for Dallas, but I did secure her telephone number and promised to call on my return.

It's surprising how much one can discover about each other in three or four hours of amicable conversation, especially if the shared "chemistry" is right. I found out that Bunny grew up in West Newton, Massachusetts, a prestigious upper middle class suburb of Boston with a strong Protestant Republican cast to it. She attended Carleton College in Minnesota and graduated with a B.A. in Graphic Arts from Simmons College in Boston. The discussion about Carleton was fascinating. For some reason she was certain that I had never heard of Carleton College. I don't think she could envision how someone who grew up in the Orient and went to school in California could possibly have any knowledge of Carleton and where it stood on the academic ladder of small American colleges. I, on the other hand, knew quite a bit about Carleton, having at one time written a paper on *The Theory of the Leisure Class* and its scandalous author and Carleton professor, Thorstein Veblen, who was unceremoniously discharged for his eccentric life style and unwillingness to conform. Somewhere in my travels and pursuit of western lore, I also learned that Northfield, Minnesota, where Carleton was located, was where the infamous outlaw Jesse James almost met his maker while robbing the local bank. I can't say exactly how much that small bit of trivial history had influenced the easy flow of our conversation, but it certainly did not hurt. In the few hours of casual chit-chat we found out that we had a number of common interests, besides skiing. We both had a preference for modern art and architecture, enjoyed the composers of the 20th century -- especially Stravinsky and Shostokovich -- appreciated political debate, liked Italian cooking, and loved the outdoors. We were having a great time getting acquainted and I didn't want to leave, but I had to return to San Francisco to catch a morning plane to Dallas the next day.

I had dated girls before. In Japan I dated a Red Cross hostess from Iowa who was a few years older than I, and probably considered me a safe temporary snare in a sea of war-weary and women-crazed lieutenants and captains who were looking for female companionship. In New York, I was often the eligible bachelor who was asked to take someone out to the theater or the symphony, but it was always so artificial that I did not even consider it part of the courtship game. This was different. The attraction was both physical and intellectual. Putting it in a few words, I was smitten and wanted to see Bunny again. Never had I had such a wonderful time.

The Dallas trip turned out to be more of a conundrum than I anticipated. Our Texas representative had taken on more side lines than our contract permitted, arguing that he had to do that because he was not generating sufficient income from the sale of our lines alone. The Nicolis, on their part, were convinced that he was not promoting our lines, and insisted that I confront him personally to find out what was really taking place. Finding a replacement on short notice was out of the question. I had to make a swing through Texas to find out what was wrong. I considered calling Bunny on the phone, but decided against it. I did not feel it was proper to call someone I had just met without a good reason to meet again.

On my return to San Francisco two weeks later, I immediately called Bunny and invited her to go skiing at Squaw Valley the following weekend. I was terribly afraid that she would say no on such a short notice, but I explained why she had not heard from me earlier, and was elated when she said yes. She had been on my mind during the entire Texas trip. I was turning over in my mind all sorts of schemes to make sure that my next move would prove effective. Inviting Bunny to go skiing appeared to be the right thing, and I was thrilled that it worked. We agreed that I would pick her up at a 4:00 AM at her apartment; in those days, the drive to Donner Summit over the old U.S. 40 took at least four or five hours and sometimes even longer.

To my surprise when I pulled up in front of her apartment, I saw not only Bunny, but also two of her Carleton classmates -- Karen Nelson and Kina Wilson -- waiting to join me. The girls apparently decided that they could not allow their roommate to go to Squaw Valley with a strange fellow they had never seen before. I had no choice but to be a good sport and agree to take all three of them, even though I was not beyond thinking that the free loaders were a little brazen in taking advantage of my invitation. Fortunately, the weekend turned out to be a real success. The weather was superb and the skiing was fabulous. We decided to ski and stay at Sugar Bowl instead of Squaw Valley because we had no reservations at Squaw. Finding accommodations in the dormitories at Sugar Bowl made better sense. On Saturday night we drove to the Nevada side of Lake Tahoe for dinner, and won enough to pay for our entire weekend. Bunny was the big winner. We were shooting craps -- a game that Bunny knew very little about, but she has always been very lucky at game tables. Twenty six years later celebrating our twenty-fifth wedding anniversary in London, we were lured by our English relatives to try a hand at chemin-de-fer. At a fancy private club Bunny placed bets at another game she knew very little about, and won over five hundred pounds in less than half an hour. The crowning insult to the club was not our winnings, but those of a group of high rolling Arab chieftains who placed their bets on Bunny's selections and won thousands of pounds, forcing the house to close the table.

The ski trip turned out to be the fulcrum of our future relationship. Following it, we saw each other regularly, as often as my business travels permitted. When I was in town, I would generally pick Bunny up after work on Friday. We would dine at Paoli's, the premier Italian restaurant in the Financial District, where Joe Paoli would personally wait on us. Joe was a friend of mine from the days at Berkeley. The only son of the restaurant's founder, Joe had an eye for attractive women, and liked to sit down with us for a few minutes and tell funny stories about San Francisco's legendary past. After dinner, we would often take in two or three shows before we called it a day. San Francisco had a vibrant night life in the 1950s, exciting enough to satisfy all preferences and tastes. Venerable Pierre Monteux was still conducting the San Francisco Symphony Orchestra. Dave Brubeck was pioneering a unique and exquisite mold of jazz at the Fairmont. At the "Bocce Ball" one could listen to Verdi, Puccini, Mascani and Leoncavalla, performed by aspiring Italian immigrants trying to break into the world of opera. In North Beach, Mort Sahl was at the "Hungry I" regaling the audience with political satire, and, at the "Purple Onion" Phyllis Diller lampooned Hollywood and everyone else she thought deserved ridicule. There was no absence of political material for comedians in 1953. With the help of the Checkers speech, Richard Nixon had survived to become Eisenhower's Vice President, but, once in office, became a prisoner of his own past. Democrats never forgave him for his dishonest assault on Jerry Voorhis in the 1946 House contest and his savage attacks of Helen Gahagan Douglas in the 1950 Senate race. California Senator William Knowland was still a power in Washington, an appetizing target of political banter and piercing partisan jokes. In Washington, the new president found it difficult to reign in McCarthy. The headline-seeking Senator from Wisconsin continued to play on the anti-Communist anxieties of the American public, viciously attacking all those whom he considered soft on Communism. The justices of the Supreme Court were also feuding. The bright ones -- Frankfurter, Black, Jackson and Douglas -- looked down on Chief Justice Fred Vinson and considered him a political hack who was willing to sacrifice our liberties in the struggle with Communism and school segregation.

On the international level, two political developments hogged foreign news. The first was the end of colonialism -- probably the most defining development of the Twentieth Century. It led to the gradual liberation of the world's former colonial territories. Starting with India and Pakistan in 1947, one colony after another broke away from Great Britain, France, Holland, and Portugal. By the mid-fifties, unfamiliar names of new nation states in Africa and Asia were spectacularly changing the maps of the world. Some new nations took sides in the Cold War, others remained markedly neutral, forcing the United States and the Soviet Union to compete for their allegiance and political rein. The other development, was the death of Joseph Stalin. He suddenly died in March 1953 under suspicious circumstances, and the world watched with trepidation who was to replace him and where the Soviet Union would move in its domestic and foreign policies. The Dulles brothers, Secretary of State and Director of the Central Intelligence, were promoting covert operations to fight international communism in places most Americans knew very little about. In August, the CIA, ousted Mohammed Mossadegh, the pro-nationalist prime minister of Iran in fear that he would cozy up to the Soviet Union. In his place, we legitimized the young Shah and the monarchy, and, together with the British, reclaimed the Anglo-Iranian Company (later renamed British Petroleum) that Mossadegh had nationalized when he was in power. Closer to home, 1953 saw the beginning of the campaign to topple the leftist government of Jacobo Arbenz in Guatemala. The success of the Mossadegh operation in Iran provided an irresistible inducement for cold war warriors to repeat the coup in one of Central America's poorest and most unstable countries. Several hundred Guatemalan exiles and mercenaries were undergoing training in Florida to implement the coup that was staged clandestinely a year later with a press black-out that Americans had never witnessed before. Listening to Mort Sahl, was like taking a course in current politics from a liberal professor with a bent for comedy. It was a marvelous diversion from the strains and responsibilities of daily life at a time when Washington was making a gradual but decisive political turn to the right.

San Francisco was also becoming the literary center of the beat generation. The City Lights Bookstore on Columbus Avenue partially owned by Lawrence Ferlinghetti, an avant-garde poet of considerable talent, was the hub of the growing anti-establishment movement. Browsing through the stacks, one could meet Allen Ginsburg and, occasionally, when they were visiting the city, also Jack Kerouac and Kenneth Rexroth. Ginsburg's *Howl* and Kerouac's *On the Road* were still several years distant, but a mood of increased restlessness and freethinking was already sweeping the American youth. It encouraged the construction of a more spontaneous and less formal consciousness and greater regard for the environment. Seeing it happen in front of your eyes was an exciting experience. Across the alley from the City Lights Bookstore was Visuvio, a coffee shop patronized by the

North Beach literati, where one could stop for a cup of coffee and an opportunity to hear the latest diatribe against conformity. A bit of a rebel who came to California to see the West, Bunny fell in love with San Francisco and decided to stay. .

But there was also something about Bunny that was closely tied to traditional values instilled by the surroundings in which she was raised. As a young girl she often volunteered in West Newton for a variety of community services, and the obligation to make the world better stayed with her and carried through her entire life. Whenever I could manage it -- and this was not always possible, because of my heavy travel schedule -- on Tuesday evenings, I tried to pick Bunny up outside San Francisco General Hospital, a neighborhood known for its high crime rate at night. She worked at the hospital once a week as a volunteer nurses' aid in the children's ward. I was terribly impressed by her dedication; so was Mama when she first met Bunny in uniform one late evening during her visit to San Francisco. I was quite concerned about that meeting. Mama could be at times difficult, but not that evening. She found Bunny to be a lovely girl whom she liked and respected from that first day. For someone whose tacit message has always been that no young woman was good enough for her three brilliant sons, this was a turn-around I did not expect. It was a great relief therefore to find out that someone whom I always thought of as a formidable obstacle to marriage liked Bunny and approved of my interest in her. I was never concerned about Papa's reaction. Somehow, I always knew instinctively that he would approve.

My travel schedule was arduous. I was on the road a good part of 1953. Especially prolonged was my summer trip to New York. On my way home I picked up a brand new Mercury in Detroit, and Bunny's brother Jim, who was on his way to the University of Washington, helped me drive it to San Francisco. We had originally planned to drive leisurely -- at least, that's what I promised Jim when I sought his help -- but I was so anxious to see his sister, that we made the entire trip in three days, arriving with a flourish after telephoning from Sacramento and telling Bunny's roommates that we were calling from Salt Lake City. It was an uncommonly warm weekend. July is usually a cold month with fog horns sounding intermittently, gusty prevailing winds blowing from the Pacific, and thousands of shivering tourists in summer wear. The day we arrived was not that kind of a day. For some unknown reason -- probably brought out by my anxiety of seeing Bunny again after almost six weeks of separation -- I have a very clear recollection of that day. It was hot, humid and the bay's waters were incredibly calm.

Bunny was wearing a light summer black and white print dress when we rang the bell at her apartment and caught her totally by surprise. I wanted to hug and kiss her, but the sudden outburst of affection had to wait. Her roommates appeared from a backroom in the apartment, and the prude in me said: this was not the time for it. I knew I was in love, but I had to wait until a more propitious moment when we were finally alone.

Separation can be a powerful benefit to courtship and to getting to know each other well. It provides time and opportunity for introspection, for examining the love relationship, and for contemplation about life together under a covenant that in the 1950s still called for "unto death do us part." And so it was for Bunny and me. Because of my erratic travel schedule, we had lots of time to think through the various obstacles that we could encounter in our life together. I was concerned about how I would fit in into a family that was so different from mine. After all, I am sure her parents never thought that their daughter whom they loved dearly would marry an immigrant, certainly, not until I came along. I am sure Bunny also must have had reservations about her relationship with my family, especially my parents. She must have known that as the oldest of three brothers I would someday have to take care of my parents. We also had to examine our political and religious preferences. Bunny was definitely to the left of me politically. I was still searching, and she helped me move in her direction. Neither of us were terribly religious. We were what many theologians today call apatheistic; we were relaxed about religion, and we really didn't mind how others thought about God. Nor did we see the world in exclusively contradicting colors of black and white. We both saw a lot of grey in the universe and we knew we would not be consumed by arguments about what was considered absolutely right or wrong. By the winter of 1953, we knew that we had similar feelings about peace, racial equality, women's rights, environmental protection, and social justice. Despite the differences in our backgrounds, we were surprisingly in agreement not only about what we enjoyed together, but also about the deeper core values that would have to serve us as partners for the rest of our lives. Besides, we were also passionately in love.

The situation at work was unfortunately very different. The world of fashion was undergoing drastic changes. Fifty year-old wives of American businessmen and professionals no longer wanted to wear the soberly tailored suits and dresses that explicitly defined their age and class. They wanted to look like thirty and thirty-five year-old young women, less formal, less ethereal, more athletic, more casual and comfortable in what they wore. Retailing was also going through a transformation. Department stores and women's specialty stores were moving away from the idea of selling women's wear by clearly defined departments towards boutique sales where skirts, blouses, sweaters, sport dresses, and even accessories were being displayed together, often by brand name, style or price. Mrs. Nicoli designed her clothes for the more affluent and older woman, but the lines were poorly coordinated; we offered a little bit for everyone, old and young. What the firm needed was to define its primary market and restructure its design emphasis toward a more casual look for which California was becoming noted. This, Mrs. Nicoli found difficult to achieve. A product of the thirties and forties, she could not adapt to new fashion trends sweeping Hollywood and the less formal and more casual California style of life. To rejuvenate our sportswear lines, we hired two younger designers in the fall of 1953. I was happy to see this development, but the results were still to be seen. My primary concern at that time was my workload that was growing by leaps and bounds. In September, our oldest and most experienced salesman who covered southern California and Arizona resigned and took on a competitive line. This meant that, in addition to everything else I was doing, I now had to fly or drive to Los Angeles several times a month to look for a replacement and provide much needed support for our showroom sales staff.

In late December, Bunny flew home for Christmas. I drove her to the airport where we exchanged Christmas presents. She gave me a beautiful sterling silver money clip with my initials inscribed on it and a handsome tie from I. Magnin. I gave her a jeweled compact decorated with opals and a silk scarf. As we were saying goodbye at the airport, I think we both knew we were ready to announce our engagement, but in the interest of family harmony, had decided to wait. Bunny wanted to prepare her parents in person before we made it public. I wanted to tell Papa and Mama that I was serious about Bunny and planned to marry her. At the airport, we hugged and kissed as if we were parting forever. To waiting passengers, it must have looked like a scene out of a sentimental Hollywood film

In mid-January, I had to fly to New York on business. On a weekend I took the train to Boston, and Bunny's parents met me at South Station. I had seen pictures of Bunny's parents, but was not prepared for the real thing. In front of me, stood a slim, strikingly beautiful white-haired lady with a rather roly-poly ruddy-faced friendly gentleman in a broad-brimmed Stetson, looking more like a Texas cattleman than a New England telephone company executive. I found out later that Bunny's dad favored Stetsons to protect his fair Northern epidermis from sun. We had a leisurely visit, polite conversation and lamb roast for Sunday dinner that Bunny's father expertly carved and served. I don't remember what I said to them exactly, but the substance of it was that I wanted to meet them so that I could personally ask for their daughter's hand. It was kind of old-fashioned, but I think they appreciated the sincerity and formality that I tried to convey. I was nursing a terrible cold, and they did everything possible to keep the conversation flowing and make me comfortable throughout the entire two-day stay.

There was something very wholesome and appealing about her parents. Their ancestral roots and family upbringing were very different from those of my parents, but their values were not that dissimilar. Her father grew up in western Massachusetts, the son of a skilled tool maker and founder of the Millers Falls Tool Company. He received a scholarship to Norwich University and, after a short stint in the army during World War I, graduated in 1920. He joined the New England Telephone Company right out of college and, by the time I met him, had moved up the executive ladder to the position of the telephone company's director of training. Warm, amiable and pleasantly articulate, he was for many years West Newton's resident scoutmaster and deacon of the socially fashionable Second Congregational Church. Bunny's mother's origins were Southern. Brought up in Banning, Georgia, a small town that had been by-passed long ago by Atlanta's growing industrialization, she was a newcomer to New England. Her parents owned Banning Mills, an old yarn and hosiery factory operated by water power on Snake Creek in Carroll County. She had lost her mother in early childhood and her father at fifteen. She could not get along with her step-mother and, at the age of sixteen, moved to Atlanta where she went to work as a telephone operator for the Southern Bell. By the time she was twenty-four, she had worked herself to the position of supervisor and, during the long New England telephone strike of 1924, was dispatched on loan to Providence, Rhode Island, where she met Bunny's father. They were married a year later, settling first in Vermont and then in Boston where Bunny's father was transferred in the late twenties. A bright, proud, and ambitious woman, Bunny's mother did not have an easy time when the family moved to West Newton. Handicapped by lack of formal college training she had always felt a little uncomfortable with the socially mobile college-educated matrons of West Newton Hill. She did not let that get her down, and gradually through responsible community work earned the respect and admiration of the entire community. Her rare good looks and soft Georgia accent probably helped her more than she gave them credit.

Like almost everyone else in West Newton, Bunny's parents were Protestant, Republican and conservative, a suburban minority within the larger population of Greater Boston that usually voted Democratic. They had voted in 1940 for Wendell Wilkie, in 1944 and 1948 for Dewey, and for Eisenhower in 1952. They resented Roosevelt's New Deal legislation, barely tolerated Harry Truman, and despised Boston Mayor James Michael Curley for his rough-and-tumble politics and the Democratic machine that he nurtured to provide him with votes. But beneath that hard-line Republican rancor, Bunny's parents held strong feelings of racial justice and believed unconditionally that African - Americans and Jews should be treated fairly on the same footing as everyone else. In the "Brown v. Board of Education" case that was being considered in the Supreme Court, they favored a decision that would end segregation, allowing black children to receive a superior education.

I believe I registered well with my future in-laws. On my return home in February, Bunny told me that they liked me and "were happy to see new blood coming to the family." I am not sure what that meant exactly, but I was glad to learn that they had no serious reservations. On Washington's Birthday, exactly one year since we first met on the ski slopes of the High Sierra, I conferred formal status to our relationship. I proposed and Bunny accepted; she had been waiting for a formal proposal since I returned from Boston. We were staying at Beacon Lodge, a rickety old ski establishment on US 40 a few miles from Sugar Bowl. The place was teeming with Stanford freshmen in various stages of recovery from giardia and too much sun. We had gone out to dinner and on the way back to the lodge, parked by the Norden General Store where I slipped a small emerald-cut diamond ring on Bunny's finger. I had planned to do that at the restaurant, but had somehow left the ring behind in the car. She was ecstatic, and we sat huddled together for almost an hour in the cold automobile restating our vows. The next day, Bunny and I also came down with giardia -- she in the morning and I on our way home, a hard lesson to learn that one has to be careful with drinking water in the Sierras because of the presence of pack animals and bovine stock. A romantic weekend turned into a medical disaster; what a way to celebrate a momentous milestone!

Bunny's mother opted for an early September wedding. She felt she needed time to get all the relatives and friends on board, and to get their large back yard ready for a garden reception that would make the wedding an unforgettable event. Getting her only daughter properly and resplendently married -- something that I believe she had missed herself -- was an "idee fixe" on which she would not budge. The year crept sluggishly like the proverbial turtle toward a goal that Bunny and I wanted to reach as soon as possible.

On the political scene, there was not much happening, except for the Atomic Energy Commission hearing on J. Robert Oppenheimer, a tragic proceeding that withdrew his security clearance and ruined the great man. It was of special concern to our family. Brother Mike was in the last stages of his doctoral dissertation in nuclear physics at Berkeley and deeply resented the methodical destruction of Oppenheimer's professional reputation and political integrity by anti-communist hysteria and the testimony of Chairman Lewis Strauss of the AEC and Edward Teller. Mike intensely disliked Teller, considered him mean, politically calculating, and not beyond taking credit for someone else's work. He was convinced that Teller's hostility was a pay-back for Oppenheimer's opposition to the hydrogen bomb which Teller promoted, and for Oppenheimer's refusal to appoint him director of the theoretical division at Los Alamos. We followed the hearings with intense interest and listened to Mike's editorial comment. Like Oppenheimer, Mike was also against the construction of the hydrogen bomb. It is not surprising that the hearing became a turning point in Mike's professional career. It was too late to change his specialty; he received his doctorate in nuclear physics, but very soon moved to other fields in physics because he was convinced that Dr. Oppenheimer was unjustly accused and found guilty He did not want to go through a similar occurrence of foul play in a field that was subservient to security surveillance and politics.

At the office, the situation was not getting better. The young designers found they could not work independently under Mrs. Nicoli and resigned after a few months. The Spring 1954 line of suits and dresses, in the vernacular of the ready-to-wear business, laid an egg, disastrously steering the firm to a second year of losses. In June, the Nicolis called a meeting that was attended by all department heads and the firm's accountants and legal council. We met in Mrs. Nicoli's large private office, with Louis Glicksburg, the firm's venerable general counsel, sitting behind her large desk, while the rest of us -- including Mr. and Mrs. Nicoli -- sat in a crescent facing him. The meeting opened with a report by the accountants who wasted no time in apprising us of the losses facing the firm. The expected losses were staggering, much larger than anyone had thought. A lively discussion followed, but there was no real merit to it. It was largely a rehash of many other previous discussions that lead to nowhere. What was needed was a voice of sensible purpose, and it came from Louis Glicksburg, Mr. and Mrs. Nicoli's old friend, legal counsel and most senior member of our group. Speaking like a judge delivering a decision and citing the essential negative features of the report, he said that he saw only two options of any merit available to the firm: close down the suit and dress departments, cut the overhead, and restructure the sportswear lines, or sell the entire business to someone else He assured the Nicolis that their real estate investments were adequate to guarantee them and their extended family a very comfortable living for the rest of their lives. "All good things have to come to an end," he said. You probably have noticed that I am no longer spending much time in my office, my daughter is handling most of your firm's legal work, you too should be thinking of retiring from business.... there is a time for everything, time to make money and time to retire before it's too late." To the Nicolis it sounded harsh and much too defeatist, but it was good advice, along the lines of what I have been telling them since the beginning of the year.

The Nicolis listened but did not heed the warnings. During the summer, they reduced some of the overhead, raised prices, but did not follow through on their counsel's advice. Money was not that important, especially to Mrs. Nicoli. Her pride and her status as a designer did not allow her to close the suit and dress departments, the most high fashion items of her design career. In the end, her ego said no to materiality, creating massive operational problems for the firm. My relationship with the Nicolis also took a downward slide. For nearly five years I had enjoyed an exceptional relationship, founded on trust and mutual regard. They never questioned my expense accounts, included me in many of their family diversions and treated me as their own son. I, on my part, had great respect for what they had accomplished as business owners and as principal donors to Russian charities in California and abroad. But the relationship was beginning to flounder under the stress of design failures and growing business losses. I believe they resented my attempts to improve what they thought did not require improvement and took exception to my increased involvement in the decisions-making process that they considered theirs and theirs alone. Mrs. Nicoli did not like to hear the truth about her designs and resented my meddling into what she considered her exclusive domain. I, on my part, was losing enthusiasm. With approaching marriage, my priorities were changing. I was tired living out of a suitcase and charging all over the country putting out fires that could have been avoided with better planning and more careful market research. I wanted to cut down on my traveling and organize my work schedule to stay more often at home. In fact, I was beginning to question the benefits of the job. Had I not been waiting to be married, I probably would have started a search for another job. I did take a precautionary step, however. In April, I moved from my fancy apartment near the waterfront to a smaller and more reasonably priced apartment closer to downtown on Leavenworth Street. I wanted to reduce my personal overhead to a minimum in the event of a full-scale breakdown of our business relationship.

Trivial conflicts have a way of reaching a boiling point and suddenly imploding when tension becomes too great. That's exactly what happened as we approached my wedding date. In mid-August, Bunny flew home to help her mother with preparations for the wedding. I stayed behind, waiting to follow her in a few weeks. In early September, a problem developed in our Texas territory. I don't remember the exact details, but it had something to do with our Texas representative who violated an exclusive arrangement that we had with the Harris Company, Dallas' most prestigious department store. Mr. Nicoli wanted me to fly immediately to Dallas to resolve the matter. I reminded him that I was leaving shortly for Boston to get married, and therefore could not go to Dallas on such short notice. He obviously did not like my answer and, in a fit of anger mixed with what I considered unforgiving callousness, said: "can't you postpone your wedding by a week or two?" I was stunned by the insensitivity of that remark, bit my tongue and, to avoid any further unpleasantness, said I would have to think it over. The next morning I submitted my resignation. In the context of our corroding relationship, Mr. Nicoli's remark was the proverbial straw that broke the camel's back. Mrs. Nicoli tried to downplay her husband's tactlessness and rebuild our precarious and tattered relationship, but I stayed firm. I was convinced it was time to make a break and move on to other work. The hardest task for me was calling Bunny to tell her that I had become suddenly unemployed. She was wonderful, one hundred percent behind me in my decision. She never really liked the Nicolis and considered them nouveau riches who put on airs and saw nothing wrong with exploiting me to attain their own pecuniary goals.

II

We were married in West Newton on September 12, 1954, two days after hurricane Edna devastated the New England coast. Nick flew in from Washington to stand up as my best man. Bunny's brothers and Bill Gale, a friend from Berkeley who now lived in New York, made the rest of my wedding party. Bunny's maid of honor and bridesmaids were college classmates and young women with whom she had grown up. Mike was in the last phase of his Ph.D. dissertation and could not take the time off to come. Papa and Mama wanted to take part in the wedding ceremony, but decided not to attend. Mama was in poor health and Papa was seventy-two. The long flight, the added agitation and undue concern over how they would adapt to unfamiliar surroundings, made them decide against the journey. It was a beautiful wedding in a magnificent church exquisitely decorated for the occasion. In an elegant long gown and a veil with a touch of fagotting, Bunny looked strikingly beautiful and deliriously happy. The wedding service, performed by a minister who was an old friend of Bunny's family, was dignified and charitably brief. In less than half an hour, we walked out triumphantly through the beautifully carved church doors to the sound of Mendelssohn's Wedding March played on the organ by another friend of my new in-laws. I was sorry that Papa and Mama were not there to share our happiness. Overwhelmed by the trappings of the ceremony I had somehow forgotten about them, but Bunny's dad came through with a Twentieth Century solution. Waiting for us on our return from church was a long distance telephone link to Monterey, California. Papa and Mama were delighted to hear that we had just left the church and were now married. They had invited friends for champagne and zakouska (hors d'oeuvres) to celebrate our wedding, and we could hear voices offering congratulations as we spoke with them.

It was a gala wedding, but not without some troubling inconveniences created by Hurricane Edna. The rehearsal dinner was held in semi darkness illuminated by candlelight, as there was no power until Sunday morning. Second Church recovered its power only two hours before the wedding, after repeated distress calls from Bunny's father asking for the return of electricity. The beautifully staged garden reception had to be scrapped in favor of the front lawn and adjoining street that was closed to motor traffic, compliments of West Newton Police Department. The garden that Bunny's mother slaved over all summer was four inches under water. The professional photographer never arrived; he could not get through Boston's flooded streets and police-erected detours. We still laugh about what happened on that memorable weekend, although we know that it was not a laughing matter for Bunny's mother who wanted to stage a perfect wedding reception that would be remembered for years to come. Our honeymoon was also not without a certain amount annoyance and disappointment. We had planned to spend a week on Cape Cod, four days in New York City visiting museums and taking in theater, fly to Denver where I left my car, and then take a leisurely tour through the Rockies on our way home to San Francisco. The weather was again an annoying hindrance. Cape God was cold, windy, clouded over, and the day we took the ferry to Martha's Vineyard a powerful storm blew in from the north-east. In New York, it rained profusely, making walking in Central Park and on Fifth Avenue out of the question. Instead, we spent a small fortune on taxi cabs to and from museums and the theater district. In Colorado, we encountered an early winter; it snowed between Leadville and Aspen on US 24. It was not until we crossed the Sierra Nevada that we finally saw sun. To our great disappointment, the planned three week honeymoon was slimmed down to only two by the early arrival of autumn and anxiety about getting jobs.

Bunny had no trouble finding employment. She landed a great job with Dancer, Fitzgerald, Sample, a large advertizing agency with national accounts within the first days of our arrival. My search turned out to be more laborious. I had an offer from Koret of California, San Francisco's largest women's wear manufacturer, but it called for more travel than I was willing to take on. Air France offered me a public relations job in its newly opened San Francisco office. It was tempting -- free air travel for Bunny and me to Europe -- but I did not see any future in it. I felt certain that one had to be French to get anywhere with Air France. I researched opportunities in real estate, security sales and insurance. In 1954, a career in real estate sales did not offer the kind of income potential that it does today, and stock brokerage firms were still fighting an uphill battle against the negative publicity created by the crash of 1929. Only the very wealthy were willing to chance investments in stocks and bonds. The demand for insurance was more widespread. The Pacific Mutual, a California life insurance company, put me through their entire recruiting cycle, but for some reason their San Francisco manager was dragging his feet. I suspect he wanted me to settle for a straight commission contract without any front-end financial support. While this was going on, I received a phone call from Evan Wild, a New York Life agent in San Francisco who had called on me at the Nicoli companies. When I told him I had left the Nicolis and was negotiating with the Pacific Mutual, he literally begged me not to do anything before I heard what he called the "New York Life story." A few minutes later he called to say that he had made an appointment for me with Inspector of Agencies, Bethel W. Walker.

I liked what I saw at New York Life. I liked Beth Walker and his Senior Sales Manager Paul Mahoney. I researched the company before the appointment and found out that New York Life had an unsurpassed reputation that went back to mid Nineteenth Century and that its San Francisco office was the Company's flagship office on the West Coast. Beth Walker introduced me to some of his top salesmen many of whom came out of business backgrounds similar to mine -- out of small closely held corporations where they had to exercise considerable independence and marketing skills. There were also no "ands and buts" about the New York Life proposal. New York Life offered me a very generous long term contract with adequate financing during the difficult first year of building a clientele. Paul Mahoney wanted to meet Bunny, and we arranged a luncheon date. He told me that his wife's name was also Bunny and that he thought it would be "fantastic" for New York Life to have two Company wives named Bunny, Bunny I and Bunny II. Bunny came dressed looking like a fashion model in an expensive suit, a designer hat from Sax Fifth Avenue and costly leather gloves. I remember saying to Bunny after the luncheon that Paul probably told Beth Walker that I had a wife accustomed to luxury and therefore would undoubtedly work hard to cover the Company's financial investment in me. Lunch was not just an added attempt to size up Bunny and me in the neutral surroundings of a nice restaurant It turned out to be a foundation for many years of business association and more than fifty years of close friendship with the Mahoney family.

On October 15, I signed an agency contract with the New York Life and started a new career. Like many other momentous experiences in my life, connecting with the New York Life was a fortuitous accident that I did not envision or anticipate. Destiny overtook the path of design. Had it not been for Evan Wild's call I would have probably gone to work for the Pacific Mutual or some other company in a totally different field of work. My early sales activity also evolved out of unforeseen events. During training for the California insurance license, I came across a book that decided my future in the insurance business. Written by a practicing attorney turned insurance agent, the book explained how life insurance can be used to fund a variety of business and estate planning needs of partners, sole proprietors and stockholders of small and medium size corporations. I read this book from cover to cover several times, applied some of the solutions to people I knew, and decided to concentrate my sales activity in the business market. Five years with the Nicoli companies provided me with a unique insight into the financial problems of family-owned firms. It was not surprising therefore that one of my first sales was to two partners who owned a women's coat and rainwear manufacturing firm. The purpose of the insurance was to fund the partnerships' buy-and-sell agreement in the event of one partners' death or disability. The sale was sizable by new agent standards, and Paul Mahoney, to whom I reported, thought I was some kind of a wunderkind. Other business sales followed, but it was by no means as easy as it first seemed. I was in competition with agents who had spent a lifetime in the business market and knew every sales trick in the book. But I persevered and by 1958, earned enough to feel confident that I had made the right choice. Becoming professional was also important, and, in 1957 and 1958, I sat in for the Chartered Life Underwriter examination, passing all five parts in three swoops. In the spring of 1958, the Company entered the pension market, and I became the first agent in the Company's Western Division to install a pension plan for a medium-size Bay Area construction firm. The sale became a basis for a four page case study issued by the Home Office to help other agents cultivate the pension market. Overnight, I had become a celebrity -- someone the company singled out as a model for business sales.

The fall of Nineteen Fifty-Eight brought another change in my insurance career. The senior sales manager left for New York to undergo some additional training in preparation for a new assignment as general manager. Two younger sales managers returned to sales. Instead of waiting for a replacement from the outside, Beth Walker decided to offer one of the openings to me. Accepting that offer was not an easy decision. I liked what I was doing, especially the feeling of being my own boss. In the four years with the New York Life as an agent I put on the Company's books more than two hundred clients, including several lucrative group life and health insurance programs. The pension case opened my eyes to opportunities in employee benefit consulting, and I was seriously thinking of making it a career. Bunny and I spent a whole week thinking and stewing about the offer and, in the end, decided to accept. The Company sweetened the offer with a promise to give me three years of additional pension credit, something that was important to me because I wanted to retire before I was sixty-five. Gone were daytime home visits, weekday excursions to the park with our two children, and occasional visits with Papa and Mama. In exchange, I was given a spacious office, fancy furniture and a partial view of California Street. Bunny and I often joked about the transformation, saying to ourselves with a twinge of mea culpa that we had sold our souls to the corporation. Fortunately, the New York Life was a decent and accommodating corporation, not a tyrant interested only in the bottom line. In the next three and one half years, my job was to recruit, train, and supervise agents who joined the Company in search of independence and superior income. At best, it was a charge to help them keep their eyes on the stars and feet on the ground; at its worst, to nurse them along when their egos were bruised by repeated rejections and other indignities that are part of the selling process.

With Bunny's parents at our wedding reception, West
Newton, September 12, 1954

On our way to the opera, San Francisco, 1955

Our Eichler, San Jose, 1963

Relaxing in Papa's and Mama's backyard, Seaside 1954

In Squaw Valley, after a day in the snow, 1953

Paul, Andy, Greg, and Buzy in our Eichler Living room,
San Jose, 1964

My first New York Life Office, San Jose, 1963

Administrative Assistant Ron Woods, Office Manager Bob Hunter
and I at my New York Life retirement dinner, December 1982.

San Jose Mercury-News   Sunday, August 4, 1963

Dedication of San Jose New York Life Office

SAN FRANCISCO CHRONICLE, Wed., July 26, 1967

Paul P. Petroff Dies at 85

Funeral services will be held today (Wednesday) and tomorrow morning, for Paul P. Petroff, a former major general in the White Russian Army and well-known leader of the Russian-American community in San Francisco.

Mr. Petroff, who died Monday, was 85.

He became an American citizen in 1953 and had taught Russian military terminology for seven years at the Army Language School in Monterey until his retirement in 1955.

Mr. Petroff graduated from the Military Academy of St. Petersburg (Leningrad) in 1906 and from the Imperial Russian General Staff College in 1913. He was then assigned to the Russian General Staff.

After the Russian Revolution, he played an important part in the early stages of the Russian civil war; he was one of the original officers of the junta which, in 1918, started military operations against the central Bolshevik government.

As the civil war progressed, Mr. Petroff received a series of important commands in the White Russian Army. He commanded the 4th Rifle Division, the 2nd Corps and the 3rd White Russian Army.

MANCHURIA

At the end of the conflict in 1922, Mr. Petroff was chief of staff of the Far Eastern Army and was responsible for the evacuation of remnants of the White Russian Army from Vladivostok. Then he fled to Manchuria, where he negotiated the resettlement of White Army personnel and their families.

He is survived by three sons, Serge P. Petroff of New York, Nick P. Petroff of Venezuela, and Dr. Michael D. Petroff of Los Angeles.

Funeral services will be held today (Wednesday) at 7:00 p.m. and Thursday morning at 10:30 a.m. at Holy Trinity Cathedral, 1520 Green street, San Francisco. Burial will be in the Serbian Cemetery, Colma.

Papa's passing July 24, 1967

Buzy and Paul relaxing after summiting Mt. Conness, summer 1969

Returning from British Columbia after tour of Northern
Canadian and U.S. parks, Summer 1971

Family backpacking in the High Sierra, Summer 1970

Family relaxing in the High Sierra, 1970

Paul and I on the summit of Mt. Rainier, September 1970

Temple Crag, Southern Sierra, Venetian Blind Arête,
First Ascent with Art Walker, August 1969

St. Joseph's College Fiftieth Reunion, Yosemite, 1991.

Our Fortieth Wedding Anniversary and Family Reunion, Florence Italy, 1994.
From left, Nick and his wife Annamaria, I, Bunny, Mike and his wife Irene.

The end of Communism, on the Moscow Barricades, August 1991

Near Pskov, Russia at the grave of Grandfather Peter Petroff

Traveling through Europe, London, 1992

Martin Cruz Smith introducing me at the book signing of
Remembering a Forgotten War, Mill Valley 2000

Bunny and I, our four children, their spouses, and grandchildren
on my eightieth birthday, Mill Valley, November 2002.

Running parallel to the business career were the demands of our family life. In the spring of 1955, we moved to a three bedroom flat on Gough Street in San Francisco's trendy Cow Hollow, a typical San Francisco railroad flat that ran the entire distance of a three-story building with a grocery store on its first floor. Owned by an Italian immigrant who died intestate, the building was managed by the trust department of the Bank of America for the benefit of the owner's two nieces who were in litigation with relatives in Italy. The rental agreement was a steal; during the entire period we lived on Gough Street -- from 1955 to the spring of 1963 -- we paid eighty dollars a month, including garage and utilities. From the point of view of our family's cash flow, it made better sense to pay rent for a flat in the city's prime living neighborhood than buy a home somewhere else in a less desirable area. All that the bank was concerned about was that we did not bother its trust officers about maintenance and repairs. We were responsible for all repairs and improvements ourselves. We redecorated the entire flat, refinished the floors, and expanded the kitchen beyond the mainframe of the building to a covered porch which became for all practical purposes a second kitchen. We loved our flat and its surroundings. For Bunny it was only a few blocks to the park where Joe DiMaggio learned to play baseball; for me a fifteen minute ride on the Union Street bus to San Francisco's financial district. Our neighbors were John and Ellie Tobin with their eight children, Robert Boyle, a journalist with Time Magazine who later became a nationally known writer and environmentalist, and the Moscones. John Tobin became our family physician and my adversary in chess, and Ellie, Bunny's good friend and "mother superior." George Moscone moved through the Democratic Party hierarchy to become San Francisco's dynamic but tragic mayor who was shot in cold blood some years later by a psychopathic supervisor who blamed Mayor Moscone for being too nice to gays. It was a great life, no lawns to mow, no morning coffee clutches, a minimum of television because our reception was extremely poor; instead, we entertained ourselves with symphony and opera and with soul-lifting reading and political lectures.

Paul was born in 1956 and Elizabeth (Buzy) in 1958. In the winter, we drove on weekends to Stinson Beach or Bolinas to play in the sand and enjoy the ocean air. In the summer, we rented a vacation home in Summer Home Park in Sonoma County to which I commuted on weekends, while Bunny and the children splashed in the shallow waters of the Russian River. In 1957, Papa retired from the Language Institute and he and Mama moved to Berkeley to be closer to the University, and to contemplate and write their memoirs. We worked hard during those early years of marriage. Bunny had her hands full with two young active children; I was trying to build a career.

Internationally, the Eisenhower years were on the whole peaceful, but not entirely without disturbing events. The war in Korea ended with an armistice -- an across the border cease-fire --that to this day has not been transformed into a permanent peace. In 1956, President Nasser of Egypt, one of the most vociferous proponents of Pan-Arabic unification, nationalized the Suez Canal. England, France, and Israel retaliated by invading Egypt while the Soviet Union threatened to back the Egyptians. Had it not been for the United Nations which insisted on the withdrawal of all foreign troops from the Suez, the crisis might have resulted in a major war. The true story of the resolution of the Suez crisis was, of course, more Byzantine. Afraid that it might be drawn into a war that could expand the Arab-Israeli conflict, the United States put the pressure on the British to withdraw from the joint military action without consulting the French. England agreed, leaving the French and the Israelis to either continue the occupation without British assistance, or end hostilities and turn the control of the canal back to the Egyptians. Outraged and humiliated, the French objected in a most vigorous manner throughout most of 1956. I am convinced that the bad blood that exists today between the French Foreign Ministry and our State Department goes back to that unfortunate slight delivered by John Foster Dulles in 1956.

During most of the Eisenhower presidency, the Cold War was in a state of cautious remission that politicians on both sides of the Iron Curtain diplomatically called "detente." But it was not a perfect loosening of tensions, not by any sense of imagination. The detente was being constantly tested and infringed upon. Stunning the entire world, the Soviet Union launched Sputnik on October 4, 1957. President Eisenhower's advisors tried to attenuate its significance, and a crescendo of excuses and incriminations followed the Soviet launch. John Foster Dulles claimed that the Soviets had an advantage because they had shanghaied the entire German scientific team, even though our own space program was under the direction of Wernher von Braun, a German rocket specialist who was in charge of Nazi rocketry during the war. Under pressure from the defense establishment, Defense Secretary Charles Wilson called it "a useless hunk of iron." But most of the world reacted differently. It saw Sputnik as a psychological victory for the Soviet Union and a scientific breakthrough with threatening military implications for the entire world. Sputnik jokes at the expense of the United States became part of everyday conversation. Someone came up with a new Sputnik cocktail: two parts Vodka, one part sour grapes. Fortunately, after a launch failure by the U.S. Navy in November, von Braun was ready to recover American prestige. On January 31, 1958, an American satellite was placed in orbit to balance the score.

Indirectly, the launching of Sputnik had a more deleterious effect on U.S.-Soviet relations. Concerned over the success of Soviet satellite technology, the CIA, with President Eisenhower's approval, vastly expanded our intelligence activities and surveillance of Soviet industrial and military sites, dispatching secret overflights of the Soviet Union by U-2 aircraft. In the interest of East-West rapprochement, Khrushchev followed a cautious policy of refraining from making too many official protests. Eisenhower also tried to improve relations, and in 1959 ordered a reduction of U-2 overflights. They were looking forward to a May 1960 Paris conference followed by Eisenhower's visit to Moscow to sign a limited test ban treaty that both thought would be a crowning jewel of their respective administrations, a genuine beginning of improved East-West relations and end of the Cold War. All of that went up in smoke on May 1. Piloting a U-2 aircraft, Francis Gary Powers was shot down near Sverdlovsk (Ekatirinburg), miraculously survived the destruction of his aircraft, and on landing was taken prisoner by the KGB. In the next two weeks we watched the U-2 drama unfold in the newspapers and on television. Outraged and embarrassed by the continuance of aerial surveillance on the eve of the Paris conference, Khrushchev laid a trap for the CIA. Holding back the information that Powers was alive, he announced that the Soviet Air Force had shot down a spy plane. Instead of coming clean about the unfortunate incident, Washington denied that the downed aircraft was a spy plane, asserting instead it was a weather plane that had somehow strayed from its normal course. On the next day, the wily Russian produced a sullen-looking Powers and aerial photographs taken by him. The CIA were caught red-handed. Like Khrushchev, Eisenhower was also outraged. While Washington officials pointed fingers at each other, the President, trying to save the summit conference, took full responsibility for the flight. But it was too late; Khrushchev and his Kremlin cohorts could not understand why Eisenhower "took the blame" To them it was not a sign of American candor, but of offense to the Soviet nation. In the end, Khrushchev was forced to walk out of the Paris conference, cancel Eisenhower's proposed visit to the Soviet Union, and seriously constrain the improvement of US-Soviet relations. What could have been the beginning of an East-West thaw in 1960 had to wait twenty-five years until Mikhail Gorbachev took the helm. Khrushchev later said that the U-2 affair was a tragic incident that was the beginning of the end of his ability to hold on to power and improve relations with the West.[29]

Closer to home two other momentous developments, superimposed chronologically on each other, held the attention of the American public through most of the second half of the 1950s. Our television reception was invariably wretched. No matter how we tried to realign our antenna, the air waves bounced off two large water tanks located to the west of our building, producing double and sometimes triple images that created surrealistic, dream like pictures on the television screen. But we didn't give up. We watched television regularly with an acute hunger for the latest bit of news. The content was so electrifying that we felt obligated to switch television on. We also poured over our local newspapers, read *Time* and *Newsweek*, and talked ad infinitum with colleagues and friends.

On May 17, 1954, a few months before we were married, the Supreme Court delivered a unanimous decision on an issue that had been a source of contention for many years. In Brown v Board of Education, it put an end to racial segregation in the nation's public schools. "Separate but equal has no place" in the field of public education, Chief Justice Earl Warren told the waiting nation. Throughout 1955 and 1956 desegregation moved slowly without any serious derailment, but in the fall of 1957 it suddenly exploded with shocking force. The explosion took place not in the Deep South as most people expected, but in Little Rock, Arkansas, a relatively moderate state capitol with one of the South's most liberal newspapers. To commence integration of Arkansas schools, nine carefully selected black children were scheduled to enter Little Rock Central High in the fall of 1957. As the first day of school drew closer, racial tensions in the community came to the surface. Politicians from the Deep South entered the fray by holding a major anti-segregation rally in Little Rock in late August, and feelings against integration steadily grew raw, especially among the white working-class parents whose children attended Central High. Under pressure from the Citizens' Councils and Marvin Griffin, the racist governor of Georgia who feared that Arkansas would start the integration ball rolling throughout the entire South, Governor Orval Faubus, a moderate populist, decided to set his pro-liberal views aside and play the racial card. He was afraid that in the growing climate of white racial protest, he would not be reelected for a second term. He therefore ordered the Arkansas National Guard on September 3 to encircle the school, allegedly to keep order, but in reality to prevent the nine black children from entering it.

Pressed by the Guard and the howling rabble shouting, "Keep the niggers out," eight black children and their civilian escort succeeded in withdrawing without suffering any physical or mental harm on the first day of school. One fifteen-year-old girl, who arrived unescorted a few minutes later, got caught up in the vicious free-for-all. She was blocked by soldiers with drawn bayonets and the mob closing in behind her, pushing and crying "Lynch her, lynch her." Fortunately, she managed to get through to a nearby bus stop where a white woman -- wife of a college professor --stood her ground and got the frightened girl on the bus. The scene was captured by movie cameramen and still photographers, and for the next three or four days we watched in disbelief on the evening news hour the chilling images of that hateful confrontation, with comments by John Chancellor and the Huntley-Brinkley team. The images were uglier and more terrifying than anything that took place during the Black bus strike in Montgomery, Alabama, because in Little Rock they involved not adults, but innocent children seeking nothing more than a decent education.

The confrontation continued for several weeks, until a vacillating President Eisenhower, finally accepted the advice of sounder minds and sent in troops of the 101st Airborne Division to protect the children and bring order to Little Rock. The images of paratroopers escorting the children and moving the frenzied mob out of the school area with rifles and fixed bayonets on the ready were chilling and difficult to forget. They kept reminding us for several weeks how difficult integration is going to be in many parts of the United States.

A less chilling but equally disturbing experience in the second half of the 1950s was the game and quiz show scandal. In 1955, a top-rated show on television was "*The $64,000 Question*", watched by nearly fifty million people. Some contestants reached the $16,000 and$32,000 plateaus, and one went all the way to the top to win $64,000 on an obscure culinary question that pertained to the menu and wines served by the king of England at a dinner for the president of France. The phrase "sixty-four thousand dollar question" became part of the American vernacular. Imitations followed and, by 1956, television was flooded with game and quiz shows. One huge success was *Twenty One*, shamelessly patterned on the card game of the same name. The hero of that show and its largest winner was Charles Van Doren who became the undisputed intellectual star of American television after ousting Herb Stempel, a previous contestant who was coached by the show's producers to lose. Scion of an illustrious American family whose roots went back to the eighteenth century, Charles Van Doren was a $4,000-a-year English instructor at Columbia University when he first appeared on *Twenty One*. His father, Mark Van Doren, was a university professor, a Pulitzer Prize winning poet, and the biographer of Hawthorne; his mother a former editor of the *Nation,* a published novelist who had an affair at one time with Wendell Wilkie, the Republican presidential candidate in 1940. Attractive, smart, and tantalizingly charming, Charles Van Doren reflected his parents' aristocratic credentials. He answered obscure questions on the show with ease and a certain amount of theatrical aplomb that made *Twenty One* into a phenomenal success.

Rumors of rigging had been circulating since the early days of the show's television triumph -- in fact, there was gossip that all quiz shows were rigged -- but it wasn't until late 1957 that charges of rigging surfaced in the press. Infuriated by Van Doren's success and fame, Stempel spilled the beans about how the show was rigged. An annoying investigation followed, first by the district attorney of New York City, and then by a Congressional committee that was looking into the practices of television game and quiz shows. The investigation focused on Charles Van Doren, and for the next two-and-one-half years we watched the high drama unravel on television and in print. At first, Van Doren maintained he received no help from the show's producers. Under pressure from NBC for whom he had gone to work on the *Today* show, he even sent a telegram to the Congressional committee in late 1959 declaring that he was innocent of any participation in the rigging of *Twenty One*. He was subpoenaed and under oath had to admit that he was "deeply involved in the deception." The confession was a traumatic moment for Van Doren and the nation. Journalists had been following the story since 1957; now they had proof, a photograph of the talented young American scholar admitting on the witness stand that he had lied about not getting help in answering questions and was part of a crooked commercial venture crafted by the show's producers to acquire top billing for the NBC.

Van Doren's confession shocked the viewing public. Like most Americans, Bunny and I trusted Van Doren and found it difficult to accept that he had been involved in something as underhanded as a rigged quiz show. Political commentators wrote and spoke about the disintegration of America's moral fiber and the cynical immorality of American culture. There may have been some validity to their statements, but, in the final analysis, what the quiz show scandal illustrated was that television had tremendous power and that the demands of entertaining the viewing public in most cases took precedence over integrity and substance. We were in a new era of the growing power of television that shaped our views on everything -- politics, ethics, business, and social change To hold on to our family standards of conduct and preserve our independence in thinking, we had to learn not to accept at full value everything we saw on the evening television show.

III

Before we knew it, the Fifties were over. Joe McCarthy, the Korean War, segregation, and the early clashes of the Cold War were now past history. By June 1960, the most important issue for Americans was who was going to be our next president: the dour and unscrupulous Richard Nixon or the good-looking but largely politically untried Jack

Kennedy. Like many young couples of the late Fifties who sought change after eight years of Eisenhower immobility, we favored Kennedy and campaigned for his election. In June 1960, we also took our first real vacation. Bunny and the children flew to Boston ahead of me to visit her parents and attend a friend's wedding. Two weeks later I joined them for a few days in West Newton and a week of sightseeing in New England. Bunny and I drove north on our first real holiday since marriage through New Hampshire, Vermont and Maine. We had a grand time. We gorged ourselves on sumptuous Maine lobster, sunned ourselves on the rocks of Arcadia National Park, visited Bunny's great aunt in Bar Harbor, and dawdled at Bunny's favorite haunts when she was growing up. On the way home, we flew to Chicago and from there took the California Zephyr, thinking it would be fun for the children to see the nation's prairies and mountains as we traveled home. It turned out to be a terrible mistake. Passenger rail travel was in its final stages of rundown neglect and malfunction. The air-conditioning system failed, the restaurant car ran out of food and beverages, and the children ran amok in the cramped and cluttered space of our compartment. Two days and two nights of promised Beau Monde travel became a pain to parents and children alike.

In November, John F. Kennedy was elected president by a narrow margin. Some die-hard Republicans even called for a recount of the Chicago vote, claiming that it had been forged in order to deliver the state of Illinois to the Democrats. Bunny and I felt very differently, especially as Kennedy and his team prepared to take office. The inaugural address, the glittering inaugural balls, the new president's youth and Jacqueline's good looks and regal bearing sent signals to the world that "the torch" was indeed being "passed to a new generation of Americans born in this century." No other inaugural made me feel so full of euphoria and gratification. I was flattered and inspired to hear the new president say: "And so, my fellow Americans, ask not what your country can do for you -- ask what you can do for your country."

Nineteen Sixty-one looked remarkably promising. The new president got off to a good start with his Alliance for Progress, a program of help for Latin America, emphasizing social reform and U.S. financial support. My business career was also beginning to show results. But the euphoria did not last very long. Mama, who had been in and out of hospitals for a variety of medical problems during the previous year, suffered a severe stroke on March 27. The president's opening program also suffered a cruel and critical shock. On April 17, a CIA-trained force of anti-Castro Cuban exiles landed at the Bay of Pigs on the south shore of the island, 90 miles from Havana. The predicted popular rising did not take place, and the CIA force was routed by troops loyal to Castro. The clandestine Bay of Pigs operation was inherited from the Eisenhower administration during which recruitment and training of the exiles took place, but Kennedy also has to take some blame for it. He could have stopped the operation if he really wanted. Instead, he concurred with Eisenhower's decision, provided no Americans were to be part of the landing. It was a dreadful mistake, in violation of the treaty that the United States had signed as part of the Charter of the Organization of American States. The reaction in Latin America and Europe was devastating. "In one day," said one prominent European newspaper, "American prestige collapsed lower than in eight years of Eisenhower timidity and lack of determination," creating a serious impediment for the Kennedy administration.

Mama's stroke was also a terrible impediment. It was hard on the entire family, especially Papa who had to take the full brunt of her confused state of mind when Mama came out of a coma that lasted nearly three weeks. In addition to the physical disability that was considerable, there was also a change of personality that made caring for her extremely difficult. Nursing aids and housekeepers whom we hired never stayed more than two or three months. For me, it created a state of constant alert and emergency. I often had to drop everything I was doing in the office and drive to Berkeley to help Papa with the chores. Bunny was an angel of mercy who often drove three or four times a week to Berkeley with the children to help Papa, sometimes staying there the entire day. I remember one mad day particularly when I called her in Berkeley from the office to find out how things were going. "Paul dropped a yo-yo in the toilet... we had to call the plumber, and Buzy swallowed a whole bunch of Mama's iron pills that looked like M&Ms.... we had to rush her to the hospital to have her stomach pumped," she told me. For twelve months we lived in a constant state of uncertainty. Nick and Mike lived miles away from Berkeley, and the burden fell on my shoulders, and those of Papa and Bunny. I am forever thankful for the love and support Bunny gave me during that difficult phase of my life.

Mama died on April 4 after suffering a series of smaller strokes, each one more debilitating and painful to manage and watch. Papa moved with us after the funeral. He was physically and psychologically exhausted; one has to read his diary to grasp the magnitude of his anguish during the last months of Mama's life. Bunny never questioned his move. "I would not have it any other way after what he had gone through," she told me, as she nursed him back to well-being in the warm surrounding of noisy grandchildren and caring adults. In September, I was informed by top management that I was temporarily transferred to the home office for additional training and orientation, pending a permanent assignment as general manager of a new office that the company was opening in northern California. For the next four months, I commuted to New York from San Francisco by air and returned home every other week for a long weekend with the family, not the most facile of family arrangements -- especially for Bunny -- but much better than moving the entire family to New York for a short period of four or five months.

I arrived in New York in mid-October during the height of the Cuban crisis. Over-flights and other intelligence sources had already established the presence of Soviet missile sites on the island, and the mood in the home office was decidedly grim, much more unsettling than in far-off California I left the day before. Some people were talking about the need of increasing security measures and making sure that the Company's policyholder data -- the life blood of the insurance business -- was properly protected from fire and enemy attack. The talk in the executive dining room centered on whether or not we should or should not make a preemptive strike. As we found out much later from researchers who studied the Cuban crisis, the debate in the White House followed much the same pattern, the hawks opting for an invasion or preemptive strike, the doves, including the president, for keeping the lines of communication with Khrushchev open in the hope of averting a nuclear war. Speaking to the nation on Sunday, October 21, a tired-looking president declared a quarantine on all military equipment being shipped to Cuba and, at the same time, warned Khrushchev that any missile launched from Cuba would be considered an attack by the Soviet Union on the United States requiring a full retaliatory response. This was a median position, argued for several days between the president and the more hawkish members of his cabinet. It was not an ideal solution, but it satisfied the hawks and made clear to the Soviet leadership that we were not going to allow the construction of Soviet missile bases in the western hemisphere. As the Soviets began turning their ships back from Cuba, Kennedy and Khrushchev negotiated a peaceful settlement under which we gave assurance that we would not invade Cuba if the Soviets agreed to dismantle the missile sites. The agreement was a face-saving measure for both sides. Khrushchev could tell Castro and his contentious colleagues in Moscow that the siting of missiles on the island was no longer necessary as the Americans had pledged not to invade Cuba. Kennedy, on his part, could assure the American public that he had forced Khrushchev to remove the missiles from an island that was only ninety miles away from the American mainland. As a kind of an unpublicized addendum, we also promised to start the removal of long-outdated missiles in Turkey, allowing Khrushchev to tell his generals that the whole thing was a highly profitable swap. Some hardliners called the resolution of the crisis an American Munich, but reality showed it to be otherwise. Facing an extremely difficult and risky encounter that could have easily degenerated into a nuclear disaster, the young president skillfully put an end to the confrontation. In retrospect, we owe a great deal to President Kennedy for the way he handled the Cuban crisis.

On October 27, I caught a 5:00 pm flight to San Francisco and returned home for my first family weekend. Lack of sleep, the Cuban crisis, and two weeks of gnawing anxiety over working in new surroundings with people whom I had never met before put me through a psychological wringer of considerable size. When I saw Bunny and the children waiting for me at the airport I was almost ready to break into tears; I was so wound up by the two weeks' experience and the sight of the family that I was speechless when we fused together in an embrace.

The four months of training and preparation flew by with colossal speed. I spent nine weeks on special projects in Montana, Utah, Washington and southern California and the rest of the time at the Home Office getting acquainted with department heads and putting together a comprehensive plan of action in preparation for the opening of the new office. In Montana, I managed to take in a snowy weekend of skiing at Red Lodge, and in Los Angeles, to visit with Mike and Irene. Even though I was technically still in training, I was invited -- as a kind of graduation present -- to attend the annual General Managers Meeting which in 1963 was in Palm Beach, Florida. Black tie, evening gowns, fancy receptions and dinners, the General Managers Meeting was a potpourri of bragging and recognition for the past year's business accomplishments and a declaration of the Company's vision and things to come. It was pretty exciting rubbing elbows with the Company's Chairman of the Board, its President and senior executives. On the way home I flew through Los Angeles where Bunny, the children, and Bunny's parents were stopping for the night after a visit to Disneyland. In the plane, I sat next to Tom McElwrath, vice president of our Western Operations, who told me in the course of small talk that he was going to schedule a meeting with me on arrival in San Francisco to discuss my appointment as General Manager of a new office in what was to become known later as Silicon Valley. Since we were flying home together, he thought he might as well ease my anxiety by telling me where my appointment was going to be. I had a hard time keeping a straight face during our discussion. I had known about it for some time through the Home Office grapevine which invariably had the right information long before anything was made public or officially announced.

In the following two months I commuted to San Jose almost daily looking for office space, and getting it ready for occupancy with a target date of May 1. In April we bought a four bedroom home in the Willow Glen section of San Jose, a one-story modern structure built by Eichler Homes along Frank Lloyd Wright's architectural lines for families with upper middle class tastes but limited means. Designed for modern living with huge overhead beams, lots of glass and open space to provide minimal obstruction, and a magnificent atrium in its center, the Eichler home was built to bring the outdoors in. It appealed to Bunny's interest in modern art and furnishings which fit in almost organically with the straight and unadulterated lines of the entire house. I liked it because of its openness and harmony with the outside greenery that looked like it was part of the inside furnishings. It reminded me of the simple and unpretentious Japanese architecture that I first encountered in Japan. We moved in May, and a few weeks later Greg, our third child, was born.

The office became operational about the same time. I postponed the official opening until August because I wanted to make certain we were fully staffed for the opening ceremony. The number of active agents assigned to my office by the Company was so small that I didn't think we had enough new premium coming in to pay the rent, to say nothing of the office staff. In the three months from May to August I worked without a stop six days a week -- sometimes seven -- recruiting and training new agents. By the time we opened officially to celebrate Charter Day on August 5, we had a total of fifteen producing agents and an office staff of four. I didn't want a conventional ribbon cutting ceremony. San Jose was growing at a tremendous pace, and everyone -- banks, insurance companies, and service organizations -- were having one almost every week. I wanted something that would have special meaning to the Company, the community, and the local press.

Less than one mile from the office, on the border between the cities of San Jose and Santa Clara, stood what was generally referred to as "Armistice Oak." Underneath this huge oak tree, on January 8,

1847, the last contingent of Californians with pro-Mexican feelings under the command of Colonel Sanchez, a Mexican cavalry officer and California ranchero, surrendered to Lt. Grayson of the U.S. Navy, ending the war between the United States and Mexico in Upper California. I thought it would be a great idea to fashion an opening ceremony around that historic event. I therefore retained Maynard Dixon Stewart, a well known local artist and art professor of San Jose State University, to render an oil painting of the signing of the armistice, based on historical material available at the University. Instead of ribbon cutting, the Mayors of San Jose and Santa Clara, the Honorable Robert Welch and Gene Burgess, unveiled the huge canvass depicting the 1847 armistice at our opening ceremony in front of television cameras and the local press. Three Company senior officers who had flown in for the occasion were interviewed and later favorably pictured and quoted in the *San Jose Mercury News.* The opening ceremony turned out to be a public relations smash -- we got more publicity out of the painting than New York Life ever received before. People who saw the ceremony on television or read about it in the newspapers came to view the canvas for days. Upon retirement, the Company presented the painting to me, but it was much too large and officious a canvas to hang in a private home, and I returned it to our San Jose office where as far as I know it still hangs in the conference room.

The Santa Clara Valley was not just growing, but exploding at the seams in 1963. From 1963 to 1966, the population of San Jose alone had almost doubled to 300,000. One had to be a business moron not to succeed. By the end of 1965 we quadrupled our initial 1963 sales. For relaxation, I started mountain climbing again, and in 1966 we bought a plot of land in the Alpine Meadows Ski area and built a 1,400 square foot family cabin for skiing weekends and summer vacations. We made many friends in San Jose, young doctors, lawyers, and engineers who flocked from all over the United States to the Valley in search of greater riches and a better life. One of them, Dr. Arthur L. Walker, an internist, became my climbing partner in the sixties and early seventies. We climbed principally in California and, in 1969, pioneered a new route on Temple Crag, a 13,000 foot peak in the Palisades area of the Central Sierra, that became known in climbing circles as the "Venetian Blind Arête" route. Two young IBM engineers whose wives were good friends of Bunny included me in a computer company start-up that eventually went public in the Nineteen Seventies to the delight of all its founding stockholders, including me. .

It was a good life with few personal material disappointments even though, politically, 1963- 1967 was a period of tragic disheartenment for Americans everywhere. On November 22, 1963, President Kennedy was assassinated as he was riding through Dallas in an open car. I was at a business luncheon at the Burlingame Hyatt when our visibly disturbed waiter in a voice afflicted by torment whispered: "the president has been shot." I rushed back to the office to get more information, and then home to Willow Glen, to be closer to Bunny and the children during this monstrous incident in the nation's history. I will never forget the scene I encountered when I finally reached home -- Papa and Bunny with Baby Gregory in her arms sitting in the family room next to each other glued to the television set with tears in their eyes. We had campaigned and voted for Jack Kennedy in 1960. He was an integral part of our generation, and now that part was suddenly and cruelly torn out of our lives. His assassination was a profoundly trying experience that took weeks to get over and restart our political lives.

That fall, the civil rights movement was also gaining momentum. In the South, thousands of blacks were out on the streets facing police clubs, dogs, tear gas, and water cannon. Despite Martin Luther King's peaceful "I have a dream" speech during the Washington march in the summer of 1963, race relations did not improve. Less than a month after the speech, four girls attending Sunday school were killed in Birmingham when a bomb exploded in the basement of a black church. In June 1964, three Freedom riders -- a young black and two white volunteers --were brutally murdered in Philadelphia, Mississippi. In 1964 and 1965, black outbreaks of civil disobedience and rioting broke out throughout the nation. Just as President Johnson was signing into law the Voting Rights Act providing protection for black voters, Los Angeles erupted in the most violent urban riot since World War II. According to Robert Conot who wrote *Rivers of Blood, Years of Darkness*, thirty-four people were killed, hundreds injured, and four thousand arrested by the Los Angeles police. Similar outbreaks took place in other urban centers of the nation in 1966. To keep order in Chicago and Cleveland, the National Guard had to patrol the streets and, in 1967, the Detroit riot demolished most of the old business section of the city. It was not until President Johnson finally signed into law the Civil Rights Act of 1968 that a semblance of order began to emerge. It was terrible. There were days when we were afraid to open the newspaper lest another outbreak would stare us in the face. Some people we knew went south to help rebuild burned out churches, others, sent donations to worthy causes. We talked a lot about what was happening in America, dispatched telegrams to our representatives in Washington in support of the Civil Rights Act that was being debated in Congress, helped financially the civil rights workers, but there was very little we could actually do to extinguish the racial blaze that was burning out of control. In retrospect, it became clear that it had to burn out by itself.

In June 1966, I was asked to move back to San Francisco as Superintendent of Training for the Company's Pacific region. This was a promotion, a crucial step up the Company executive ladder that could lead to a bigger office or a vice presidency in New York. By then we had four children; Andy was born on our tenth wedding anniversary in September 1964. Accepting that position was not an easy decision. Both Bunny and I had a love-hate relationship with our life in San Jose. We loved our design-wise modern house, we made lots of good friends whom we did not want to lose, and I was beginning to make the kind of money that would be very difficult to duplicate in a more sophisticated and competitive business climate of a large urban center such as San Francisco. There were also lots of investment opportunities in the fast-growing electronics industry in what eventually became known as Silicon Valley. But the other side of the coin carried a more negative and disapproving assessment. In 1966, San Jose still had a small town air of mediocrity and artificialness that Bunny and I found not to our tastes. It was culturally a barren desert; for decent dining and entertainment; we had to drive sixty miles to San Francisco. Bunny also often complained that the children's section of our local library never seemed to have more than fifty books on its sparse shelves, and the adult section suffered from neglect and lack of discernment about what was being read by educated Americans.

In the sixties, the Santa Clara valley was undergoing a major transformation from a sleepy agricultural community to a sprawling industrial complex of cities and towns with San Jose as its business center and principal retail hub. The expansion occurred without any regard for the physical environment, without any thought for professional urban planning. With it came shopping malls, discount houses, and quick order eating establishments. Bunny loathed what was happening in the valley. There was no true downtown to which one could relate as a citizen. "Most people," Bunny maintained, "identified with their closest shopping mall, not the historic center of town." Papa, who always had a sharp eye for the aesthetic, for equilibrium and symmetry, found it very difficult to accept the wholesale cutting down of prune and cherry orchards and their replacement by huge home developments without any consideration for city planning and beautification of the newly created thoroughfares. "San Jose," he would often say, "is out of balance with its natural environment; it has gone berserk in its attempt to become a large urban center in one of the most beautiful valleys of California."

In the end, aesthetics and big city sophistication won the day. I decided to accept the new position and move somewhere closer to San Francisco. In the spring of 1967 we put money down on a brand new architect-designed home in Mill Valley with a panoramic view of the San Francisco Bay. We could not have made a better choice. A suburban community with its own distinct identity only thirteen miles from San Francisco's financial center, Mill Valley had retained much of its pre-World War II charm and way of life. Bunny used to tease me that my rationale for settling in Mill Valley was the presence of a first class deli in the downtown section of Mill Valley and a beautiful new library amidst the Redwoods of Old Mill Park. But there was more than that to Mill Valley. It had polish and depth to lure us to its tree-lined streets and old-world charm. It had a well educated and politically conscious populace that was child-oriented, one of the best public school systems in the county, and miles of hiking trails on Mt. Tamalpais. The house was finished during the summer, and we moved into it at the end of August. Our only disappointment was that Papa did not live to see how we settled in our new home. He had fallen several times in 1966 and 1967, and never really fully recovered from the last fall. He died on July 24, 1967 at the age of 85. All Bay Area dailies carried column-length obituaries to commemorate his long life. He was, after all, a historic figure -- one of the last senior commanders of the White Russian Army.

Although on the whole I liked what I was doing, I did not stay long in my new position, only about a year and a half. My principal responsibility was administering a system-wide training program for New York Life's Pacific region. I had to plan and run company meetings, travel the entire length of our assigned territory, from Alaska in the north to Bakersfield in the south, and through northern Nevada and Hawaii, helping local managers train their sales staffs. Periodically, I also had to fly to New York to attend conferences on new products and programs that were being readied for introduction to the sales force. The position gave me an inside view of American corporate life and its many drawbacks. It did not take long to realize that Bunny and I did not really belong in its upper levels of management. We were much too liberal in comparison to most company executives; we also had too many outside interests to allow for the kind of dedication that corporate life demanded of its senior leaders. Besides, I did not play golf and was not interested in learning the sport. One of our boys when asked in school what I did in my spare time, said I skied, climbed mountains, and read history books. What I was really looking forward to was running my own sales agency like I did in San Jose.

An opportunity presented itself in December1967. Beth Walker who headed the huge San Francisco flagship office where I started was retiring, and the Company had decided to split the office in three. I put in a strong bid, and in 1968 took the helm of a new office that we located on the sixteenth floor of the Wells Fargo Building in the heart of San Francisco's financial district. In-house Company architects designed the office space, but Bunny and I decorated it in a modern constructionist motif. I had a large corner office with a view of the bay and the northwestern skyline that stretched to the Bay Bridge and the cities of the East Bay. I was forty-five. I was doing what I wanted and I felt like I was on top of the world.

IV

Paul was eleven, Buzy nine, Gregory four, and Andy three, when we moved to Mill Valley. I commuted daily to San Francisco -- first by auto and then by bus, when the children finally convinced me that it was environmentally more sensible to use public transportation. For exercise, on my way home, I often walked the 740 steps of the Dipsea trail -- the start of the famous race from Downtown Mill Valley to Stinson Beach and the Pacific Ocean. The idea was to arrive home around 6:30 in time for dinner, a family ritual that Bunny insisted we uphold as often as possible when I was not traveling out of town.

The business prospered beyond my wildest expectations. By the mid nineteen seventies, I put together one of the largest and most up-to-date life insurance agencies in the San Francisco Bay area. I also served as president of the San Francisco General Agents and Managers Association and chairman of the city's Chamber of Commerce anti-inflation committee. The GAMA position had a salient facet that Bunny and I still laugh about. In May 1975, at a GAMA convention in Hawaii I had to deliver the opening address with my right arm tied in a sling, recovering from a stupid accident of the same day. I did something I should have avoided, considering I knew very little about surfing. I got rolled by a moderate-size wave that dislocated my left arm at the elbow, bruising it unmercifully against the hard-packed sand of the ocean floor. It was Wednesday afternoon and local orthopedists were not to be found; they were all probably golfing because it was such a beautiful day. Bunny and I finally located one at 5:30 PM, early enough to set the arm properly and rush by taxi to the hotel for the opening night dinner and my address,

Our community life also flourished. It did not take long for Bunny and me to build a new circle of friends and settle down to a life of plenty in one of the more socially aware small towns in northern California. Bunny immersed herself in community work almost immediately. While the children were growing up she participated in PTA work, took part in all of our children's social and athletic endeavors, and ran the UNICEF booth at the annual Mill Valley Fall Art Festival. I also lent a hand to Mill Valley's community activities. For two years I was scout master of Mill Valley Troop 34 and then headed an Explorer Post that specialized in backpacking and mountaineering. Running a scout program in the Seventies was a trying endeavor, to say the least. The Vietnam War and the protest movement that it engendered traumatized American youth. Even eleven and twelve year-olds resisted the wearing of uniforms and rebelled against a rigid following of organizational rules. It took a great deal of imagination and versatility in the early 1970s to develop a program at the local level that was acceptable to county Scout headquarters, parents, and also to the boys. Most Mill Valley parents understood the problem, and I was therefore able to fashion a program that placed less emphasis on rules and ceremony and more on group games, camping, and outdoor skills. Our boys were permitted to wear scout shirts and jeans instead of full uniforms. Almost every month we had a long hike or camp-out. The boys participated in trail management and clean-ups on Mt. Tamalpais, and every summer we ran a ten day wilderness camp in the high Sierra where the boys learned to store and cook food, build bridges and shelters, and develop rudimentary climbing and survival skills. Greater informality notwithstanding, we still managed to have one or two older boys -- including our oldest son Paul -- earn the coveted Eagle Scout award each year.

Nations invariably experience high and low points in their histories. For America, the sixties and seventies were a decidedly low point in theirs. Not since the Civil War had America experienced so much violence, grief, turmoil, dissent, and humiliation. Three national leaders -- the president, his politically prominent younger brother, and the leader of the black civil rights movement -- were assassinated within a short period of less than five years. The sixties witnessed a continuum of civil rights demonstrations and outbreaks of disobedience in America's larger cities that often turned into police mayhem, rioting, looting, and fire- bombing of property. The nation was also involved in a hopeless twelve-year war that was not just a war against an outside enemy but also a war with the nation itself. And worst of all, by the early nineteen seventies, we were in a constitutional crisis that eventually brought the resignation of a president for the first time in two hundred years.

The war in Vietnam had its origins in our reluctance to support independence in Indo China. Ho Chi Minh wrote a number of times to President Truman reminding him of the self-determination promises of the Atlantic Charter, but neither Truman nor his successors were willing to antagonize France and Great Britain who were continuing to pursue their colonial policies in Southeast Asia. The prevailing thinking in Washington, confirmed years later by the famous *Pentagon Papers,* released to the public by Daniel Ellsburg, was that Ho Chi Minh was not a nationalist leader seeking independence but a hardened communist who was trying to bring Indo-China into the communist camp. For eight years after World War II we therefore backed the French against the Viet Cong insurgency and, when the French finally left Indo-China in the wake of the Vietnamese victory at Dien Bien Phu, we allowed Vietnam to be split into two parts along the 17th parallel, creating two Vietnams, one in the north with Hanoi as its seat of government, and the other in the south, with Saigon as its capital. Half a loaf is better than none to keep the French and the Americans out, Chou En-lai told Ho Chi Minh during the negotiations for a cease-fire; besides, he was sure the north would gain the whole loaf before too long. And that is exactly what happened, even though it took hundreds of thousands of civilian lives. Before the ink was dry on the Geneva-negotiated agreement, pro-communist guerrillas in the south were already testing the defenses of the Saigon government. The Diem government in Saigon was corrupt, inept, and incapable of rallying its forces against the communist insurgency, and it did not take long before the newly elected President Kennedy, fearing that he would be criticized by the far right in Congress for being soft on Communism, stepped into the vacuum created by the French withdrawal. In the first ten days in office, he approved the liquidation of the Diem government and a counter-insurgency plan that eventually gave birth to MACV (Military Assistance Command Vietnam). By April 1963 there were 17,000 U.S. support and training troops on the ground in Vietnam. In

August 1964 President Johnson followed through with what became known as the Tonkin Resolution that gave him the power to initiate hostilities without a formal declaration of war. By the spring of 1965, 200,000 American combat and support troops were deployed to the war theater, and by early 1968, 500,000 American soldiers were on the ground engaged in a life and death struggle against not only Viet Cong guerrillas, but also North Vietnam's regular army.

With half a million troops in South Vietnam, the war now entered a stage of intense brutality, that affected both the North and the South. It has been estimated that we dropped twice as many bombs on Vietnam as we did during World War II, causing hundreds of thousands of civilian casualties. We also executed nearly twenty thousand communists and civilian sympathizers without trial under a secret CIA program euphemistically called "Operation Phoenix." The Viet Cong struck back with booby traps and harmless-looking village encampments, carrying out thousands of ambushes that massacred American front-line patrols. North Vietnam's regular army units raided American positions, one such raid penetrated all the way to our embassy in Saigon. By 1968, nearly 40,000 American soldiers were dead, 250,000 wounded, and there was still no end in sight. President Nixon, who campaigned on the promise to end the war by declaring "peace with honor," began withdrawing troops in 1969. By the spring of 1972, we were down to only 150,000 front line soldiers, but the bombing did not stop. We were now following a new policy of "Vietnamization," using South Vietnamese ground troops and our air power to pursue the war. The new policy did not bring about an end to hostilities as Nixon and his generals had hoped. North Vietnam refused to accede to a peace based on the permanent separation of north and South Vietnam. In an attempt to improve our negotiating position by cutting off the north's supply lines through western Cambodia, Nixon invaded Cambodia in 1970 and expanded the heavy bombing of North Vietnam. Except for a few short months of de-escalation, the Cambodia maneuver did not change the course of the war. The war lingered on for another four years with continuing military and civilian losses until April 1975 when North Vietnamese troops finally entered Saigon, as Chou En-Lai had predicted, uniting North and South Vietnam into one nation, the Democratic Republic of Vietnam.

For nearly twelve years the world watched the carnage on television and read about it in our newspapers and weekly magazines. We saw protesting Buddhist monks dousing themselves with gasoline and burning to death in the streets of Vietnam. With great sadness in our hearts, we watched our dead being readied for their solemn journey home. We saw nineteen-year-old soldiers whose limbs and faces had been shot away by gunfire being nursed on the field of battle, and viewed maimed Vietnamese women and children crying for help. We also witnessed on television, the North's offensives in Hue and other South Vietnam cities, including the very heart of Saigon. War is never the heroic experience perpetuating the mythology of war that one reads about in novels. It's a foul and utterly disheartening ordeal patiently endured by a suffering youth sent to fight the nation's wars. Seeing it happen day in and day out, even if it's in the privacy of one's living room or local tavern rather than the blood-drenched rice fields and jungle hollows, does something to one's sensibilities and mood. It's not surprising therefore that by the mid-sixties, anti-war protest became an everyday occurrence in our cities and towns. Some of the first signs of opposition to the war came from the civil rights movement still very much alive among the black youth of the South. It then moved to the clergy, especially the priests and nuns of the Catholic Church. Philip Berrigan, a Josephite priest and World War II veteran, was first to dramatize the injustice of the war. In the fall of 1967, he broke into a draft board office in Baltimore, Maryland, removed their records and set them on fire in the presence of the public and police. The opposition movement then migrated to big city streets and college campuses. Students protested against ROTC, organized anti-war campus teach-ins, and burned their draft cards on street corners, government squares, and university commons. The University of California and the city of Berkeley were under siege for many weeks. Windows on Telegraph Avenue were smashed, store fronts and parked automobiles were savaged, and restaurants and coffee shops were trashed. To bring order to the streets, the National Guard had to be summoned, but the protesting crowds continued to grow. Across the nation, peace rallies became an everyday occurrence with hundreds of sustained injuries and thousands of needless arrests. The climax came in 1970 after President Nixon decided to dispatch an invading army to Cambodia and expand the bombing of Hanoi. At a peaceful rally on May 4, 1970, at Kent State University in Ohio, four students were killed by National Guardsmen who fired indiscriminately into the protesting crowd. The picture of a young college student kneeling in agonized disbelief over the body of a dead companion flashed on television screens, becoming a hallowed icon of the protest movement around the world. Anti-war declarations and protest statements proliferated and, on a more personal level, a 1970 Gallup poll confirmed that sixty-five percent of those questioned wanted all troops withdrawn from Vietnam within a year. Closer to home, a Marin county referendum asking for the withdrawal of U.S. forces from Southeast Asia passed in 1970 with a majority vote. Our high school also became a scene of student protest. Juniors and Seniors carrying anti-war posters and an effigy of President Nixon, demanded the immediate end of the war. Paul and Busy, our two older children, were old enough to identify with the protesters and bring their strong anti-war feelings home. The nation was fighting a war not only in the rice fields, mined pathways, and the sun-scorched brush of Southeast Asia, but also in the cities and towns of our tormented land

For me, the war in Vietnam was an onerous conundrum, a difficult issue to resolve. Unlike Bunny who, very early in the war, recognized it for what it actually was -- a nationalist war of independence from years of colonial rule -- I continued to see it in the context of the "domino theory" and struggle against Communism throughout the world. My anti-communist upbringing heightened by strong feelings about honor and country acted as a powerful bulwark against a diplomatic settlement of the war. I found it difficult to disregard the surge of Communist expansion -- Soviet and Chinese -- that seemed so obvious in the fifties and sixties; nor did I feel comfortable questioning the war policy of a nation to which I had only recently pledged my allegiance. In conversations with friends and family there were times when I even condemned the press and the protesting public for the one-sided view they presented of what was obviously a very distressing and ugly war. I denounced the war for its grotesque and barbaric conduct, but I found it difficult to speak against our intentions of stopping the spread of communism in Southeast Asia. It was not until I recognized that nationalist Vietnam with its strong historical proclivity against Chinese domination could serve as a far better barrier against massive Chinese expansion on the Asian continent that I finally became opposed to the war. Only then it became clear to me that the war was not in our national interest, and therefore should be ended as soon as possible. I am not sure when this change of thinking actually ripened to its obvious conclusion. I believe it finally came sometime in 1971. Nixon's blatantly dishonest and unconstitutional decision to expand the war to Cambodia and increase the bombing of Hanoi in 1970 caused me to re-examine the entire course of the Vietnam War. About this time, the *New York Times* came out with the secret *Pentagon Papers* which threw an entirely new light on our conduct of the war. I also read several histories of Southeast Asia which convinced me that Vietnam -- communist or otherwise -- would never accept Chinese domination. Debates at home with Bunny and the older children also had something to do with my conversion, probably more than I gave these discussions credit. In retrospect, I wish I had recognized the futility and immorality of the war earlier and had accepted that they were right and I was wrong.

The war was still raging when another obstacle to political stability, this time a scandal - a disgraceful ignominy that became known as "Watergate" -- erupted on the Washington scene. It began during the 1972 presidential campaign, when five burglars, carrying wiretapping and photo equipment, were caught in the Watergate apartment complex burglarizing the offices of the Democratic National Committee. It did not take long to connect the robbery to the White House, as one of the burglars was James McCord Jr., a former CIA operative who, as security officer for the Committee to Re-elect the President, reported directly to the White House. At a press conference a few days after the burglary, President Nixon denied any connection to Watergate. This did not stop the press or the victimized Democratic National Committee from continuing the investigation. Before long, a number of senior officials of the Nixon administration, including Attorney General John Mitchell and senior Nixon aides, Robert Halderman and John Ehrlichman, were indicted on the basis of testimony offered by lesser officials in the White House to a Senate investigating committee. As if that were not enough to blacken the reputation of the Nixon administration, in September 1973, Nixon's Vice President Spiro Agnew resigned after being indicted in Maryland for receiving bribes while he was governor of that state.

The investigation spread to the White House staff, and finally reached the president himself, when a witness told the Senate committee that President Nixon had made tapes of all his personal conversations. Arguing that disclosing his conversations to the public might jeopardize national security, Nixon refused to surrender the tapes at first. When he finally did turn them over to the investigating committee, it was discovered that they had been tampered with -- eighteen and a half minutes of one tape had been erased. It was now clear that the president was in serious trouble. He was either directly involved in the break-in or lied to cover it up. A house committee drew up a bill of impeachment, but it never came up for a vote. On August 8, 1974, Nixon resigned ending nearly two years of sensational exposures of political deception that the entire nation watched on television. In a mood of relief and hope for a national reconciliation, Vice President Gerald Ford, who was sworn in as the new president, had to admit that "Our long national nightmare is over."

The day that Nixon resigned has stayed forever in my memory. Bunny and I were traveling in Europe, and wherever possible were trying to stay au courant on what was taking place at home. At an outdoor restaurant in Cannes, France, we struck up a conversation with a young French architect and his wife who were having dinner at a table next to us. "Ce tres triste, n'est-ce pas (it's so sad, you know) that your president had to resign," our new friends said, trying to be as diplomatic as possible. Neither Bunny nor I had the guts to tell them that we had been waiting for Nixon's resignation for weeks, and were relieved to find out that the "national nightmare" had finally come to an end.

Gerald Ford, who took Nixon's office, was not re-elected. Instead, Jimmy Carter, a little known Georgia governor, became president in 1977. Some commentators blamed the Republican loss on Ford's decision to pardon Nixon, but I always thought there was more to the defeat. My opinion was and still is that, enough Americans had become so disillusioned by the outcome of the war and the Watergate scandal that they no longer wanted a Washington insider and instead voted for a new face outside of the center of power in the hope that this would bring political tranquility and reform. Jimmy Carter's primary task was to restore faith in the system and solve the economic problems generated by the war. Liberal magazines commented approvingly on Carter's domestic policies, but there was actually very little that was accomplished domestically by the president himself. *Roe vs. Wade,* the right of women to choose abortions, and the affirmative action law against past discrimination were achievements of liberal Supreme Court justices William Brennan and Thurgood Marshall. Carter's principal accomplishment, for which many years later, he received the Nobel Prize, was in foreign relations. He was astute enough to realize that Anwar Sadat and Menachem Begin were tired of fighting and were ready to bury the hatchet. Acting as a catalyst and umpire, he prevailed on them after what seemed like unending negotiations to sign the Egyptian-Israeli Peace Accord. In all other respects, he was probably the most unlucky president in many years. His vast energies were constantly diverted by contingencies over which he had very little control. Anti-American riots in Panama, the Soviet invasion of Afghanistan, double digit inflation and oil shortages, and the Khomeini revolution and ensuing hostage crisis, sidetracked Carter's other concerns during a good part of his presidential term. From November 4, 1979, when militant Iranian students in Teheran seized fifty-two American Embassy employees as hostages, right up to January 20, 1981 when Ronald Regan was inaugurated as the 40th president, the world and the American people watched with consternation as an exhausted and despondent President Carter tried everything possible to get the hostages out of Iran. He even authorized a military rescue operation which was botched up by our Special Forces. The last year and a half of Carter's presidency was a humiliating experience for him and for the American people, one of the darker moments in our history.

For us, it was the period during which we watched our four children grow to adulthood. It was also a period when our American youth looked daily at rebellion on the nation's campuses, saw the shattering of family solidarity, and witnessed the denunciation and destruction of authority, particularly the authority of the President and our system of government. In an upper middle-class community such as Mill Valley it was fashionable for teenagers to flaunt opposition to all authority and lambast anything and everything connected with the establishment. The military were especially subjected to ridicule as almost no one wanted to serve in Vietnam. There were also drugs, alcohol, and cannabis, in quantities that surpassed their previous use. Almost every teenager -- and some even younger -- had at one time or another tried to smoke pot. I remember Bunny telling me that one of our four children was growing marijuana plants in a container on our outside deck. This was not an uncommon occurrence in Mill Valley of the Nineteen Seventies.

Most of our friends who had children were unprepared for the cultural and political climate spawned by the Vietnam War and Watergate. We, too, had to feel our way through it. Looking back at all the difficulties we had to surmount, Bunny has often said we were incredibly lucky that all four of our children turned out so well. There was, of course, some truth to that observation, but there was also more than just luck. We were lucky that all four of our children were academic and smart enough to stay out of serious trouble when it stared them in the face. I suppose we were lucky that all four were physically late bloomers; their social and moral values were largely set by the time the hormones began to assert themselves. We were also lucky that the friends they picked came from families that cared. But beyond that, I believe, we can also take credit for all those things we did to help them overcome the hurdles of growing up as teenagers at a difficult time. To begin with, we thoroughly enjoyed our children and had great fun seeing them grow up. We actively participated in their various activities and took great pride in their accomplishments. This is not to say we didn't have our share of painful confrontations that often lasted for hours and even days. Our strength as parents was in the unanimity of our thinking. There were times, of course, when we may have differed in the way we conveyed our reservations and authority, but not in the substance of our response. All four children knew that Dad's reaction would be no different than Mom's, even though I often articulated it in a gruffer and blunter manner without room for further discussion. Bunny was more diplomatic and willing to talk things out, in the hope of reaching a mutually acceptable result.

I think our willingness to accept non-traditional solutions to the early training of our children also played a positive role. Despite our structured and rather authoritative upbringing, Bunny and I recognized very early in our relationship that unalterable and inflexible structure had serious limitations, and tradition for the sake of tradition had no place in an unstable environment characterized by the decline of authority and rise of secular thinking. We did not wait for problems to develop; as much as possible, we tried to anticipate them. Our family developmental policy -- if there is such a thing -- was therefore one of adaptation to the changing patterns of cultural and spiritual behavior in a world that was becoming rapidly less traditional and more experimental. In San Francisco, relying on my Russian Orthodox heritage, we attended the Green Street Russian Orthodox Church that was only two blocks away from our apartment in Cow Hollow. In San Jose, the children went to Sunday school at the First Congregational Church of Willow Glen. Neither experience brought us or the children the kind of fulfillment we were looking for in our busy and multi-faceted lives. We therefore decided to rely on our instincts which moved us in the direction of raising our children without the help of organized religion. We were not atheists who denied the existence of God or a higher being. Simply put, the established religions and their sectarian derivatives were for us too structured, too distant from the reality of life in the Twentieth Century. They did not speak to us as they did to others. We wanted our children to find their own way in life without the help of the clergy and a rigidly constructed credo based on doctrinal precepts often no longer entirely relevant to everyday life.

Our action was clearly a rebellion against authority -- even if we did not think of it that way. We were reacting in defiance of precepts and traditions practiced by our parents who observed established religious principles and never gave up the binding security that faith offered to them. We were very much aware that casting off that security is a risky tactic, but the idea of individual choice was for us more important than the security of a common faith. We also suspected that our four children would gladly welcome the less structured and free-wheeling approach. Together, we searched for answers not only in the Bible or other religious texts, but in history, family experience, and the shifting paths of every day life. We did not hide from them that there were other established religions. On the contrary, we had a beautifully illustrated History of Religion folio that described not only Christianity, Islam and Judaism, but also Hinduism, Buddhism, and Confucianism that the children could scan and read at their leisure. We also emphasized the notion that although the doctrinal and ritual aspects of the various faiths were very different, the moral principles were for the most part the same. We preached religious and racial tolerance. For a whole year, Paul and Busy attended Martin Luther King Primary, a predominantly black school in Sausalito, where they met many African-American children who are still their friends today. We talked about human values, about how they should be preserved and sustained, about great men and women in history who were honorable, unbiased, and uncompromisingly just. We allowed the children to make up their own minds about what was right or wrong, or in some cases simply irrelevant. We did this informally, by example, sometimes at home, sometimes at our cabin in Alpine Meadows, sometimes on a mountain top during one of our many backpacking trips. All four grew up to be exemplary citizens with strong feelings of what is right or wrong and an earnest tolerance for the beliefs and practices of people who were ethnically, racially and politically different from them.

We also kept our children very busy, sometimes to the point of physical exhaustion. In the fall, the boys played soccer, and, in the spring, little league, while Busy ran track and participated in theater. In her junior year in high school, *Tom Payne,* a play in which she had a leading role, won the state prize for excellence, and she toured with it through the larger cities of California. In the winter, the entire family skied together and, in the summer backpacked. Busy was the youngest girl to have signed the register on the summit of Mt .Dana where we lingered too long before a torrential rainstorm with lightning and thunder sent us virtually flying down the mountain to our campsite at Tuolumne Meadows. All four children were active in Scouting, some longer than others, but always willingly and in the spirit of congenial companionship that Scouting offered. There were days when Bunny made as many as ten trips down the mountain from our eagle's nest on Castle Rock Drive ferrying the children from one activity to another, while I sat through wind-swept little league games suffering from hay fever and other allergies that often lasted through the entire spring. We were an exceptionally close family -- we played, entertained, and traveled together. In the summer, I would often spend my entire vacation backpacking with the family in the High Sierra or traveling to Yosemite or other American and Canadian national parks. Bunny was a great sport; she loved the mountains and didn't mind being deprived of modern comforts. Her only condition was that every four or five days we had to stop in a motel or some back country hostelry to take a shower and become, as she often said, "a civilized human being again."

We had very little time for ourselves during this time in our lives. Occasionally, we would manage to take in an opera or a concert. Bunny would sneak in a tennis game or two, and I would take a long weekend with Art Walker climbing the peaks of the central Sierra. As Paul turned older, he took Art's place and became my climbing companion. Together, we climbed the mountains of California. One summer on a family trip to Yellowstone, while Bunny and the rest of children anxiously waited at Jenny Lake in the Grand Teton National Park, we summited the Grand Teton via the Petzold route where Paul got a chance to lead his first long pitch up the southern face of the mountain and take a one hundred foot free rappel on our descent. It was a great two day adventure, except for our packs and sleeping gear that we left behind at a bivouac the night before we made the final assault on the summit. A hungry marmot chewed through our packs and sleeping gear, leaving a permanent memento of our successful climb A year later, Paul, Art Walker, the Kings -- friends from San Jose days now living in Seattle -- and I made an early fall ascent of Mt. Rainier via the Gibraltar Rock route from the south, a relatively easy route compared to the routes from the north. It turned out to be a greater challenge than we had expected, as we ran into trouble almost from the very beginning of the climb. The stone hut where most climbers spend the night before making the final push for the summit was occupied by a joint British-American Air Force mountain rescue team overseeing the evacuation of a temporary meteorological station that had been placed on the summit during the summer. We therefore had to establish our base camp on the glacier and spend an uncomfortable night in tents that quivered and sang all night. The weather report when we put on our crampons and roped up for our push to the summit at 4:30 in the morning said "unstable weather expected," but nothing about snow or high winds. About half-way to the summit it started snowing and before we knew it, we were enveloped in a "no horizon" white-out that brought visibility almost down to zero. Fortunately, I came prepared for bad weather, and we were able to place enough wands to mark our route. To make things worse on reaching the summit, Art began showing signs of hypothermia. Accustomed to climbing in warmer and sunnier California, he did not come prepared for a howling snow storm. A climb is never over until you're in the safety of base camp is the most crucial rule of mountain climbing. We had to get Art down to warmer and less exposed slopes as soon as possible through a snow storm that became less threatening only after we dropped about 3,000 feet. The descent could have turned ugly had I not placed wands during the ascent.

When Paul went off to college, Greg and Andy became my climbing companions. Together we climbed Mts. Ritter and Banner, summited the 14,000 foot Middle Palisade, and often worked out on School Rock located off the old US 40 near Donner Summit, and the granite walls of the Rockbound Wilderness where MGM filmed *Rosemarie* in the nineteen-thirties. The climbing rope has a way of coupling the climbers psychologically as no other human endeavor can. Allowing one's offspring to lead a hundred foot pitch on a challenging rock face builds confidence and reinforces the physical bond between child and parent. Reaching the summit is also a psychologically satisfying experience that is often not without strong spiritual connotations. There is something about sitting on top of a sky-piercing spire with adrenalin still running high and seeing in front of you the snow-covered peaks, stiletto pinnacles, and a dark blue sky as far as the eye can see. In the peaceful silence that is around you, the summit is a perfect site for quiet meditation, and can even be a place of profound spiritual experience brought on by a feeling of harmony with the awe-inspiring vista extending in all directions.

Fifteen wonderful years of exceptionally close propinquity and kinship flew by too fast Paul was first to break the family circle. In 1974, he left for Boulder and the University of Colorado where he majored in mathematics, graduating in 1978 with a double major in mathematics and economics out of which he fashioned a career as a consulting actuary. Together with a friend he was the owner of an employee benefits consulting firm which they recently sold to Standard Insurance Company of Oregon. Busy left for the University of California-Berkeley two years later, graduating from University of California-Santa Barbara in film and theater after a year of "casual wandering" and a year as an exchange student at the Sorbonne in Paris. She has made a career out of her film major and, among many other accomplishments, was a member of the team that won an Oscar in 1990 for *The AIDS Quilt*, a documentary film about AIDS. Greg left for college in 1981 and Andy in 1982. Both graduated from the California Polytechnical University in San Luis Obispo, Greg in architecture and Andy in horticulture. Greg went on to UCLA for his masters in architecture and, after practicing in California and Connecticut, is now a member of a high-powered team at SAP in Palo Alto, California that specializes in solving complex information and design problems. Andy is the proud owner of New Leaf Landscaping, a landscape design and maintenance company in the Santa Clara valley. All four are doing what they enjoy doing in fields that interested them since early childhood and all four are now married. All four never lost their love for the mountains, and all four remain free spirits with a strong predilection for social progress and free thinking. As of this writing, we are proud grandparents of eight grandchildren, ranging in age from a precocious five-year old to one who is a senior in college – five beautiful girls and three active boys. My two brothers have seven grand-children, making Papa's and Mama's total contribution of fifteen great-grandchildren to the world beyond the Russia that they had abandoned in 1922.

6
SENIOR CITIZEN OF
THE WORLD

Our life, exempt from public haunt
finds tongues in trees, books in the
running brooks, sermons in stones ,
and good in everything.
Shakespeare

I

With all of our four children established in their professions, Bunny
and I could now devote our time to projects that we dreamt about
but never could find enough time to undertake. Bunny actually began
earlier. In the spring of 1978, she joined the Docent Council of the
deYoung Museum of Art in San Francisco, spent two years in training in
the arts of Africa, Oceania and the Americas that had always interested
her, and in 1980 began docenting in the museum. The new endeavor
brought new friends, an opportunity to participate in special exhibits,
and a keen interest in the art history of African and Meso-American
cultures. In the fall of 1980, I also embarked on a new quest. At first
at random, and then more systematically, I began taking courses in
history at San Francisco State University

In the fall of 1982, New York Life came up with an early retirement
program for all employees in executive positions who were over the
age of sixty. I turned sixty in November and decided to accept the
offer. It wasn't quite the golden parachute that most of us old-timers
expected, but it was a generous enough settlement that made it possible
for me to retire at sixty instead of waiting until sixty-five. I was ready
for it. The past two or three years had been extremely demanding.
The delivery of financial services had undergone tremendous changes,
and competition from smaller companies and brokerage firms offering

one-stop shopping of financial products was eating into our sales and profits, particularly in the financially more sophisticated markets of California's larger cities. Top management did very little to help us cope with the new trends; they dragged their feet in making any comprehensive changes, waiting for the financial revolution to stabilize. Like a huge ocean liner plowing through high seas in bad weather, the New York Life found it difficult to alter its course. It made sense, therefore, to disembark earlier and begin pursuing other interests that had been patiently waiting for greater leisure and retirement.

In 1982, I also made my last serious climb. Bunny had been after me for some time to curtail my mountaineering activity. Retirement seemed like the perfect time to hang my ropes and climbing equipment permanently in the garage or give them away to someone who was younger than I. On my last climb, Paul, Greg and I – Andy was recovering from an accident – started out to summit the North Palisade via the U-notch. It was a low snow year. The bergschrund separating the glacier from the rock face was too wide and menacing, and we did not bring any ice climbing equipment to guarantee a safe transfer from ice to rock. Since this was to be my last serious climb I was not about to take a chance. Instead, we summited Mt. Sill, another fourteen thousand footer, an easier and much safer climb in the Palisades. The mountains had been an important part of my life for nearly forty-five years, and it was not easy to give up what I loved so much. I knew I would miss the snow covered peaks, the challenge of a strenuous and difficult climb, the solitude and the feeling of being on top of the world. But all good things have a beginning and an end. It was time to confine my romance with the mountains to trail hiking and snow skiing which I also finally gave up when I reached eighty-two.

Retirement invariably causes a certain degree of discontinuity which is often difficult to surmount. Routines established by years of fine tuning have to be abandoned, business friends and associates no longer play the roles they did before, and everyday life, especially if one held a position of responsibility and high visibility, becomes less stressful and more relaxing, a state of mind that many executives often find difficult to embrace. But there is also a certain amount of personal liberation that comes with it. In my case, it was certainly wonderful to know that I no longer had to coddle recalcitrant salesmen, pacify irate clients, and suffer the stress of satisfying annual production goals. But above all, I felt liberated from the oppressive regimen of the clock. I no longer had to get up at an ungodly hour each morning to reach the office before anyone else arrived so that I could prepare for the coming onslaught of people, meetings, and phone conversations with a home office separated by a three hour difference in time. Bunny once asked our young son Andy, after his visit to the office, what he thought of Dad's work. "Why," he said, "he doesn't work.... all he does is he talks to people, attends meetings, and spends too much time on long lunches." Now that I had retired I no longer had to do any of that, but best of all, I could now stay up late at night doing whatever pleased me and not worry about getting an early start on the following day.

Endings also often lead to a new beginning. In the fall of 1982, I became a full-time student, majoring in European history with a strong concentration in Twentieth Century Russia. Over the years I had done a lot of reading in Russian history, listened to the accounts of my parents, and acquired a storehouse of data on the Revolution, the Stalin years, and the Cold War. Now was the time to sort all of this often disjointed information and come to some kind of a conclusion on why the Russia that my parents knew and cherished had come to such a tragic end. San Francisco State accepted my transcript from the University of California-Berkeley, and a year later, on May 28, 1983, I graduated Magna Cum Laude with a Bachelor of Arts Degree in history, the oldest student in the department. The baccalaureate was just the beginning. What I really wanted was to learn how to write history. I therefore enrolled in the Master's program which I completed in 1986 with a dissertation on Mikhail Suslov, the venerable Soviet politician and ideologue whose fierce devotion to Communism brought both stability and stagnation to Soviet society. Slightly modified to meet the demands of a more general readership, the dissertation came out some years later in book form as *The Red Eminence.* I don't know how many Americans had taken the time to read it, but at a Chicago conference on the Russian mafia, in the 1990s, a young CIA operative singled me out to say that it was required reading for analysts working in the Soviet field.

The two and a half years during which I was working on my Master's were in some respects the most rewarding years of my life. I began attending lectures and brown bag lunches offered by the Center for Slavic and East European Studies at the University of California-Berkeley. I also joined the American Historical Association and the American Association for the Advancement of Slavic Studies whose annual conferences I attended regularly. I made new friends and regularly read at least three or four scholarly journals on Russian, Soviet, and post-Soviet studies. It was a case of total immersion into a field of study that became part of my life in retirement. Bunny did much the same at the museum. Liberated from the care of children, she joined the Docent Program at the Fine Arts Museum of San Francisco in the field of Africa, Oceania and the Americas. We began traveling to archeological sites in Mexico, Peru, and the American Southwest. For a number of years she served as Training Chairperson of the museum's AOA (Africa, Oceania, and Americas) gallery. We also began to devote more time to travel throughout the rest of the world.

Our first big trip was to the Soviet Union, a five week grand tour, visiting Russia, Ukraine, Georgia, Uzbekistan, and Estonia, all under the well-honed eye of Intourist and the KGB. This was my first trip to Russia – a heart-rending journey – and what I saw there was extremely disillusioning, despite the propaganda machine's tireless efforts to display the enshrined accomplishments of Communism. Except for the pre-revolutionary landmarks of Russian history and the young children still untouched by the distortions of communist society, it was a land of grotesque and tasteless architecture, outrageous billboards extolling communism, and unhappy and ill-mannered people trying to survive the indignities of a callous bureaucracy with which they had to deal every day. It was not the wondrous land that Tolstoy and Turgenev wrote about, or the elegant *Vieux Russie* that Papa and Mama described to us. In fact, it looked conspicuously unattractive, mis-developed and retarded in comparison to the United States and Western Europe. This did not prevent us from visiting such attractions as Peterhof, the Hermitage Museum, the Bolshoi, St. Sophia in Kiev, and the Blue Mosque in Samarkand built by Tamerlane. But in Red Square, at the Lenin mausoleum with its goose-stepping sentries, extravagant bouquets of red and white carnations, and curious tourists and Communist faithful, I refused to enter the tomb and view the embalmed corpse. I just could not do it. Something inside of me said this would be an act of unforgiving irreverence to Papa and Mama who spent the best years of their lives fighting Lenin and Bolshevism. The whole thing – the cuing crowds, the woodenly stiff guard of honor, the grotesquely constructed monument, Lenin's embalmed corpse which the revolutionary poet, Vladimir Mayakovsky, called "more alive than all the living" – seemed to me conspicuously ecclesiastical and medieval in its rendition, too sanctified, too pretentious for my taste.

In the years that followed we crisscrossed the globe a number of times. We listened to Byzantine chants in the Peloponnesus and folk songs in the Ukraine. In Lisbon, we heard Fado, Portugal's sad melody of unrequited love. We went to the opera in London, Paris, Munich, and St. Petersburg, in Puccini's lakeshore estate in Tore de Lago, and in the incredibly beautiful opera house in Sydney, Australia. We hiked in the French Alps and the Dolomites, and stood on the summit of Mulhacen, Spain's highest mountain in the Sierra Nevada. We toured China and Japan - for me a journey of rediscovery -- where I retraced my childhood and early adulthood. We stood in respectful silence at Hellfire Pass in Thailand where thousands of exhausted British, Australian and Dutch POWs cut a passage through solid rock for a railway made famous by the film *The Bridge on the River Kwai,* and retraced on a cruise ship Magellan's epic journey in 1520 through the strait that now bares his name. We spent several quiet moments in the narrow defile of Thermopylae where a tiny Greek army held the Persians at bay in 480 B.C. until it was outflanked and massacred. At Borodino, we relived the battle that slowed down Napoleon's advance on Moscow, and at Waterloo, in southern Belgium, stood where Wellington and his officers watched Napoleon lose his last battle. By the time of this writing, we had visited forty-one countries, staying in some for only a short time, in others, for weeks, sometimes even months.

As a history major, I could not pass up opportunities to combine history with travel, but there was more to our travel plans than just cathedrals, palaces, museums, battlefields, and music halls. We were genuinely interested in the social and economic conditions of the countries we visited, their educational and health systems, their treatment of retirees and unemployed, and their attempts to cope with the demands of a growing global economy. Except for Europe, Japan, Australia and New Zealand, and a few isolated spots in the Americas, it was obvious that most of the world still had to go a long way to catch up with the development at home, despite the economic and social dislocations of the 1980s and 1990s.

The Reagan years, for all the sound bites to the contrary, spanned a decade of political swaggering and unprecedented industrial decline. It was a period characterized by junk bonds and takeovers, commercial and government fraud, and unmitigated greed, and moral slackness not very different from that of today. On the surface, the new president appeared to have gotten off to a good start. He was successful in recapturing the optimism and confidence of the nation after twenty years of failed war, domestic political crisis, and international embarrassment and dismay caused by Iran's take-over of our embassy and its staff in Teheran. But the optimism was largely superficial, much like the President himself, a product of Hollywood fantasies and ostentation.

Privatization, deregulation and competition forced millions of American workers on the street in the 1980s, while communities in the Rust-belt – the backbone of industrial America – became ghost-like islands of mass unemployment, shut down store fronts, and deep despair. A whole way of life had suddenly disappeared for millions of American working families in Minnesota, Michigan, Illinois, Indiana, Ohio, Pennsylvania, and the inner cities I had visited in the early 1950s. Not all of this dislocation was the fault of President Reagan. Much of the industrial decline and the misery that it caused, came long before Reagan was elected President. The fault lay not in the dislocation – a good part of it was the result of changing markets and foreign competition – but in the unwillingness of the President and the cabal that came with him to Washington to do anything positive to reverse the trend and improve the lives of those who were suffering.

Instead, on the recommendation and urging of his supply side advisors, President Reagan lowered the tax rates. The theory was that lower taxes would lead to a higher level of investment, creating jobs, increased spending, and greater economic activity that would generate higher tax revenue for the government. Convinced by the hawks in Washington that Communism and the Soviet Union were again on the offensive, he also vastly increased defense spending. The net result of these wildly extravagant and faulty policies was the creation of the largest budget deficit in years. Neither action produced the results that the supply-siders and hardliners hoped to achieve. Lower taxes put money in the pockets of the rich and famous, while increased defense spending – uncalled for because the Cold War was already winding down – forced the government to reduce its spending for other government programs, especially social welfare.

Lowered taxes did not produce the trickle down effect that propagandists of supply side economics had anticipated. Instead, they contributed to the widening of the gap between the "haves" and the "have-nots," precipitating a wave of rampant materialism, corruption, and greed, not seen since the free-booting days of the Roaring Twenties. Making money became the only thing that counted, regardless of how it was done or who got hurt in the process. Insider trading on Wall Street became a regular practice, business schools began teaching how to make money through elaborate financial schemes instead of how to manage a business enterprise. Mergers, and take-overs proliferated without any consideration for the workers who were suddenly displaced by the process of reorganization. Until they were finally exposed and prosecuted for fraudulent investment banking, arbitrageur Ivan Boesky and junk bond dealer Michael Milken became the new grand princes of high finance, while corporate predators, T. Boone Pickens, Carl Icahn, Oscar Wyatt, Sir James Goldsmith, and a new crop of lesser names became the take-over kings of American corporate life.

The same kind of disdain for the law, and the end-justifies-the-means mentality pervaded the higher circles of executive government. Protective measures put in place during the New Deal were either summarily dismantled or simply bypassed and disregarded in the interest of the market. I was still working in 1980 and remember how the Federal Trade Commission that was looking into certain questionable practices in the insurance industry suddenly put a stop to further investigation within two or three months of President Reagan's election. In the interest of purported national security, Congressional oversight became something to get around. CIA director William J. Casey thought nothing of undertaking extensive covert operations without prior notification of the Congressional Select Intelligence Committee. His decision to start the mining of Nicaragua's harbors in 1984 was the most flagrant infraction of Congressional oversight. The president also saw nothing wrong with bending the law in the interest of what he considered national security. The whole Iran-Contra scandal was a dramatic violation of presidential executive power. From everything that had come to the surface in the Iran-Contra hearings, it was obvious that Ronald Reagan had authorized the diversion of funds from the sale of Iranian arms to the Nicaraguan contras, an impeachable offense according to the Constitution. He was clearly not the detached and uninformed president that some people tried to make of him. He knew what was going on, approved of it, and did not take any steps to put an end to it, even when he was not officially informed on all of the details, as Admiral Poindexter maintained when he testified during the investigation. The hearings lasted two weeks, and what I remember of them most vividly was Ollie North's testimony. In full marine uniform, his chest filled with campaign ribbons and decorations, standing ramrod straight, Lt. Col. North absolved the President, admitted that he had made mistakes and obstructed the investigation, and reminded the committee that it was all for a higher cause -- the national interest of the United States. In a remarkable show on television, he came out as a national hero harangued by unpatriotic committee members and the unpatriotic press. The whole scene was a calculated insult to the rule of law and the practice of Congressional oversight. .

The defense build-up was another deception. It was justified on the grounds that we had to stand up to the growing Soviet military might, defend Europe, and maintain parity in our nuclear armaments. Conservative Cold War warriors demanded the defense build-up and, when the Soviet Union began unraveling, they defended the build-up, maintaining that the collapse of the Soviet Union took place because it could not keep up with our level of spending, and therefore was forced to go into bankruptcy. We spent the "Evil Empire" out of existence, Reagan and the super hawks in his administration told the press. In reality, this was nothing but a deliberately devised justification. By the time Reagan came to Washington, the Soviet Union was in unstoppable decline, choking under the weight of its own contradictions. If our intelligence organs and specialists did not anticipate the crash that took place under Gorbachev in the 1980s it was only because they did not want to see it. Andrei Sakharov saw it already in the 1970s when he said: "If a course of democratization is not taken, we will fall behind the capitalist countries in the course of the second industrial revolution and be gradually transformed into a second-rate provincial power." Even members of the Politburo saw it in the 1980s. Between the lines of their optimistic and stilted communist rhetoric, one could detect admissions that not everything was going well.[30] By 1985 – during Reagan's second term -- the admissions were out in the open. Mikhail Gorbachev openly acknowledged that the Soviet Union could not survive the gradual collapse that started in the 1960s, and began dismantling the Warsaw Pact and introducing social and economic reform that eventually led to the fall of the Berlin Wall and the freeing of Eastern Europe.

Traveling through the Soviet Union in the 1980s, even I saw the downward slide of Soviet power and authority. On the Arbat in Moscow, street poets openly criticized the government. "We need less communism and more sausage," a long-haired balladeer sang in a deep basso. In 1983, in Tallinn, Estonia, our guide fearlessly talked about Estonia seceding from the Soviet Union. In Pskov, when we changed out travel plans in 1989, the young travel agent – an attractive young woman of liberal views – nonchalantly told us not to worry about informing the authorities regarding the new itinerary. "Don't worry," she said, "no one really cares anymore where foreigners are going." Three days later, at the Yaroslavl railway station in Moscow, a well-dressed young man – a KGB operative – greeted us politely saying "Mr. and Mrs. Petroff, where have you been? We lost you (My Vas poteriali), and that was the end of it. But the most convincing incident of the growing disorganization and loss of military preparedness took place in1989 at the Mineral'nyi Vody railway station in the North Caucasus.

We were waiting to catch the 6:00 P.M. Moscow-Baku express, but it never came. I made several attempts to find out from the station master when we could expect it, but was never able to get a satisfactory answer. Sitting next to us was a railway engineer with whom we struck up a conversation. He turned out to be a Caucasian native from Nal'chik in the Kabardino-Balkarian ASSR. He tried to be as helpful as possible, and when I returned to my seat in the waiting lounge at about 10:00 P.M., he asked me what they told me at the station master's office. "There was a wreck north of Mineralyi," I said, "and it doesn't look good." "Rubbish," he laughed, our guys (nashi rebiata), the Chechens, probably dynamited the tracks to stop a military train, They do that all the time to seize military supplies which they either stockpile or sell on the black market.... if I were you I would go back to the hotel in Piatigorsk while there are still taxis around. I don't think your train will come until they clear up the mess."

The final collapse of the Soviet Union came during Bush Senior's administration. I was privileged to witness it when I was in Moscow. I was invited by President Yeltsin of the Russian Federation to attend what was billed as the Congress of Compatriots, a conclave of overseas Russians who Yeltsin and his staff hoped could become a supporting network of foreign businessmen and professionals during the Russian transition from communism to capitalism .I felt a powerful pull to attend the congress. I had traveled to the Soviet Union regularly since 1983, and was anxious to find out who Yeltsin actually was. Was he a democrat, a populist, a Westernizer, or a Russian nationalist? In 1991 there were still no reliable answers to these questions, and the Congress of Compatriots seemed a perfect point of reference, particularly since many of Yeltsin's supporters were scheduled to participate in the program.

I arrived in Moscow on Sunday evening August 18th with a long list of questions on the state of the Russian society and its progress toward democracy only to wake up the next morning to the rumbling of tanks and the news that a self-appointed Emergency Committee of communist hardliners had staged a coup, shut down all television and radio broadcasts, arrested Gorbachev who was vacationing in the Crimea, and taken power of the government. They made two serious mistakes, however. They underestimated the reaction of the people and failed to arrest Boris Yeltsin, the President of the Russian Federation. By 9:00 A.M., Yeltsin was at the Supreme Soviet of the Russian Federation – the White House, as it became known during the putsch – on top of a tank denouncing the unconstitutional action of the Emergency Committee and calling the Russian people and the army to resist the coup. It was a courageous step taken by a leader who was not afraid to move decisively at a time when the future of Russia hung by a thread. In the next three days the dramatic outcome of the confrontation was played out in front of the Russian White House. There, tens of thousands of Great Russians, Ukrainians, Belorussians, Muscovites and people from the provinces, businessmen, professionals, academics, Orthodox priests and Seventh Day Adventist ministers, Afghan veterans in soiled fatigues, officers in crisp uniforms, groups from the new democratic parties had gathered in support of Yeltsin. Fed up with Communism, they represented a powerful mixture of democratic anti-communist and Russian nationalist sentiment, ready to lay their lives for Yeltsin. During the night of the second day three young men had died in an unfortunate encounter between the pickets defending the outer barricades of the White House and the armored personnel carriers of the 27th Brigade.

I was inexplicably drawn to the crowds in front of the White House and the barricades that were erected for its protection. I wanted to see for myself what was taking place at the center of defiance. For two days I slept only a few hours, subsisted on energy bars that I brought from California, took hundreds of photographs that were later displayed at the University of California, Berkeley, and tried to ascertain for myself the extent of support for Yeltsin.[31] By the end of the second day it was clear that there was a large enough critical mass to topple the Emergency Committee. The attitude of the troops, the vitality of the crowds supporting Yeltsin, the rapidity and thoroughness with which Moscow had mobilized its anti-putsch forces, the continuing transmission of clandestine radio stations, news from the provinces, and the dissemination of Yeltsin's declaration to resist, all pointed toward a Yeltsin victory. The climax came at 3:00 P.M. on the third day. Surrounded by his aides and supporters, Yeltsin came out on the balcony of the White House to announce that it was all over and that the "traitors" who tried to turn the clock back had surrendered and were being placed under arrest. A thunderous yell went up from the anxiously awaiting crowd. Some people laughed, others cried. I had a difficult time controlling my emotions. I thought of Papa and Mama and how they never gave up hope that some day Russia would free itself from communist oppression. Standing in front of the White House with the Russian tricolor waving in the wind, I wondered how they would have felt had they lived to see what I had witnessed.

The formal dissolution of the Soviet Union had to wait for another four months, but for all practical purposes the Soviet Union died on the barricades of the Russian White House in August. At the ensuing victory celebrations to which I was invited, I met many prominent Russian leaders, established business connections and, on my return home, decided to start a consulting business. Unfortunately, nothing concrete came out of it. The new Russian businessmen – many of them former high ranking Party members – were poor prospects, interested primarily in fast money, not in building a viable long-term relationship. It's not surprising, therefore, that the American firms I represented gradually lost interest. During that period I traveled extensively through Russia. For some mysterious and unknown reason, I always managed to arrive in Moscow at a time of imminent crisis, including the September 1993 upheaval that led to the October 4 attack on the Russian parliament by troops called in by Yeltsin to dislodge the insurgent deputies who had organized to topple him. The coincidence of my visits with Russia's political imbroglios caused a Russian friend visiting me recently in California to remind me in jest that it was time for me to take another trip to Moscow so that the Putin government could face up to another much-needed revolution.

An exciting and touching development did come out of my visits to Russia. After the failed putsch I was interviewed on Russian radio and television. There were also a series of articles in *Izvestia* about Papa's connection to the gold left on deposit with the Japanese military mission when the remnants of the White Army crossed the Chinese border in 1920. A retired school teacher, daughter of Papa's younger brother, correctly identified me as her first cousin, after seeing the interview on television. An outgoing and confident woman in her early eighties, she wrote *Izvestia*, and the newspaper forwarded her letter to me in California. On one of my junkets to Moscow I had a free weekend, and I took the night train to Pskov where I was met at the railways station by my two first cousins, Sergei and Valentina and their extended families with flashing cameras and a big sign that said "Welcome to Pskov." Bunny and I had visited Pskov and Papa's village in 1989 but failed to find anyone who remembered the family. Sergei and Valentina put together a sumptuous dinner with traditional Russian singing, countless toasts, and a video of the reunion. But the most touching and emotional experience was a visit to my grandfather's well-cared grave at a cemetery surrounding an old church undergoing renovation. At the grave site, the family had organized a picnic with *zakuska* and vodka, some of which was poured ceremoniously on my grandfather's grave. Someone said a short moving prayer, and we bent our heads in reverence to the family patriarch. I asked to see where my grandmother was buried, but was told that her grave could not be found, as part of the cemetery was destroyed by a bomb explosion during the retreat of the German army.

II

Bush Senior's presidency somehow left only a passing memory, largely because I was too preoccupied with my own life during his stay in the White House. I was busy traveling to Russia, and I was also doing research on a book that eventually came out in 2000. The first Persian Gulf War also remains a sketchy and passing incident. Bunny and I did not vote for George Bush in the 1988 elections, but we supported him in his decision to oust Saddam Hussein from Kuwait. It seemed like the right thing to do, considering that the war was against a tyrannical aggressor, was sanctioned by the United Nations, and was being paid mostly by Japan and Germany. For President Bush, the Gulf War was the most important event of his public life. For me, it was largely overshadowed by an event that was, in my opinion, far more significant than anything else that took place about the same time – the dissolution of the Soviet Union and the end of the Cold War. It's not surprising, therefore, that the four years of George Bush's presidency slipped by without leaving a more permanent mark. After all, one tends to remember only that which he or she wants to remember, and the past is never simply what one remembers of it.

President Bush was not re-elected, despite his immense popularity after the war. The huge deficit that he inherited from the Reagan administration remained a collar of thorns around his neck. The economy sputtered and then took a sudden dive, and the American people voted their pocketbooks to elect a Democrat. Bunny and I had great hopes for Bill Clinton. He was young, smart, better educated than most of our recent presidents. As governor of Arkansas he had mastered the art of politics, and he was also a "people person" who could charm almost anyone with whom he came in contact. But to most conservatives and self-righteous practitioners of the far right he was a dangerous upstart from the wrong side of the tracks, a representative of the pot-smoking, draft-dodging, womanizing counter culture whose ideas were in conflict with what they considered true American values. Their intense distaste for him was almost visceral.

They hated everything for which he stood. To make things worse, his wife, Hillary Rodham Clinton, a strong-willed and bright career woman who reminded me of my own "power house" daughter, did not fit the image of a pliant and unassuming First Lady. She was too outspoken, too committed to the task of righting the world's wrongs, too different from her predecessors to be a desirable consort. There was no usual honeymoon period for the Clintons. From almost the first week, the new president was hounded and vilified by an ideologically disconnected conservative juggernaut.

To defend themselves, the President and the First Lady constantly had to battle and rebut allegations of the conservative right wing. They were young and proud, and they made their share of mistakes by trying to avoid direct and unequivocal answers to Travelgate, Whitewater, and all the other alleged presidential indiscretions for which the hostile and embittered opposition tried to denounce them. The reaction of the opposition to the Monica Lewinsky affair was the culmination of the bitterness and resentment that had built up during their years in the White House. What Bill Clinton did was obviously wrong, immoral, indecent, and stupid. Bunny never forgave him for his indiscretion and breach of national trust. "He could have been such a great president," she often reminded me, "if only he had been able to control his sexual drive." She is, of course, right, but he did not deserve the impeachment that his antagonists meted out in a final paroxysm of vengeance and hate. His ill-fated liaison with Monica Lewinsky was a personal affair, not an affair of state, and Congress had no right to impeach the President, equivocation and perjury notwithstanding.

In the final analysis what is important to remember are not the political distractions and partisan battles waged in the name of conventionally accepted behavior, but what President Clinton actually accomplished during his eight difficult years in office. If we think about his presidency impartially, we will find that he did much better than most people are willing to give him credit. He kept us out of serious foreign entanglements, approving the Bosnia and Kosovo military engagements within the framework of the United Nations only after getting material support from our European allies and Russia. He turned the ailing economy around that he inherited from Bush Senior, and for the first time in many years of fiscal mismanagement delivered an annual surplus and reduction of the national debt. What was especially important to me because of my interest in the preservation of our wilderness, he refused to give in to special interests, designating vast portions of our pristine forests and open spaces as wilderness areas. Finally, what is often entirely overlooked was Bill Clinton's relations with post-Soviet Russia at a time when it could have easily turned fascist or communist again. He helped Yeltsin build not only a democratic Russia out of a bankrupt totalitarian regime, but also reached an agreement on thousands of nuclear weapons still scattered in silos throughout Russia and pointed toward the West during more than thirty years of turbulent Soviet-American relations.

When emergencies developed – and there were many – he would simply tell his aides: "Don't worry, I will speak to 'Ole Boris,' and we'll work it out." The end of the Cold War and the break-up of the Soviet Union was the most significant event of the second half of the Twentieth Century. Its realization had to be nursed and maintained steadily on course lest it deteriorate into political anarchy with nuclear implications that could be extremely serious and calamitous for the entire world. Bill Clinton understood the gravity of the Russian internal political situation and acted resolutely to keep the lines of communication open. I am not the only one to acknowledge Clinton's contribution to Russian-American relations after the collapse of Communism and the break-up of the Soviet Union. Strobe Talbott, Clinton's classmate at Oxford and Deputy Secretary of State during Clinton's two terms in office, wrote an outstanding book about the ups and downs of Clinton's personal diplomacy with Yeltsin.[32] As a Russian-American keenly interested in the democratization of Russia and the establishment of friendly Russian-American relations, I feel greatly indebted to President Clinton for his help in making that possible.

In September 1999, Bunny celebrated her seventieth birthday and, in November 2002, I reached the venerable old age of eighty. In both instances, our entire progeny gathered in Mill Valley for a family hike, family dinner and, in Bunny's case, for a gala surprise party attended by more than one hundred friends, some of whom came from as far as Los Angeles and the East Coast. Our daughter and I managed to create the surprise by bussing the guests to our eagle's nest on the mountain from downtown Mill Valley while Bunny was away for a few hours. But the early years of the twenty-first century were not without tragedy. My brother Nick died in July 2000. Bunny and I flew to Italy to spend a week with him and his family during the last months of his life. He had developed prostate cancer in the late 1990s that was in remission for a number of years, but kicked up again in 2000. He fought it with humor, impassive determination, and matchless control. He even did not hesitate to fly to Southeast Asia on business against the advice of his physician. He never returned. He died in a Singapore hospital of complications. In 2002, we had to live through another family tragedy. My brother Mike died in February 2002 in Ojai, California, where he and his wife retired after nearly half a century of research in the field of physics. He had a massive stroke from which he never recovered, leaving me to be the last Petroff alive out of that closely knit immigrant family that journeyed through China and Japan to a new life in the United States. Mike's premature death was a hard blow for me to accept. In the last ten years of his life we came closer to each other than we had ever been before. He was a kindred spirit in many things – politics, view on science, and life itself. I found it hard to come to terms with the fact that he was nearly five years younger, but died first. As always Bunny understood the extent of my sadness and helped me to alleviate the mental and psychological pain for which I am profoundly thankful to her.

There was one compensation to the grief and feeling of sudden estrangement – the discovery of Mama's relatives still living in Russia. During the summer of 2004 I met a young Russian historian at the Hoover Institution in Palo Alto who was working there on a research grant from the South Urals State University in Chelyabinsk. We became acquainted, and somewhere in the course of our many discussions about the history of the Russian Civil War I mentioned to him that my mother was from the Chelyabinsk region of Russia and that I had been trying to find relatives for a number of years, but never succeeded because the southern Urals region was off-limits to foreigners during the Soviet and early post-Soviet years. Three months after he returned home, out of the blue, I received an e-mail from him informing me that he had found Sonya Stepanova, grand-daughter of Mama's youngest brother, a divorcee still living in Troitsk where Mama was born. I called her on the telephone, found out that she had two sons, had recently graduated from law school, and was currently clerking for a judge of the regional court. In May, Busy and I flew first to Moscow and then Chelyabinsk where I delivered two lectures at the university, and then to Troitsk to spend a long weekend with Sonya and her family. After nearly seventy-five years of silence between the two branches of the Stepanov family – those who remained in Russia and those who escaped after the civil war -- I did not know what to expect from my newly discovered relatives. I found it difficult to control my emotions when I first saw Sonya at the Chelyanisk airport standing on the tarmac with a bouquet of flowers waiting for me. She was almost a carbon copy of my mother in her forties, a little taller and bigger in frame, but the family likeness was remarkable. The Stepanovs who remained in Russia after the revolution did not have an easy life. My grandfather died in 1927, the family was repressed and Sonya's grandfather, Mama's younger brother Alexander, was arrested in March 1938, during the height of the purges as an enemy of the people, allegedly for offering asylum to White guard officers. Like many others during the great purges he simply disappeared and the family never saw him again. In the 1950s during the thaw that came with Khrushchev, his son filed for his rehabilitation in order to improve his chances of getting into a good engineering school, and found out that he had been shot in 1938, his only affront to communism being that he had an older sister who married a White Army general. Mama's sister and two other brothers apparently anticipated the possibility of arrest and harsh treatment, changed their sir names to conceal their identities and, like many other Russians from wealthy families, disappeared into the wide expanse of the Soviet state.

The trip to Troitsk was an unexpected eye-opener. It not only allowed me to reestablish contact with Mama's family, but also gave me a much better insight into the role played by Russian entrepreneurs in the expansion of the Russian empire in the Nineteenth and early Twentieth centuries in western Siberia and along the empire's borders with what is today Kazakhstan and Uzbekistan. Like the Crockers, the Hills and the Stanfords in California, the Stepanovs were a pioneer family who arrived in Troitsk when it was still a stop on the Silk Route and a front line military outpost from which expeditions ventured south and southeast into Central Asia. Over the years, the Stepanovs, like many other settlers, built a commercial empire on which pre-revolutionary Russia depended for its flour, lumber and railroads. Rummaging in the city archive and the regional museum for clues about the early years of the Stepanov family, I found old photographs of the family homestead and their steam-powered flour mill, a variety of commercial papers, and even documents ordering the expropriation of their real estate holdings by the Soviet government in 1919. My favorite document of the new Soviet power in Troitsk pertaining to Mama's family was the implausible and bizarre Order No. 2, dated 13 August 1919. According to it, "all musicians residing in Troitsk and its surroundings" were to "appear on August 16 at the Kommissariat's headquarters located in the Stepanov home on the corner of Monastyrskii and Markov streets to register and receive pertinent documents." The house still stands today on the same corner amidst an overgrown cover of trees and sad-looking bushes that must have been planted many years ago; it is the house where Mama was born. It has been abandoned by the government, a conspicuous example of a dysfunctional municipal system brought to its demise by the hemorrhaging Soviet state. It is a large two-storied commanding structure with a widow's walk, a windowed basement built out of local granite, large intricately carved windows on the first and second floors, and a spacious backyard containing a stable, a garage which I understand housed a Studebaker run-about, a flower garden and what was at one time probably an orchard with apple and pear trees. The widow's walk is gone, the window frames have lost their luster, the imposing granite entrance looks like someone had used a sledge hammer to make the stone stairway a walkway for disabled persons, and the roof has been patched many times by galvanized iron and copper plate. Sonya told me that a local entrepreneur had purchased it recently from the government and, in a true spirit of the new capitalist awakening that has gripped Russia and its newly emancipated citizens, plans to restore and convert it into separate apartments.

It has been a long life, and as I look back at it, I cannot but notice that the world of today is very different from the one into which I was born. Gone are the colonial empires and the arrogance and exploitation with which they subdued the natives of Asia, Africa, and the Middle East. Gone are the post World War I "isms" – fascism, communism and Japanese militarism. They failed to deliver the utopias they promised and instead turned into ugly and immoral tyrannies that had to be liquidated by a policy of resolute containment and application of force. The bi-polar world of the second half of the Twentieth century has been supplanted by a single all-powerful United States that has emerged after the collapse of the Soviet Union. Except for China that may at some future date begin to offer political and economic competition – the verdict is by no means clear yet – we are the only true global player remaining today. Most of the world has also moved closer toward democracy. The "end of history"[33] that Francis Fukuyama had led us to expect after the collapse of the Soviet dictatorship is still beyond the world's political horizon, but impressive advances in democratic governance and political pluralism have come to Russia, Eastern Europe, a large part of South and Central America and east and south Asia. The world is now a global economy with goods and services moving efficiently with a minimum of interference from recalcitrant dictators and uncooperative nation states. Communication is instantaneous. I can talk to my editor in Russia by dialing his home or office whenever I please. Via the internet I can also transfer whole files, important photographs and complex graphs and schedules almost anywhere in the world, and, not the least of it, I can access my brokerage account twenty-four hours each day from my home in Mill Valley, California or any other place while traveling in the United States or abroad.

The social framework of United States and many parts of the developed and developing world has also undergone a profound and irrevocable institutional transformation. The role of women in our society has been vastly improved since World War II. Today, women raise families and compete with men in business, government, and academia, and many reach the zenith of their professions to become presidents of Fortune 500 companies and renowned universities. Some become prominent legislators, high court justices, and heads of government. Racial prejudice, although still in existence, has been largely tamed by civil rights legislation, far-sighted activism of the NACP and the Anti Defamation League. African Americans today are government officials, community leaders, presidents of universities and large corporations. So are Jewish-Americans who as late as the 1950s were still barred by "gentlemen's agreements" from the more fashionable and desirable districts of our cities and suburbs. An even more important measure of social development in the past fifty years has been the transformation of a large number of our people into open minded thinkers and doers who recognize social progress for what it actually is. They are not willing to go back to the inequities that were previously pervasive, nor are they willing to bow to the crude political and social rhetoric of arch conservatives who, under the guise of trying to reinstate standards of moral behavior, want to take us "back to the good old days." Our world today is less rigid, more fluid, more flexible, and our relationships are now predominantly based not on questionable beliefs and prejudice, but on knowledge and the dictates of public interest. Advances in technology, hygiene, medicine, transportation, and delivery of information have also vastly improved our lives.

The advances did not come without a certain amount of painful mischief and unintended consequences that have created complications in international relations and our daily lives. In the political realm, decolonization, often along ethnic and religious lines, created a collection of underdeveloped nation states warring internally and with each other. The collapse of the Soviet Union and the emergence of the United States to the position of world dominance have undermined the legitimacy conferred on U.S. power and leadership during the Cold War by a Europe no longer in need of American military support. Western Europe no longer feels it has to kowtow to Washington and its power brokers. Globalization, although desirable in the long run, has in the short run contributed to the loss of American, west European and Japanese jobs to countries with significantly lower labor costs. Advances in science and technology begot cheap habit-forming drugs, biological weapons of mass destruction, and the threat of nuclear armament proliferation by terrorist networks and rogue states. In the arena of social change, we now experience higher rates of divorce, breakdown of family, and urban crime. The unintended consequences are hardly restricted to the examples cited by me. Reformers, academics, and pundits have been inventorying them and offering a plethora of solutions, some well-founded, some less applicable, and some decidedly dubious.

But if we put everything together and construct a comprehensive and truthful balance sheet, I think we will have to come to the conclusion that, in spite of the cries and detractions of the doom-sayers, the world of today is a much better place than it was when I was born. The lives of the vast majority of people throughout the world, sadly except for sub-Sahara Africa, have vastly improved in the past eighty years. In the United States, Europe, the Americas, and many parts of East and South Asia the improvement has been towering, especially for the middle classes, and not only in living standards, but also in the freedom of expression. Today, people are freer, safer, and have greater access to information and participation in civic activities. The changes that took place in the twentieth century have been constructive and profound. I had never thought I would some day live in such material luxury and freedom of movement and expression.

III

I, too, have changed. Some of the change came about as a result of age, experience, maturity. Some resulted from exposure to varying environments. Some arose as a consequence of reading and philosophical deliberations. In the Preface to my memoir I noted that *Life Journey* was a story of six stages of my life; in fact, they were more than stages. They were six lives in one, because they were so distinct, so indispensably disconnected, and so idiosyncratic. Born to Russian parents in China, I was brought up as a Russian. Papa and Mama had not yet completely lost hope of returning to their native land, and raised us during their early years in exile as they normally would have had they remained in Russia. I spoke, wrote and read in Russian, played with other Russian-speaking children, attended Russian Orthodox church services, recited Russian poetry, celebrated Russian national holidays, and dreamt that one day I would travel to St. Petersburg where Papa would undoubtedly be a member of the Russian government. I might as well have lived in Moscow, St. Petersburg, or some provincial Russian city

We moved to Japan when I was nearly eleven, and everything changed almost overnight.

From the Russian environment of Mukden and Shanghai we found ourselves in the international surroundings of expatriate Yokohama, in a new aggregate of social and cultural conditions that govern life and human behavior. Our American teachers at St. Joseph College became our role models, our friends were the children of American, British, and French expatriates, we read English-language newspapers and American magazines, watched Hollywood films, listened to the latest American popular music, and rubbed elbows with American and European nationals at the Hachioji Swim Club and the Yokohama Country and Athletic Club. I continued to speak Russian with my parents, but among ourselves we spoke English – American English. By the time I had reached fourteen, I had become a different person from what I had been in Mukden and Shanghai, and the transformation was irrevocable. In an effort to keep up with the transformation, Papa and Mama also changed. They lived a bifurcated life of socializing with their Russian friends and with the English-speaking parents of our friends. Mama mastered English, speaking it with a pronounced German accent, while Papa stopped reading émigré newspapers in favor of the Japan Times and Advertiser and the Christian Science Monitor.

This international and expatriate setting continued until the Japanese bombed Pearl Harbor and war was declared. For nearly four years, until the end of the war and the occupation by the United States forces, we lived in a state of cautious seclusion and constantly fluctuating anxiety, hoping that the war would end soon. Gone were our contacts with the American and British residents, gone were the American magazines and films that described life in the United States. The emphasis was now on learning Japanese as without it one could no longer exist in Japan. Under the pressure of false patriotism, and super-nationalist rhetoric, English – the lingua franca of the Orient – disappeared from daily usage on billboards, at railway stations, and business firms. The personal goal was to survive--especially after Japan began to suffer defeat. To survive, one had to speak Japanese, and this meant one had to adapt to the new conditions. For me, it was also a time of meditation and serious thinking about the world and the exigencies of life. What else could one be doing when there was nothing else to do as the bombs fell almost every day after November 1944. The occupation of Japan by U.S. forces was, therefore, a welcome diversion. It put an end to the isolation and brought us back into the stream of relations with the Americans, this time on a much more intense basis than prior to the war. We now socialized with our American co-workers: officers, GIs, and civilian employees of the occupation. They accepted us as their own, and shared their war-time experiences and their family histories willingly and without any reluctance. It was a complete immersion into the American culture

In May 1947, my brother Nick and I left Japan, arriving in San Francisco on an immigrant visa. As new arrivals and immigrants, we were suddenly thrust into the crucible of Russian immigrant life among Papa's and Mama's friends and civil war colleagues who arrived in the United States many years earlier. Except for a few who moved to the suburbs and became partially Americanized, almost every one of the Russian immigrants living in San Francisco continued to follow the precepts of the Russian culture they brought with them to America. They spoke Russian, --some never learned English—shopped at Russian-owned stores, read Russian émigré newspapers, belonged to various émigré social and cultural organizations, and had a very limited understanding of American politics and social life. The second generation, that grew up already in the United States and received their education in American public schools, spoke English among themselves, but were only superficially Americanized, They, too, were raised in a predominantly émigré culture of their parents. They were the product of the slow and sometimes harsh process of acculturation that was part of the American experience from one generation to another. They retained many of their parent's attitudes and views on American life. The melting pot theory that sociologists used to explain the process of Americanization did not apply to them. They remained a clearly defined part of an ethnic mosaic that made up the American social and political scene. After years of expatriate experience in Japan and intense Americanization during more than a year and a half of the occupation, my brothers and I found it very difficult to become part of this immigrant assemblage. It was not surprising, therefore, that within less than two years we escaped it to pursue our own objectives. Nick left for southern California, and, later, for the high desert of the state of Washington, Mike found a home within the confines of the Department of Physics at the University of California, Berkeley, and I left for New York.

It would take another three years before I could legally become a U.S. citizen, but I never felt like an immigrant. I spoke faultless American English without an accent, and was accepted by everyone I came in contact as an American. Using New York as a base I explored New England, the South, and the Mid-west. By the time I was called in to take my citizenship exam to became an American citizen I had crisscrossed America several times, seen the good and the bad of my chosen country from a number of vantage points, and probably knew as much about America as most educated Americans. And then, I married not an immigrant but a native with roots in pre-Revolutionary America, a bright and curious New Englander from an upper middle class family who introduced me to her friends and college classmates, helped me find my way through the vicissitudes of life, and steered me through the difficult spots of parenthood. After ten years in San Francisco and San Jose in an environment isolated from the Russian immigrant community, we settled in Mill Valley, one of the most charming tree-lined suburbs of San Francisco with a distinct small town American identity, took on an active role in the community's social and cultural life, and raised four children amidst a well-educated and politically conscious populace.

In Mill Valley, we saw our four children grow to adulthood in the culturally and politically difficult climate of the Vietnam War and Watergate. We saw them graduate from college, and then settle down and start their own families. Having fulfilled our parental obligations, we now were free to pursue projects we dreamt about, but never had enough time to undertake. I went back to school and earned a master's degree in history, and authored three books that were published. Bunny joined the Docent Council of the deYoung Fine Arts Museum in San Francisco, and we began traveling extensively. As of this writing, we visited forty-two countries and all of the continents.

I also underwent other changes that were not directly influenced by the environment in which I found myself throughout my life. These were changes that came about as a result of philosophical and political deliberations that I came face to face in the course of every day life.

I was never very religious. I was a questioner, a sceptic from the early years of my life, but we attended church and followed the precepts of Eastern Orthodox Christianity, although more out of habit than any deep conviction. Because there was no Russian Orthodox church in Yokohama until 1937, periodically, we even attended services at the Episcopalian church. But I was drifting away from participation in organized religion. Christian faith, with all its rituals, myths that had been transformed into doctrine, prohibitions, and admonitions did not bring the kind of fulfillment that I was looking for. Eastern Orthodoxy and Catholicism seemed to me to be medieval in their structure and direction -- not suited to life in the Twentieth century. Protestantism, in its many forms, placed too much emphasis on the Bible which I refused to accept as an answer to everything. The whole concept of an all-knowing and omnipotent God appeared to me to be contrived, and created by humans to explain what was really not explainable. I was slowly becoming an agnostic with a more secular view of life. I refused to accept religion on faith alone. By the time I reached age thirty I had opted out of organized religion, although I had not yet completely resolved the question of whether or not there was one supernatural being to whom we owed our existence. That took another ten or so years when Bunny and I started raising a family and began thinking how to structure our children's moral and religious training. There were a number of determinants that influenced my thinking. My parents also were not very religious, and did not demand that we attend church regularly. Like me, Papa was a questioner with a fundamentally analytical approach to knowledge. In his search for the reality of existence, he even considered humanism and the possibility of human experience and achievement rather than faith in a revealed religion. In college, I took anthropology and geology for my science requirements. I did a lot of reading in cultural anthropology, which I believe caused me to form a more pantheistic view of the universe. *Haseiden* (The Temple of the Eight Wise Men) in Honmoku may have also left a lasting impression about the need to tolerate all creeds, and accept the reality that Christ was a historical figure –a teacher of morality—not a divinity. Visiting *Haseiden* was an experience I was never able to extricate from my mind.

In my forties and early fifties I also changed my attitude toward the Vietnam War. It was a hard and disturbing decision to make. With my strong anti-Communist upbringing I found it difficult to disregard the surge of Communist expansion, but the war was going on too long, and becoming grotesque and barbaric. Bunny and our two oldest children, who were old enough to identify with the anti-war demonstrations, debated the war daily. Slowly but surely I was moving to the side of the anti-war majority. I am not certain what caused the change, but I suspect that the killing by the national guard of four students at Kent State University in May1970 was what tipped the balance in favor of an anti-war position. The arguments offered by Paul and Buzy, who brought their strong anti-war feelings home, reinforced any doubts that I may have had. Also, I was doing a lot of reading on the history of the Vietnam war which convinced me that the domino theory was not applicable to Vietnam because Vietnam –communist or otherwise—would never accept Chinese domination

The transitions from one life to another were remarkably painless. I was able to adapt myself to new circumstances in most cases without suffering any psychological trauma. As I look back, I can single out three major reasons for this. First, of course, was the guidance and direction that all three of us children received from Papa and Mama. They were able to instill strong feelings of independence and recognition of what is right and wrong. Through discussions and by example they also succeeded in fostering an approach to life that was essentially analytical. We were conditioned from a very early age to collect the facts, analyze them, and then only react rationally, not emotionally and dramatically. This made the transitions easier and more harmonious. The nearly fourteen years of life in Japan, in an expatriate culture with strong American influences, also played a crucial role in making the transitions we had to make upon arrival in the United States. The Japanese experience gave us a proficiency in language and idiom, and made it much easier to accept the American culture with which we were already familiar. Our position was very different from immigrants arriving in America without language and only a limited knowledge of what life in America is going to be. Finally, I have to include my wife, Jane Amidon Petroff – Bunny to her friends and family—as a crucial positive influence in my development and ease with which I was able to adapt to new circumstances. From the very beginning of our fifty-four-year-relationship of marriage she created a family atmosphere of cohesion and support in grappling with the numerous transitions that I had to undertake as a husband, parent, breadwinner, retiree. Politically and socially, she was a little to the left of me, but as time went on we moved in each other's direction, resolving our differences permanently. We were extremely fortunate. Despite our different backgrounds we had an awful lot in common. We liked the same things –art, music, an informal life style, the outdoors, and our political preferences were almost identical. We were also not afraid to experiment and recognize that tradition for the sake of tradition had no place in an environment characterized by the decline of authority and rise in secular thinking.

This made our decision to opt out of organized religion and the structuring of our children's moral education along secular humanist lines so much easier. Bunny enjoyed travel as I did, and, when I decided to retire and devote my life to intellectual pursuits, she encouraged me and lent support to the projects that I undertook. Her love and warm support of my years in retirement made them the happiest years of my life, at peace with myself and the world around me.

POSTSCRIPT

In all things it is better to hope than to despair.
Johann Wolfgang Goethe

Except for some family desiderata that spilled over to the 21st century I had hoped to end my memoir with the 20th century. Bunny and I greeted the new century with such hope and exaltation that it did not seem there was any necessity for additional comment or critique. Unfortunately, the exaltation did not last. Vice President Gore, whom we supported and voted for in 2000, was not elected our next president; the election was stolen from him. Instead, George W. Bush, the eldest son of George Bush Sr., became the forty-third President of the United States. The new president won the presidency not through the age-old election process prescribed by the constitution, but by a five-to-four decision of the Supreme Court on a controversy that developed because of a malfunctioning in the Florida voting procedure. For Bunny and me, Bush's election and reelection for a second term were dark days in American history.

Billed as a centrist and compassionate conservative, Bush brought with him to the White House a cabal of arch conservatives, hard-line hawks from the Reagan administration, evangelical activists, and a bevy of ambitious administrators willing and ready to enforce the neo-conservative agenda articulated by Vice President Richard Cheney and his neo-conservative support team. Within months of the inauguration, our conjecture turned real. The administration repudiated the Kyoto protocol on the environment and declared Clinton's signature on the International Criminal Court null and void. According to the president whose unilaterist instincts were never in doubt, we were just not going to get involved in any international agreements that he and his aides felt were not in the interest of American business. Many administrative directives on the environment were also rescinded. Especially regrettable was the reopening of lands designated by President Clinton as wilderness areas for business exploitation and motorized public use.

But the most dramatic reversal came in the field of foreign relations following the terrorist attack of September 11, 2001.

I missed the initial television broadcast describing the attack. I was on my way to the Hoover Institution Archive at Stanford University, and heard about the attack on my car radio. Except for statements of profound indignation, there was no immediate response from those who were at the archive that morning. Everyone was so stunned by what had happened that there was a strange and eerie silence, as if by mutual agreement. At 9:30 AM, Pacific Time, the University sounded a terrorist alert. The entire complex – archive and offices – was evacuated, and the historic Hoover tower and adjacent buildings were cordoned off as a precaution against, what the campus police called, a possible act of terror. Suddenly, some fifty or sixty Hoover associates, foreign scholars, researchers and staff found themselves on a grassy plot outside the Hoover tower speculating on who masterminded the attack. One senior Hoover fellow with connections in Washington was convinced that an attack of such magnitude could not have been carried out without the help of a hostile foreign government, most probably Iraq. I found the comment somewhat flippant, obviously influenced by the growing belief of many neo-conservatives in Washington that the Iraqi regime was the main source of trouble in the Middle East. The remark was an early harbinger of things to come. The neo-conservative leadership in Washington was chomping at the bit to put the blame on Sadam Hussein, the brutal dictator of Iraq, and use the occasion to occupy Iraq.

The suicide attack on the World Trade Center and the Pentagon on September 11 was by no means the first terrorist assault on American people and property. On April 18, 1983, a Moslem suicide bomber attacked the U.S. Embassy in Beirut killing 63 people, and on October 23, 1983, 241 U.S. marines were killed in Lebanon by a suicide truck bomber who succeeded in penetrating their encampment. Over the ensuing years, there were other terrorist attacks that resulted in American casualties, but there were two significant differences between all previous attacks and the attack of September 11. They took place in remote corners of the world that many Americans never heard of. The Nine-Eleven assault was on home soil, in New York City and the nation's capital – two symbolic centers of American economic and political power. For most Americans, the attack was the most horrifying event they had ever experienced. It was also not something they read about or heard on the radio. They actually watched it on television in real time as the twin towers burned and hundreds of innocent citizens flung themselves to their deaths from the towers' upper floors. It was an excruciatingly emotional experience for everyone: the unfortunate occupants of the towers, the police and firemen who arrived with help, the neighbors and casual passers-by, the millions of stunned viewers who watched it on television, and the public servants whose task was to protect and defend the nation.

Bunny and I flew to New York two weeks later to spend a week with our son Gregory and his family in Westport, Connecticut, and took an afternoon off to visit the still smoldering site in lower Manhattan. The burned out and decapitated steel carcasses of the World Trade Center were still standing, but the demolition crews were already working to take them down. Surrounded by armed National Guardsmen to keep the public out, the violated ruins looked foreboding, almost surrealistic, like something out of a post-World War I expressionist painting portraying the shocking destruction of war. It was not the first time I saw devastation on such a severe scale. In bombed out Tokyo and Yokohama it was horizontal, sometimes stretching as far as the eye could see. Here, among the skyscrapers of lower Manhattan, it was vertical, massive, localized, a shocking reminder of what can happen to an undefended urban center in the event of war. Even though the attack had taken place two weeks earlier, the air around the smoldering ruins was still fetid, saturated with dust and gaseous refuse. The surrounding grounds and buildings were covered by ash and debris. The stench from the still smoldering remains of rubber, plastic, artificial fabric and burned furniture was overpowering. It reminded me of the terrible smell permeating the bombed out streets of Tokyo after the air raids in 1945. Along the rim, pinned to a wire fence surrounding ground zero and to buildings on the periphery, were hundreds of photographs of innocent victims, firemen, policemen, messages from friends and relatives, and bouquets of flowers, testifying to the grief and feelings of sympathy for those who died in the attack, an unsung requiem for the World Trade Center and all those who worked and died within its walls. We were both deeply touched by the experience of seeing the devastation brought about by the terrorist attack. Bunny, especially, found it hard to accept. For her, as for many Americans who had never witnessed destruction and loss of life on such a massive scale, what she saw that day in lower Manhattan left an indelible impression of the ravages of war.

The reaction to the attack was swift and powerful. President Bush reassured the stunned nation that he would do everything possible to insure the safety of Americans against future attacks by terrorists.

Security at airports was tightened as soon as they were reopened, a new Department of Homeland Security was established to coordinate the activities of the intelligence services with Immigration and Naturalization, the Border Patrol, the Coast Guard, and the various state and municipal security organs. The Treasury Department began closing down Islamic foundations suspected of funneling funds to terrorist organizations. Even the decision to go after the Taliban and close the al Queda terrorist training camps in Afghanistan made sound sense. President Bush acted decisively with genuine compassion for the enormity of the human tragedy engendered by the attack. The vast majority of Americans – both Republicans and Democrats – praised him for his leadership and stood behind him. The civilized world offered sympathy and condemned the terrorists for the horrible crime they committed. The French newspaper *Le Monde* dramatically underscored the feeling of compassion with a four word headline "We are all Americans." But beyond that, his response to the Nine Eleven incident was a poorly conceived over-reaction that should have never been allowed to take place. Congress hastily passed what became known as the Patriot Act – a shameful repeal of protection guaranteed by the Fourth Amendment. The Justice Department began holding prisoners indefinitely in secret detention without access to lawyers and disclosure of why they were being held. Especially excessive was the decision to send Taliban and al Queda prisoners to Guantanamo where they were denied the protection of the Geneva Conventions, interrogated constantly, humiliated, and held incommunicado under conditions of maximum surveillance and extreme stress.

The over-reaction became even more implausible when a cabal of neo-conservatives with messianic aims to democratize the world -- Richard Perle, Paul Wolfowitz, Douglas Feith, and company – decided to link up Middle East terrorism with Iraq and its brutal dictator, Saddam Hussein. They had tried to convince Bush Senior in 1990 during the first Gulf War to capture Baghdad and remove Hussein, but the president refused to go beyond the mandate extended by the United Nations, and confined the war to the liberation of Kuwait. In 1992, Paul Wolfowitz authored a new memorandum on the Middle East urging President Bush Sr. to remove Saddam Hussein and establish a pro-American democratic Iraq, but the president was not re-elected, and Bill Clinton showed little interest in it. Now, with the groundswell of emotionalism brought about by the Nine Eleven tragedy overtaking all rational thinking, they went to work first on Vice President Cheney and then on the president himself. Appealing to the president's overblown evangelical fervor and predilection to see the world in terms of "good" and "evil", they declared Saddam Hussein the cause of all evil and instability in the Middle East. Remove him, they said, and establish a permanent pro-American state in Iraq from which we can deal with the rest of the Middle East without having to worry about the collapse of the Saudi monarchy and the stoppage of oil deliveries for our gas-guzzling consumers in the United States. Saddam is a tyrant; the whole world will be glad to see him toppled. With him gone, we will build a model Muslim government from which we can democratize the entire Arab World. His father's advisors – the more cautious Scowcroft and Baker – went on record against such a risk laden strategy, but the more reckless and inexperienced George W. fell for it. He was certain that removing Saddam Hussein would win him a prominent place in history and secure his re-election in 2004.

The rest is history. Unable to secure the approval of the UN Security Council and without serious thought about the consequences of military occupation, we began to plan for a unilateral military campaign against Iraq, hoodwinking the American public to support the war by insisting at first that Saddam had weapons of mass destruction, and when none were found, by trying to link al Queda with the Saddam Hussein regime in Iraq. We're tough, our hawks sang in unison, we don't need the help of the United Nations and the sclerotic nation states of old Europe, besides the spirit of democracy is on our side. The United Kingdom did commit one division, and a number of minor players sent a token force, making the "Alliance of the Willing", a last minute attempt to give our action a degree of international respectability.

The military phase of the campaign was brilliantly executed and went remarkably well for the American and British armies. With but a few exceptions, Saddam's legions simply dropped their weapons, changed to civilian clothes, and disappeared into the shadows of the hot desert and the crowded cities of central and northern Iraq. Intense missile bombardment and superior military technology allowed us to reach Baghdad in three weeks, but they did not prepare the misguided leadership and the American people for the long-term task of rejuvenating and democratizing the devastated nation. No one among President Bush's immediate advisors anticipated how difficult and costly it will be to rebuild the damaged infrastructure and to provide power, water, and oil to the traumatized citizens of the larger cities. No one who promoted the war had foreseen the looting, the sabotage, the violence, and breakdown of security that came with the end of Saddam's rule. No one expected Saddam's loyalists to reappear as urban guerrillas menacing our convoys and killing our soldiers, nor did they anticipate the angry reaction of the Muslim world. Our war planners – Dick Cheney and company – had thought we would enter Baghdad as liberators who had freed the Muslim world of a universally hated dictator. Instead, we found ourselves in the position of hated invaders scorned and vilified from Indonesia to Morocco, across the broad expanse of the Moslem world. The spin is that we emancipated the Iraqi people from a terrible dictator and that we are making progress, but the facts on the ground tell a different story. We urgently need help from the international community of nations, but our inflexible president does not want to admit that he made a serious mistake by acting without the support of the United Nations. In campaign-style rhetoric for domestic and foreign consumption, he and his lieutenants continue to pledge "no retreat" in the war against terror with belligerent declarations meant to strike fear in the minds of Iraq's neighbors, and add powder to the anxieties and frustrations of American citizens at home.

We are into the second term of the Bush presidency. No other presidency in my lifetime has been as disastrous to the American people. President Bush has failed in Iraq because he and his advisors acted precipitously and failed to foresee the consequences of the Iraq campaign. Despite the formation of an interim government, national elections, a fragile constitution, and the beefed-up surge of our troops, the war in Iraq goes on without any prospects of a possible end. Our casualties in the past six months have diminished appreciably, but the slaughter of innocent Iraqi men, women and children continues without any end in sight due to suicide bombings and a civil war that has sprang up between competing Shia factions seeking regional control. Exacerbating the political situation is the struggle between the Kurds and the Arabs for the control of Kirkuk and the oil fields of the north.

Our attempt to gain a secure outpost in the Muslim lands of the Middle East is clearly in jeopardy, and it does not look like there is an easy solution, short of tripling our troop deployment and increasing our financial commitment beyond the level of what the nation could sustain. I don't want to end my eighty-four year chronicle on a pessimistic note, much less on a condemnation of America, a shining ideal throughout my entire life. America has been awfully good to me and my family, and I don't want to see it mired again in another long-term confrontation from which it is difficult to disengage without suffering a domestic trauma and losing international respect.

But I distinguish between America and the radical ideologues who captured our government to pursue a neo-conservative agenda that is in contradiction to America's national interest. I condemn them for starting a war without any serious thought of its cost and consequences. We could have avoided it. For more than fifty years we collaborated successfully with Europe to prevent the expansion of the Soviet Union, a balancing act considerably more difficult and risk-laden than any conflict with Saddam Hussein. It was a strategy of containment that every president since Harry Truman followed scrupulously. George W. Bush also emphasized its effectiveness when he first ran for president, saying that he was against the idea of "nation building" and promiscuous use of force. And then, Nine-Eleven happened, and we suddenly scrapped our proven strategy of containment and successful cooperation with Europe, and proclaimed a hare-brain policy of "unilateral preemption" on the urging of a small clique of radical hawks and neo-conservatives who had infiltrated the higher circles of our government. Never in the history of the United States had a small group of radical zealots – a self-styled government within a government – done so much damage to our foreign policy and our relations with the rest of the world.

I was against the war because I foresaw that it would stir up a hornet's nest of Arab extremism and set the entire Muslim world against us. If our leaders had read more history, they would have recognized that this was bound to happen, as acts of terrorism are invariably a reaction to inconsistent and unsound policy. It was rampant during the French and Russian revolutions, the Spanish Civil War, the Irish and Chechen struggle for independence, and the African wars of the second half of the Twentieth century. It was even a factor during our own War of Independence. Encouraged by a radical Muslim ideology, it's not surprising that it also became an integral part of our experience in the Middle East. Widespread Middle Eastern terror is a reaction against a failed foreign policy that has become dangerously tilted toward Israel and the support of corrupt Arab regimes that refuse to be democratized. Calling Muslim urban guerrillas murderers, nihilistic lunatics, and evil killers who hate America for its culture and freedom, as President Bush reminds us constantly, will not eliminate terrorism. Such moralistic rhetoric inflames the mujahadeen to commit even more acts of terrorism. To pale the fire of terrorism and eventually bring it under control, we have to go beyond security measures to the root causes that make killers out of marginalized Muslim nationalists and fanatic true believers who firmly believe that they have a sacred duty to undermine an American foreign policy that decries their aspirations, just like their fathers had done in the1980s against the Russians in Afghanistan and their grandfathers and great grandfathers against British rule before that.

The establishment of more intense security measures with the help of improved intelligence and the searching out and killing of suspected terrorists will not put a stop to terrorism, nor will the enactment of legislation to protect our borders and way of life. They may reduce the number of terrorist incidents and therefore should be undertaken, but they will not eliminate the use of terror by extremist groups seeking the end of occupation and a long-term change in American foreign policy What is needed is a new and more imaginative and productive American foreign policy that recognizes the discontent of the Muslim world and the levers that trigger and encourage the radicalization of its true believers. President Bush and the neo-conservative elite that surrounds him are incapable of crafting such a policy. They are too caught up in the dialectic of good and evil and the geopolitical rationale of the war. Only a new administration can regain the respect of our allies and, with their support, reach out to the moderate Muslim world with a foreign policy that is committed to the settlement of the Israeli-Palestinian conflict, the democratization of the corrupt and despotic states of the Middle East, and an end to the occupation of Iraq. Without the help of our traditional allies and a moderate Muslim leadership committed to the eradication of extremists we will not see the end of terror.

As I look deeper at what has taken place during the Bush stewardship and where it is taking us, I have great concerns for our nation. Fifty-five years ago I pledged my allegiance to a nation that I considered the most perfect model of sound governance and impartial administration of justice. I found especially attractive America's observance of separation of church and state and the doctrine of checks and balances. I was impressed with America's adherence to the rule of law and to the internationally accepted practice since the end of World War II of not going to war unless attacked. At the level of everyday behavior of our civil servants, I found their openness and truthfulness an inimitable virtue that I never expected to find in government. All of these democratic institutions and traditions have been seriously compromised by the Bush administration after the Nine Eleven attack. Almost every week, we are reminded by the self-righteous president that the war on terror is a struggle of biblical proportions, and that the good will triumph over evil if we persevere in bringing democracy and our Christian values to the Middle East.

Implicitly and explicitly, the doctrine of checks and balances has been pushed aside because Congress is polarized and congressional power has been vastly reduced by executive power with the help of carefully crafted propaganda and spin. The doctrine of checks and balances has been further compromised by the appointment of conservative judges to the Supreme Court who think like the president does on crucial questions affecting our lives. For the first time in one hundred years of our history we went to war before we were attacked, and our leaders are threatening to do it again if Syria and Iran do not fall in line and accept the Bush-constructed *Pax Americana* in the Middle East. What is perhaps most tragic and alarming is that in the interest of gaining intelligence on terrorist activity we have desecrated our established code of ethics. We allowed our interrogators in Guantanamo and Abu Chraib to use dogs, sleep deprivation, confinement of prisoners in fetal positions, beatings, partial suffocation, and sexual humiliation, all in violation of the Geneva Conventions, rules of war, and our long-established American tradition of human rights. We have acted no better than other brutal dictators who have justified the use of torture by their intelligence services on the grounds that it was necessary to rid the nation of enemies, a sad and immoral inference that the end justified the means. As to openness and truthfulness of our leadership, the Bush regime has been the most secretive, uncommunicative, and concealing U.S. administration in my lifetime, dedicated to the idea that what takes place in the higher levels of government is not the people's business, a dangerous tenet that we know from history can lead a democracy to authoritarian and totalitarian rule.

Some students of American history have ascribed the behavior of the Bush administration to the fact that we are currently in our conservative cycle and that the pendulum is bound to swing back before too long. I hope they are right, even though demographics and geography are not on the side of those who seek moderation and reform. Evangelicals, hard-line war hawks, and Wilsonian neo-conservatives who think they can democratize the entire world have infiltrated the upper rungs of our government and deceitfully created an electorate that fell for a carefully crafted political message based not on economic and social reality, but on spurious ideology and dissemination of anxiety and fear. It will take time before the gullible electorate recognizes that it has been deceived. That is a sad consideration, but I have not given up hope that a spark of reason will somehow lighten up the sky and bring this great country back to its senses to show the world that the Bush presidency was an anomaly, an aberration, which like McCarthyism, will be disowned and laid to rest.

I did not mean to end my eighty-five year chronicle with a tiresome tirade, but I love my country and feel strongly that I have to say something about what transpired during the twilight years of my life. I don't want to see the United States bogged down in another Viet Nam quagmire that will continue to drain our human and material resources and sap the energy and spirit of the American people. Even more important, I don't want to see the undermining of the principles that have made this country great. The concept that there has to be separation of church and state for the nation to function impartially, the doctrine of checks and balances applying to our three branches of government, the rule of law that safeguards human rights, and the transparency and openness of our government have served America well, and should be protected, not debased. Nor do I want to see a further escalation of foreign negative attitudes toward the United States because of the way the Bush administration pursued the war in Iraq and handled detainees and prisoners it incarcerated in Guantanamo and Abu Chraib or rendered them to less ethical regimes for interrogation under conditions of torture and unscrupulous intimidation. In many parts of the world today, our leaders are looked upon as arrogant, hypocritical, self indulgent, and selfishly calculating to achieve objectives that suit only our geopolitical and domestic business goals. A recent Pew Survey in forty-four countries has gone even farther in its assessment of unfavorable attitudes towards America. According to it, the negative attitude now applies not only to our leaders but to the American people. There may be an element of exaggeration in that indictment, but it is not too far off the mark from the truth. Besides, perception is what really counts when we try to understand why our image abroad has suffered so drastically since George W. Bush became president. I want our image to be positive, constructive, characterized by respect and reverence, the kind of image America projected when I first arrived in San Francisco sixty years ago and pledged my allegiance to the United States. Being an American then was something special. America could do no wrong. It had saved the world from fascism and militarism, and was considered a shining example to be emulated by the rest of the world. In the years that followed, the United States stood firm against Communism and was universally looked upon as leader and defender of democracy during the Cold War. I want to see that admiration restored for all to see again. I want my country to be a respected world leader, exercising its power not with force and intimidation, but intelligently with compassion, diplomacy, and through a collective security system which, for all its weaknesses, has more to offer than the brute use of unilateral force promoted by the radical clique that has hijacked the inner circles of our government.

I believe reason will replace miscalculation and obliquity. By electing a new leadership in the fall of 2008, the American electorate has recognized that we must end the Iraq undertaking and the debasement of our core principles. I have not lost hope in the bright future of America. The Bush and Reagan eras have come to an ignominious end. As in 1932, when President Roosevelt stated that "The day of enlightened administration has come," it has also now come in 2008.

END NOTES

[1] Palm leaves were not available in Russia. Russia used pussy willow branches instead, and Palm Sunday was known as *Verbnoye Voskresenie* (Pussy Willow Sunday).

[2] Serge P. Petroff, *Remembering a Forgotten War -- Civil War in Eastern European Russia and Siberia, 1918-1920,* East European Monographs, distributed by Columbia University Press, N. Y., 2000.

[3] Some foreign scholars of Russian military history incorrectly refer to the Imperial War College (*Imperatorskaia Voennaia Akademia)* as the General Staff Academy, a name that it held prior to the military reforms after the Russo-Japanese War.

[4] The so called *Kirilovtsy,* followers of Grand Duke Kiril, considered by many Russian émigrés as the heir apparent of the Romanov dynasty.

[5] Named after the Kwantung peninsula in Manchuria that Japan occupied in 1905 after the Russo-Japanese War.

[6] An all-Russian military unit made up of cadets from former Russian military schools and young officers who fought as mercenaries in the ranks of Jan Sun-chan's armies during the Chinese Civil War.

[7] Victor Petrov, *Shanghai on the Huangpu,* Washington, D.C., 1985.

[8] California-Russian Émigré Series, Univ. of California, Berkeley, "Interview with Filipenko."

[9] Victor Alexandrov, *The Tukhachevsky Affair,* New York 1963.

[10] For more information see Serge P. Petroff, *Remembering a Forgotten War,* Columbia University Press, New York 2000.

[11] *Komitet Uchreditel'nogo Sobraniia* (Committee for a Constitutional Assembly) Created in June 1918 to demand the convocation of the Constituent Assembly that Lenin dissolved by force on January 18, 1918.

[12] Literally, meaning big wind in Japanese, taifun is the Asian equivalent of hurricane in the United States.

[13] Lafcadio Hearn. *Selected Writings*, New York, 1949 and *Japan, an Attempt at Interpretation*, Rutland, Vermont and Tokyo, Japan, 1959.

[14] Japanese in blood and culture, the *Burakumin* did the dirtiest tasks in old Japan and were the lowest of the lowest in Japan's social structure. The word *Burakumin* is an abbreviation for the expression "the hamlet people" or "ghetto folk."

[15] Dmitri I. Abrikossow. *Revelations of a Russian Diplomat*, Seattle, 1964.

[16] Rosemary and Donald Crawford. *Michael and Natasha*, New York, 1997.

[17] Edwin O. Reischauer. "Imperial Japan: Democracy and Militarism," in John K. Fairbank, Edwin O. Reischauer and Albert M Craig. *East Asia*, Boston, 1978.

[18] Joseph C. Grew. *Ten Years in Japan*, New York, 1944.

[19] Edwin O. Reischauer in John K. Fairbank, Edwin O. Reischauer, and Albert M. Craig. *East Asia – Tradition and Transformation*, Boston, 1978.

[20] A Japanese colloquial expression meaning "going back to negotiations."

[21] Joseph Grew. *Ten Years in Japan, 1932-1942* (New York, 1944).

[22] Barbara W. Tuchman. *The March of Folly* (New York, 1984).

[23] For details on the Sorge case, see Chalmers Johnson. *An Instance of Treason* (Stanford, CA, 1964); D. F. Deakin and G. R. Storry, *The Case of Richard Sorge* (London, 1966); Robert Whytman, *Stalin's Spy* (New York, 1996).

[24] Marina Tsvetaeva returned to the Soviet Union in 1939 and two years later committed suicide by hanging herself because she could not adapt to the horrors of the Soviet regime.

[25] Takafusa Nakamura, translated by Edwin Whenmouth, *A History of Showa Japan, 1926-1989* (Tokyo, 1993).

[26] Pacific War Research Society, *Japan's Longest Day* (New York, 1968).

[27] Tsuyoshi Hasegawa. *Racing the Enemy: Stalin, Truman, and the Surrender of Japan,* Harvard University Press, Cambridge, Massachusetts, 2005.

[28] In order to increase its political power at the Convention and to avoid internal dissention, California delegates agreed to vote as a group for Governor Earl Warren on the first ballot.

[29] Nickita Khrushchev. *Khrushcev Remembers,* Boston/Toronto, 1970.

[30] Serge Petroff, *The Red Eminence,* Clifton, N.J., 1988.

[31] For details of the coup see my account in Victoria E. Bonnell, Ann Cooper, and Grgory Freidin, Eds. *Russia at the Barricades, Eyewitness Accounts of the August 1991 Coup,* New York, 1994.

[32] Strobe Talbott. *The Russia Hand,* New York, 2002.

[33] Francis Fukuyama, *The End of History and the Last Man,* New York, 1992.

Made in the USA
Las Vegas, NV
07 May 2022